Lure of Service:

My Peace Corps Adventures at Middle Age

Diane Shugrue Gallagher
Returned Peace Corps Volunteer

The Republic of Cape Verde, West Africa
1990 - 1992

Gallagher Associates
83 Harvard Avenue
Brookline, MA 02446

For information about special discounts for orders over 100 books, please contact
Gallagher Associates at our website **www.LureofService.com**

For speaker bureau requests, please contact the speaker bureau's email at the book's
website www.LureofService.com

ISBN-10: 0615710239
ISBN-13: 978-0-615-71023-5

Printed in the United States of America

For additional information please go to
www.LureofService.com

Cover: Picture taken by Chief Abu of Diane during training in Guinea Bissau, West
Africa

Second Edition

New York   San Francisco   Boston

It would be dishonest to pretend that
I went because
I wanted to turn the desert into a garden
      or to realize dreams that were
      thousands of years old.
I went because it was different, because
I wanted to go, because it was a road
      that might have an end.
I knew I would not stay forever;
I never thought of tying my future to this newness;
I knew I would take the road back one day,
      but perhaps carrying with me a particle
      of the night's silence,
      or the day's honesty.

                    adapted from "Dust"
                    by Yael Dyan

INTRODUCTION

Peace Corps has just celebrated their 50th anniversary and, by all accounts, the program that John F. Kennedy envisioned has been a success for the US and the countries that have been served. But the real human story is the impact on the individuals who were served and those serving as the PCVs (Peace Corps Volunteers). Armed with language, cultural and sector based training given in a three month intensive program by PC and the vision of improving human life, the PCVs, the unsung heroes, have done so much for so many. In return, they have experiences that will forever shape who they are and how they will approach life; adding true humanity, depth and a commitment to service to often rich and full lives. The Lure of Service is but one offering to the day to day experiences of a not so typical PCV. But then, there is really no stereotypical PCV.

Diane, or Deana PACIM, as she became known to her Cape Verdean friends and co-workers, took a path to service much less traveled. Inspired by John F. Kennedy's speech in 1961 launching the Peace Corps, Diane and her new husband Bill, applied to the Peace Corps, but were not accepted because Diane became pregnant six months after marriage. Dream deferred. It has been said: life happens when you plan for something else. While raising her children, she pursued careers in acting, running an art gallery, writing, and archiving. Along the way, she divorced her husband after 20 years of marriage, moved in Massachusetts from the south shore town of Scituate to the city town of Brookline and successfully "launched" her four kids in meaningful careers and lives. After all of that, she started to explore how she could give back for all of the wonderful blessings of her life. "The Peace Corps is not designed as an instrument of diplomacy or propaganda or ideological conflict. It is designed to permit people to exercise more fully their responsibilities in the great common cause of world development".

She never abandoned her dream, 29 years later, at age 53, she applied for the Peace Corps and got her assignment to serve in West Africa. Opening the fateful package from the Peace Corps in 1990, she admitted to a full range of emotions ranging from her usual sunny optimistic view to sheer panic at learning new languages and cultures. Upon her first arrival in Africa, her hands had to be "pried" from the airplane seat in sheer terror. In 1990, she would serve in Cape Verde, West Africa without running water, electricity, cell phones, internet or other modern conveniences and would use the ocean for her bath. She left behind her children, friends and family and even the cat. What was she thinking?

The reward for her taking this huge leap of faith and living every moment to the fullest was the permanent imprinting of her personality with patience, tolerance, humility, and respect for the value of all humans. She developed a pace of approaching life that is to be envied by all who get to know her. Her story is an account of a strong willed woman who uses her age, maternal and corporate experiences to her advantage and sees no barriers, rather, interesting challenges to be tackled. In her two plus years tenure in Cape Verde, she establishes a children's library, a sewing guild for the financial benefit of the poorest of families and educational materials for HIV prevention. She left the US feeling that she was too old to do many things and feel deep love for others. She quickly learned that one is never too old to love, to cry, to dance all night, to experience the moon and stars of another continent and to touch so many lives around the world. She fell in love with Vitorino, and brought back to the states a little Cape Verdean boy, Paulino, to be adopted. Her story is an inspiration for all who are considering taking the challenge of serving in the Peace Corps and is a must read for anyone traveling to developing countries for service of any kind. To all fellow sojourners in lives of service to others, Diane's experiences will inspire, encourage and motivate people of all ages to follow the path least traveled with openness, love and faith for the vision of improving life for those less fortunate.

Beverly A. Brown, Ph. D, Director of Development
Center for Global Health and Development
Boston University School of Public Health

DEDICATION

To my four amazing and spectacular children; Katherine, Claire, Maura and Bill – Gallaghers all.

The entire Peace Corps Family; current Peace Corps Volunteers, Returned Peace Corps Volunteers, and the Peace Corps Volunteers who will be serving in the future.

ACKNOWLEDGMENTS

I shall begin my list with sincere thanks to my four children; Claire, Katherine, Maura and Bill who top the list of those who supported me unconditionally. Bill and Maura visited me and learned about the soul of Cape Verde. Along with Maura and Bill, Katherine and Claire now love and understand the music of the Cape Verdean singer Cesaria Evora.

The Bare Cove Gallery girls: Jean Cain, Sue Packer, Yvonne Trilsch, Pauline Sly and Anne Garton.

Longtime friends Ellen and Hank Baer who shipped hundreds of books from the NYPL for the school library in Mindelo.

Dear friends who pushed me continually to finish the manuscript; Claudyne Wilder, Roberta Benjamin, Vita Paladino, Nola Geraigery, Win Hall, Sheryl Bono, Julie Hatfield, Pamela Galgay, Nedda Casei (who sent creative libations), Jacqueline Knapp who drew scary skulls on libations from NYC, Joan and Sam Scali, Saranell De Chambeau who told me how to start a children's library, Ellie O'Rourke, Jane Cusack, Jack Alexander, Jack Anderson, Jack White, Amy Buckley, Betsy Farley, Penny Fuller, Lynn Pitchford, Helen Rees, Liane Brandon, Jim and Jill Gabbe who gave me all the information I needed to know about publishing, Mary Ann and Ed Pires, Arthur Hurley (kept my financial status on the up and up), Evalynne and Jack Hajjar, Eunice and Joe Hoover, Sonya Hamlin (my tutor), Tim Hollingworth and Vin O'Neill, Katherine Jolluck, Mary Blumenthal, John Kramer, Leslie Di Russo, Lee Dunne, Ed Washington and Arlene Nunes.

Great thanks to Elizabeth Philipps for her excellent skills who became my final editor; was gentle and firm at the same time.

Dr. Walingunda who got me in good health for the odyssey, Dr. Di Maggio who repaired the damages after no dental work for three years, Carolyn Fuchs, Margie Collins, Terry and Margie Keith, Terry Ann Lunt and Tom Sellers, Duncan MacDonald, Kandace McKinney. Agostinho Nunes and David Bair who explained to my children that the Peace Corps process was a life changing event and I would not be the same mom when I came back.

Ruthie Shapiro, Enna Kutz, Nancie and Chris Weir, Michael Wood and Natalie Woodward, Becky and Bill Ezzard, Bernard Borman.

My brother Terry Shugrue and his wife Kathi, Father Michael Shugrue, Ellen Shugrue and Steff Berardesca, Peg and Rob Schwarz, the Finlayson clan, and the Traphagen clan. The South Shore tarts; Faith Bowker - Maloney, Lisa Tompson, Carol Swain, Pat Baker, Polly Pyne, Elaine Murphy. Colby Sawyer College girls: Kim Whitely, Suzanne Vanderveer, Emily Lovering , Elaine Kutrosky, Bibby Deal, Robin McDougal, and former President of Colby Sawyer, Peggy Stock and David Morcom. My longtime and most loyal friend Rya Zobel and James C. Curvey who sent me my second Christmas card.

Karen Hook who reconstructed my all "in caps" manuscript, Aileen Kelly, Cynthia and Heather Lang who visited me, Clementine Brown, Kay and her mom Mary Lennon.

Bill Gallagher, Senior, who gave me the courage to leave everything behind and serve.

The people who took care of me in Cape Verde are all in the book but special thanks to Maryann and Pedro Almeida who became my sister and brother. Bernice Powell, at the U.S. Embassy, who attained sisterhood and always had fresh baked peanut butter cookies at the ready when I went to the capital city, Francisco Silva who got me through the PC bureaucracy and his wife Kristin, Suzette and Carlos Da Cruz. Thanks to all the PCVs who served then and continue to serve!

Heartfelt thanks to Dr. Beverly Brown for her stirring introduction and thanks to Tom McCann, Norman Moyes, Julie Hatfield, and Tad Jankowski who wrote their sensitive endorsements.

Thanks to Paulino Beach for coming into my life.

Final thanks to my brother Richard Shugrue, who gave me a compass and was my true north, Vitorino who carried me through all the good times and tough times with his love, Aunt Millie Husted with her constant lecturing on how a lady must behave, Phil Nutting who got me over my fear of writing, Corita Kent who told me to just go and serve, Jay Veevers. Cesaria Evora, who became a treasured friend, all of whom looked down from their perches up in the clouds and sent me protective prayers.

Am most grateful to my son Bill, who shepherded the manuscript to book despite his mother's nattering; he did an amazing job.

I thank them one and all.

Diane Shugrue Gallagher, 2012

LURE OF SERVICE:

MY PEACE CORPS ADVENTURES AT MIDDLE AGE

Diane Shugrue Gallagher

TABLE OF CONTENTS

SEIZE THE DAY
"WHILE WE'RE TALKING, ENVIOUS TIME IS FLEEING:
SEIZE THE DAY, PUT NO TRUST IN THE FUTURE"

Horace

My Peace Corps dream started forty-five years ago. Let me take you back. We were young, life was good and we were together. It seemed indeed the age of Camelot. My husband Bill and I married in June of 1961. In March of that year, a young, slightly brash U.S. Senator named John Fitzgerald Kennedy was flying around the country asking the nation to vote for him in the upcoming national presidential election. Somehow, he caught the need, the heartbeat of the people and began to raise a stir amongst a nation tired of the "business as usual" syndrome. Maybe, just maybe, there could be someone to do the job of leading our nation to different, exciting, forward thinking.

On an October night in 1961, Kennedy's campaign plane had landed on the Ann Arbor campus of the University of Michigan. Waiting to greet him was a crowd of ten thousand students who wanted to hear his message, his hopes, and his dreams. His speech was a call to arms, not the arms of war but the arms of peace, a peace corps. "How many of you are willing to spend two years in Africa or Latin America or Asia working for the United States and working for freedom? How many of you who are going to be doctors are willing to spend your days in Ghana? Technicians or engineers, how many of you are willing to work for the foreign service and spend your lives traveling around the world? The answer to whether we, as a free society, can compete depends on your willingness to contribute part of your life to this country. I think Americans are willing to contribute, but the effort must be far greater than we have made in the past." He then said "Ask not what your country can do for you, but what you can do for your country." This was the beginning of the grass roots movement towards a Peace Corps.

When Kennedy was a student at Harvard University, he had read the work of the noted essayist William James. In "Essays in Religion and Morality" James said that perhaps there should NOT be a war corps but a corps made up of young men who would work towards peace and that the war against war would be no holiday excursion. "If now, and this is my idea, there were, instead of military conscription, a conscription of the whole youthful population to form for a certain number of years a part of the army enlisted against nature, the injustice would tend to be evened out, and numerous other benefits to the commonwealth would follow." This essay was written in 1908. Our elder military man, General Dwight D. Eisenhower said in 1956, "Beware the military industrial complex." It made me thoughtful that the oldest president and the youngest president would strive for peace. Hubert Humphrey had mentioned a type of Peace Corps, others thought of it, but Kennedy hung it out for all to see and then he did it.

When Kennedy won by a narrow margin in November of 1961, the Peace Corps light had been ignited and America responded. Thousands of potential volunteers sent letters to the White House asking how they could answer the call. Organizations rallied groups of people and a Gallup poll indicated that an overwhelming percent of the people were in favor of the concept of the Peace Corps. Bill and I were part of that enthusiastic national audience; he a brand new medical doctor, and me, the activist daughter of Dwyer William Shugrue of New York City who told me, over and over again, "if you don't like what is happening in the world, don't complain, do something about it!" Activists, yes, and we were doers as well. In the days when Bill was at Dartmouth, one had a military obligation and as a reservist in the Navy, he was scheduled to go to Paris Island as a doctor to the Marines. He also chose to see if the Peace Corps was interested in him. They were, and grabbed him. Our daughter Maura was conceived in September of that year, and by the time Peace Corps and Bill got their act together, it was December of 1961 and I was three months pregnant. "No, you may not take a pregnant wife with you to your post in Free Towne, Sierra Leone, West Africa" where we had been assigned. The Peace Corps rejected our application of the grounds of my pregnancy. I'd have to wait ... but it was a dream that did not go away, it just got shelved.

Dream deferred, put on hold, put on the back burner, have our four children finish college and make them comfortable in the world of being on their own.

2

Twenty nine years later, I called Bill. He was living the good life in Bangor, Maine as a successful dermatologist. We had been divorced for ten years. I told him I was going to apply for the Peace Corps and if accepted, I would go. "Do it," he urged and for all the frustrating time it took to be accepted into the program as an older volunteer, he continued his encouragement. I secretly thought he wished he was going as well.

Later on, during the application process, Bill had to write a letter explaining a medical treatment I had. His letter got me accepted. The Peace Corps nurse called me and told me I had been medically cleared. "We receive many letters in the Medical Department about potential volunteers but the letter I received from your doctor explaining the situation around your allergic reaction to penicillin was one of the more unique letters I have received. In fact, if you give me permission, I will put it up on the bulletin board so that everyone in the department can have a good laugh." I asked what the letter had said, she read it to me, "I, Dr. William F. Gallagher, Jr., graduate of Dartmouth Medical and Harvard Medical Schools… blah blah (all his impressive credentials) did indeed treat Diane Gallagher for her allergic reaction to penicillin …."Fine," I said, "copy and put it up on the board." "But wait," said the nurse, "he had one more sentence, Diane does suffer from a plethora of freckles, which, only adds to her charm. If you have any further questions…" I laughed, the nurse laughed and the letter went on the bulletin board.

WOULDN'T A WEEKEND IN VERMONT DO JUST AS WELL?

In the autumn of 1989, nature was beginning to show her skeleton; everything was being stripped bare. I decided to strip bare too, only it would not be my skeleton, but my soul. After all, four of my "bright as shiny new pennies" children had graduated from college, were living in homes of their own, had good jobs and had found their niche, so I could comfortably give myself permission to leave my nest, follow the dream born so long before and apply for a two and a half year stint in the United States Peace Corps. The reactions to this dramatic choice were varied, from positive to disbelieving to "you must be on heavy drugs to do that." So I counseled myself with to hell with the shocked friends and family - just do it. I called my four children on the telephone. "Come for dinner," I said with a serious tone to my voice. I knew I would miss them desperately.

I set the dining room table, put the flowers in place and lit the candles. Somehow, I felt light headed, euphoric. I knew it was not going to last, but that was a great first feeling. One by one they trooped into my apartment. Everyone got a drink, I put on some mellow Dave Brubeck jazz and we sat down to dinner. I cleared my somewhat dry throat. I found out how the moisture goes away just when you need the lubrication to get the hard words out, "I have been thinking about applying for the Peace Corps as a volunteer." Looks from each of the children were fast, next came silence, and then the questions came pouring out. The reactions: Maura, eldest, tall, straight and French elegant said, "I hope you won't be killed for your feminist views." Bill, handsome, serious and inquisitive, queried, "how about the degenerative arthritis in both your feet?" Katherine, intelligent, savvy and lovely said "awesome, Mom", Claire, youngest, bright eyed, pretty, curious said, "that's wild." I heard four wildly different reactions from my four children.

Every time I would start the sentence in which I would try to explain to others what I was going to do, why I was going to do it and when I was going to do it, I would receive a look of bemusement, disbelief or just plain "hey, are you kidding?" The responses ranged from bold choice, to bully for you, to you hot ticket you. Clementine, longtime friend, got quiet. Being a Brooklyn-born kid, she started doing her usual data collecting procedure. Where would I be going, what would I be doing, who would I work with, and then the killer of all the questions, how long will I be doing this exercise? "Umm," swallowing, "two and a half years will be the time frame." "I see," long pause, then the twinkle returned into her face, "wouldn't a weekend in Vermont do just as well?" We both roared with laughter. After all, laughter would pull me through all the bad times and the tough times that would come. There were going to be many of those times in the next ten months as I went through the process of getting my act together. The former beloved, Bill in Bangor, said, " you know what really worries me about going into the Peace Corps is not knowing what's going to happen, but what really appeals to me is not knowing what is going to happen." Old lady in a doctor's waiting room said, when hearing me talking to my friend about my decision, "in the old days, I hear, they measured you for a coffin and it arrived with you."

Then there was Aunt Millie, my mother's sister, straight laced as a Victorian corset, rigid as a catboat sail in a full blow, kind when it suited; Mildred Burt Husted, who was then living in a nursing home. I had admitted her three winters before, this frail shell of a former career woman from the New York City world of fashion. I called up the director and explained what I was going to do and wanted to come and explain to my beloved aunt. "Fine dear, I will make sure her favorite nurse, Bathsheba, will be with her." When I walked into her room that autumn day in 1989, I was struck by her smallness. In her former life, she always filled up a chair with her perfect posture, her perfect manners, and her perfectness. Now, huddled into a metal wheelchair, she looked tiny. I knelt at her knees. "Aunt Millie, it is Diane, your niece, Leona's daughter. I have something to tell you. I have decided to apply for the Peace Corps, an organization of the American government that responds to requests for volunteers to serve in a developing country." The verbiage went on, I watched her watch me, nodding, smiling, touching my hand from time to time and saying, umm, yes, oh, my, my. Then I said, "I'm going to be gone for two and a half years and will not see you during that time. Your grandniece Maura and grandnephew Bill will visit you and your grandnieces who live in California will write you lots of letters." Bathsheba's big, ample hand, resting on Aunt Millie's shoulder, patted Aunt Millie from time to time. Bathsheba untied the restraining belt and encouraged Aunt Millie to give me a hug. Aunt

Millie leaned over, and with a strength that belied her frailness, gave me a hug; cold, sparse, but none the less a hug. I felt my throat constrict, no tears came to rescue my emotions that had been building. She whispered into my ear, "that is so nice of you to do, dear, but I have a question, just who are you?" Bathsheba made a sound that was a cross between a chuckle and a sob. Millie looked clearly at me, she was not joking. I held her hands with her dark freckles in mine as the afternoon sun filtered through the gauze curtains creating patterns on Aunt Millie's wheel chair. No tears came at that moment, but many months later when a shaft of West African sun filtered through my shutters, I remembered and cried. I'll always remember Aunt Millie being so brave, so courageous, so sensitive to someone she had forgotten she had ever known.

THE ENVELOPE PLEASE
NOTHING HAS BEEN ACCOMPLISHED IF THERE IS STILL SOMETHING TO BE DONE

On a dreary day, June 1, 1990, I came home after work to my condo in Brookline around dusk, noticed the flowers blooming in my neighbor's window boxes, but no flowers in my boxes. I used to plant white flowers (Coco Channel said - "always have white flowers for they reflect the moonlight"). My thinking was now focused on going into the Peace Corps, not about summer in Brookline. Pushed open the heavy, wooden door to our vestibule, I saw a large envelope on top of my mail box, too big to fit into my box. The bright logo of the Peace Corps was in the upper left hand side of the envelope. I tucked the envelope under my arm as I reached the second door with the brass lion knocker, wondering if there would be lions in the country I would be assigned to - or maybe I would be told I had not been accepted into the Peace Corps. I picked up my cat, put the envelope on my hall hat rack and walked into my living room. As I sat on the sofa looking out the windows that faced a row of town houses, I wondered that if I went, what would my view be – what would my house be, what would my life be like? The cat snuggled into the crook of my arm and we both fell asleep.

That envelope stayed on the hat rack for three days. For the next three nights, I came in my back door. The mail piled up, I ignored the front hall. Finally, June 3, I went into the kitchen, made a large pot of tea, went to the front hall, got the envelope, cat, and glasses and sat down in the living room. The envelope opened easily, the letter said, "You are invited to serve as a Peace Corps Volunteer in The Republic of Cape Verde, West Africa. Please call this number with your decision". Their line was busy, dialed again; busy again, dialed again and heard "Peace Corps placement, may I put you on a hold?" Drat. Person came back on the line, "social security number please," gave it and she said, "Diane Shugrue Gallagher", "yes", "do you accept the placement?" "yes" "congratulations, I am making a record of your acceptance, and you will be leaving on Monday, July 9, 1990. Tickets will be put in the mail for you to fly to Atlanta, Georgia, enjoy the experience." Hung up, took the cat back to my sofa and started to cry, a soft, weak cry that led me into a deep sleep. When I awoke, I felt drugged, it was night time and the street lights were peeking through my shutters, I dragged myself up as the cat stretched and thought, will miss you Chin Chin. I knew he was a survivor, but the question was, would I survive this experience?

When I thought of my four fabulous children, I wondered how I would face each day not seeing them or talking to them on the phone. I would lose touch of their daily lives, of that I was sure. That made my heart heavy with the thought.

LEAVING MY HOME FOR ATLANTA, LISBON AND GUINEA BISSAU

A July Monday morning in Brookline was as gray as my heart. Too little sleep, too much still to be done, I thanked God for daughter Maura, son Bill and his friend Mary. Two duffle bags, stuffed, lay next to the front door. All the furniture was gone: the oriental rugs, the hat rack, all gone. At six am, the alarm clock jangled us awake, an hour later a horn blared - the cab had arrived. The telephone rang "did you forget me?" Clementine asked. "No, we are on our way," I replied. Bill drove, Maura, Mary and I were quiet as we picked Clem up and went to Logan airport. I spied Arlene Nunes, a young 21 year old Peace Corps trainee from New Bedford. Her mother was standing alone; her father could not make the journey (Arlene told me later it was too tough for him to say goodbye). Maura gave me a hug and said; "See you in '91," Bill hugged. Arlene and I grabbed hold of each other. I didn't turn around: if I had, if don't think I would have left.

Three hours later we arrived in hot and muggy Atlanta, Georgia. We went to the hotel to meet the group that was going to West Africa and began the bureaucracy dance. Registration staff - friendly and upbeat - the words to the song I danced to in New York City in my salad days come to mind, "This could be the start of something grand." The paper blitz began: fill this out, make a decision about that, fill this in; the trainers were all business. We went into our first seminar. There were two married couples, and three other trainees about my age, we smiled and nodded with a slight hint of relief that there were others in our age group. We went to our assigned country groups; I was elected to do a presentation about our expectations for the twelve of us who would be going to Cape Verde. Four countries would receive this group of trainees: Guinea Bissau, Sao Tome and Principe, Guinea and The Republic of Cape Verde. That night all of the 55 trainees went out to an Italian restaurant; I wondered when the next time would be for spaghetti and garlic bread.

Day two was filled with lectures, role playing, and cross culture lessons. My brother Richard had remarked when he called me in Boston the night before I left, "just go with the flow," came back to me. He was a Marine in Viet Nam; he must know I thought as I felt the metal mirror he had given me in my purse as well as the glow in the dark watch on my wrist. We were given malaria pills. I asked which members of the staff would be flying with us to Africa and was told we would be on our own from JFK airport. They asked for volunteers to take different pouches over to Africa and I said I would take our medical records. The sheer weight of the pouch made me feel comfortable, like I was doing something constructive towards the process. My friend Jay had given me a gray canvas bag, and into that bag went the medical pouch. For the second night's dinner, we chose McDonalds and went to bed on a junk food high.

The day of our departure, after shots and more medical lectures, we got the bush taxi lecture. This consisted of putting five people on five chairs, adding five more people but no more chairs, adding five more people, still no more chairs and then we were instructed to "go with the flow" because this was what the bush taxis would be like. Cartons and waste baskets representing screeching baby goats, crying infants, dying chicks were heaped upon us. Ten of the trainees, never having been out of the country, got a little bent out of shape with this exercise.

Our last dinner in the States was at a Steak & Ale restaurant where I ate my last filet mignon, and a huge baked potato slathered with sour cream and chives, and drank a Dewar's very slowly, savoring each drop. Back at the hotel I made my final telephone calls home, which, as I no longer had my own credit card number, were collect calls to my family - a new experience. My two brothers, Richard and Terry, and my stepmother Peg and stepfather Rob wished me well. I thought there would be long conversations, but found there was not a lot to say when you just have to say goodbye. Sleep came, but it was not an easy sleep.

Morning and the telephone rang in our hotel room - it was Win, an old beau, saying goodbye; my outward strength began to falter. I went down to the lobby and called Nedda, a dear friend who had traveled the world over, "see you in Europe." Joanie, a friend from the "having babies together days" called, "remember, if it is unbearable, you have a safety hatch - my home in the south of France." We giggled and then the telephone calls were over. As I was finishing up my conversation with Joanie, I heard a very sad young woman's voice on the telephone next to me. When I looked I realized it was one of the trainees, Amy, and she was crying. She hung up, I asked her what was wrong and she said she could not go with us to Africa, she had to return home as her doctor had seen a shadow on her chest x-ray and wanted to do more tests. I told her it would be just fine, doctors see shadows all the time so there was nothing to worry about. Amy got very silent and said, "My mother died of breast cancer." I said, "I am sure you will be joining us in Guinea Bissau and I will save a place for you." We hugged and she went off in a taxi. I wondered if I ever would see her again. Our group milled around in the hotel, milled around at the airport, milled around and around. We would do many mills around so best to get used to it now. As we boarded the plane, Donna, another trainee about my age, told me to sit next to her in the business class. She had been upgraded and there was an extra seat next to her. I did, and we had white wine, linen napkins and good food. The other young trainees in the tourist seats gave us dirty looks and we felt just a tad bad. We saw the movie "Stanley and Iris", poignant story about an unusual love. I wondered if I would find any love. Nah, I didn't need that, I was going to do a job. Besides, I was 53 and that part of my life was over.

We arrived in Lisbon, Portugal on Friday, 13th. In the States, this date involved a superstition; here it was just a day on the calendar. A taxi took us to the Alpha Hotel where I found I was to share a room with fellow trainee Brian. Being a gentleman, he politely said he was going to check out the town and left me to my bubble bath which might have been the last one for a very long time; it was delicious. In the lobby I joined some other trainees for a visit to the old part of Lisbon. I heard another language, was told it was Portuguese and got a sinking feeling in my stomach. Could I learn this at my age? I had a divine glass of Port to quiet my now nervous stomach. We went down to the ocean because one of the trainees, Ross from Kansas, and had never seen an ocean so I delighted in taking him to the harbor where he got his first glimpse. Afterwards I took a nap by the huge columns abutting the harbor and dreamed about the Portuguese explorers who discovered Cape Verde in the 1400's. As the younger trainees climbed to the top of the famous fort, I remembered that I must pace myself, and not get caught in the "I can do it just as well as they can" number. Back at the hotel, the luggage shuffle, then Air Portugal took us off to Africa and the country of Guinea Bissau, where we would live and be trained for three months.

We were landing in a torrential rain storm. When I looked out of the tiny windows I knew one of the reasons it was called the "dark continent":

there was absolutely not one light in sight. Rain pelted the plane, we circled twice before landing. It was exciting and scary to hear the wind, to see the rain and trees dancing with joy to the rain. On the ground we came to an abrupt halt and the adventure, which, had terrified me from the first, began.

The country was Guinea Bissau, West Africa, the town we would live in was Mores, and the feeling that I had in the pit of my stomach was sheer terror. What in the world had I done to myself? Who did I think I was ... anyway? I remembered that Georgia O'Keefe once said "I've been absolutely terrified every moment of my life and I've never let it keep me from doing a single thing that I wanted to do." All the trainees, full of adventure, rushed down the plane's small aisle. I began to walk slowly and then clutched the back of the seats and froze. I could not move, my mouth went dry, legs did not work and I stood there, not moving. The pilot looked at me, said something to a person at the bottom of the stairs and I heard "Welcome to Bissau." A very dark face with a wide smile beamed at me and somehow made me feel that I was truly welcome. The young man was tall and elegant, and walked towards me, took both of my hands gently in his hands and again, his rich voice said, "You can come off the plane with me now" and I went. He put up an umbrella and, with my arm under his, we headed towards the darkness. A large shed, with a big sign, WELCOME CORPO DA PAZ", homemade chocolate chip cookies and real American Cokes laid out on a huge wooden table made us feel welcomed. The young man named Chico, would become an important part of my PC life.

We did the luggage "wait and shuffle" and then took off in two buses into complete darkness. We were all quiet until the people in the front of the bus, on one side, started screaming at the top of their lungs. It was impossible to see but I noticed that the screams were going aisle by aisle, first one seat, then the one behind. Then I saw the creature, I mean it was a big, black sucker and it was moving right toward me without a sound. All of us were in an uproar as the driver stopped the van and turned on a tiny light. We gasped in dismay and chagrin when we saw the cause of the terror. The rubber stripping that covered the tops of the windows had come loose and fallen off. As quiet returned and the nervous laughter subsided, I wondered how many more adventures were ahead. Then the bus got stuck. We all hauled out; Melanie and Cheryl dragged back huge stones to put under the tires. I laughed as I thought where was Triple A? As first light began to peep through the thick trees and vines of the jungle, we noticed a village about fifty feet from us where the roosters had begun their crowing, the children their crying, and the fires their crackling. We watched in fascination as the village came to life on this amazing and unknown African morn. The first bus came back for us and we proceeded to the compound where we were told that after we found a bed to sleep in we were to get up at the sound of the bell. Boys went to one end and the girls went to the other end. I was so bone tired that I was devoid of all feeling when Donna motioned me into her room. I went without question. Two other women trooped in and took the remaining beds: Frances from Chicago, Rebecca from Virginia, Donna from mid-west and me, New York City. We all fell onto the bare mattresses and sleep was instantaneous.

The bell awakened us, the nurse gave us a tetanus shot and the staff told us what to expect next. We, of course, were in a daze and it all was jumbled together: lunch, unpacked, ate dinner, unpacked, talked, unpacked, and slept. The next day, Sunday, and the US Ambassador came to welcome us along with a group of Bissauans who provided us with our first look at African dancing. Their costumes were wild and full of thatch that made them appear wooly and bigger than life as they whirled, dipped, gyrated. I thought about my dance teacher, Martha Graham, who told a story about Henri Cartier Bresson, the famous French photographer, whose wife was a famous Thai dancer. An automobile accident had cost her the use of her legs, but, undaunted, she became a famous hand dancer. My thoughts came back to the present and I wondered what Miss Graham would have thought of these exquisite dancers so far removed in so many ways from the American techniques that she taught me. The next weeks were filled with health lectures, meetings, and the never ending tests on language. I asked the doctor what side effects the malaria medicine might have. "Well, loss of memory and some pretty strange dreams," was the retort. I then asked the language guru, "How difficult do you think it will be for someone my age to learn a new language?" "Well", was the slow response, "almost impossible after the age of about 14 -16 years." When I asked him what I had to learn, he told me twelve tenses in Portuguese. Great, along with memory loss, wild nightmares, being sure as hell over 16, I had twelve tenses to learn. I considered quitting. I considered it a lot in the weeks that followed. We were told we would have language classes seven hours a day for the first few weeks. We were a class of six, the bottom of the language pile: Donna, Gary (male nurse and sharp), Mame, (African American who was in the Peace Corps many years ago and decided to do it again), Kathie from Alaska, Brian, the engineer, and me who never had another language. We were told we must pass a verbal test at the end of training or we would be sent home; that did have a certain appeal. Every morning we would awake to the call of the small yellow birds that lived in the huge tree outside our window as they left at first light. Then the roosters from the nearby village got into their act, then the goats, the pigs, braying donkeys and always the mosquitoes. One particular morning, a rooster had decided to bellow his call under my very window. The first morning, I let it go by. Three mornings later, it became too much so I grabbed my machete, (we were all given one to use in tramping through the jungle) and lit out of the dorm with murder on my mind. Missed that beast by a hair - he never came back.

Breakfast served at 7AM was peanut butter and jelly sandwiches. The jelly had a curtain of yellow jackets surrounding it so we learned to bob and weave to get the jelly without being stung. Remembering the time daughter Katherine was stung and rolled down a hill with the pain, I gave the bees a wide berth. Lunch was rice, sometimes fish or chicken, but always rice, cooked by three ladies over huge rocks outside the kitchen. We nodded to each other in recognition of our senior status. We might have become friends but for the language barrier so I smiled and did a lot of sign language. One afternoon I walked to a health lecture. It was pouring so I put the thick medical book on my head; the water cascaded down my back but it felt good in the heat of the day. I arrived and the nurse told us to open to page 19, the lecture on the poisonous animals we would see. I opened my book and there, on page 19, was the biggest scorpion I had ever seen. It was about to scurry away when I slammed the book closed and said, "I have a dead scorpion." It was the star of the lecture.

Daily we walked to the village where we were bombarded with "too-bob" from the villagers, an expression that literally meant white person but it was not meant to be complimentary. I bought some candles, a thread bare towel that might last a few washings, and splurged on a can of pineapple juice which tasted so good, not Dole, but good. To pay for these things I used our "walking around money", an allowance we were given by staff.

The rain that greeted us at the airport weeks before had not lessened and now I understood what "the rainy season" meant. We learned a new and appropriate word, guarda cheuva, umbrella - to guard against the rain. Saturday came, no classes. I took a long nap as I was now an old hand at diving under the protective mosquito net without letting my legs or arms hit the netting, the mosquitoes can't reach you, and I slept like an Egyptian mummy.

The training only lasted three months, but it seemed a lifetime. I don't remember ever being so discouraged and down in the dumps one day and then on a high the very next day. Language had a lot to do with my state of mind. They say that Portuguese is the language that is closest to Latin. I found that my high school Latin kicked in (thank you Sisters of Mercy on Long Island.) The nuns could never have devised a training program as hard as this. All in all the adventures and experiences that I had during our guerilla training stood me in good stead. The impossible did seem to be doable. At least I prayed that it would!

There was a dance that first Saturday night and all the trainees preened and got gussied up but I stayed home to study those damn irregular verbs. Arlene and Frances came back to my room - grabbed me and dragged me to the dance. The music sounded very good, but I still felt I should be studying so when Arlene and Frances were whisked off to the dance floor, I started to head back to my studies. However, at that moment, a tall, very tall, man came over, bowed from the waist and extended his hand. I accepted it cautiously and we moved to the dance floor. The beat was easy, but fast and he graciously took his time allowing me to get the feel of it. His arm brought my back into alignment with him and although the music had a different rhythm, we moved well to his strong lead. Then they played a slow number and I was at once aware of his different position. I felt all of his body next to mine and we moved as one, as dancers should, but so few American men do. I did not pull away for it felt good and I had not felt like this for a very long time. When the band broke for a rest, I left him and went for a soda. The stress of the week disappeared and I felt light and happy, even the irregular verbs faded away. Chico, the first man I met in Guinea Bissau, came over and asked me to dance and we danced in silence until after 2 AM to the band, named "Tabanaca Jazz". I had not danced that long for years and with the African moon guiding us, Chico and I walked back to the dorm. Still not a word was said. He nodded a goodbye.

AN AFRICAN GIFT

It was midnight. The children of the village had been tucked under their protective mosquito nets, the cows were in their rickety corrals, the mother hens had pushed their chicks into hollowed-out places in the soft dirt, and the sound of sleeping Africans filled the air.

I had spent the day being ushered around by my host for the weekend and was exhausted by the effort of being up, friendly, responsive and alert, and yes, weary from trying to speak their language. Now it was night and the hugeness of the African sky lulled and calmed me, and I relived what had happened to me that day.

As part of our three-month training, each trainee was to spend a weekend with a host family in the interior. When our trainers first mentioned this exercise, many felt a little apprehensive; I was just plain scared. I was told I would be by myself and my host family would take good care of me. God, I could only hope so. They gave us a list of phrases in Crioulo, the local language, and as I looked at the letters strung together, I wondered how in the world I would ever be able to be fluent. At this point, the words of advice a returned Peace Corps volunteer gave me came into my head, "don't be afraid to make a fool of yourself, keep the ability to laugh at yourself with you at all times."

As we packed for our adventure, I looked apprehensively at the few items I was bringing with me: a small bottle of bleach to treat my drinking water, a package of Gatorade, a rolled-up mosquito net, my Swiss Army knife, a cotton nightgown and my sandals. This was all that I would need. The skirt and blouse I wore would be changed only once. Practicality was to be the order of the day.

Before going to our villages, three trainees and I were driven to pick up the President of the region. The first person we saw was a large woman coming up the broad cement steps of an impressive building. We were invited inside, where the favorite game played in Africa began: hurry up and wait. Men scurried in and out, talking with the woman. When she rose and told us to leave, I realized that she wasn't the wife of the President: she was the President. The four of us piled into the falling apart truck, the President in front, of course. Then, much to my amazement, a group of young men and old men climbed into the back with us. There had barely been enough room for the four of us. Now there were nine, and no one batted an eye.

At each village along the way, we dropped off a Peace Corps trainee, the President making introductions and smoothing the way. The very last stop was the village that would be my home for the weekend. A crowd gathered, the President swung into action with the rituals of protocol, and then suddenly the truck and the President were gone. The man who had been introduced to me as the Chief, Abu, bowed towards me and gestured for me to follow. We walked towards a sturdy structure of dusty orange bricks all piled neatly in place and topped with thatch. Abu motioned to the room at the end of the hall. There was a huge double bed and a wooden bureau and the ever present mosquito net. Small wooden stools lined one wall and a gazelle skin hung on the other wall. This was to be my home for the next three days and nights. I unpacked my small backpack, took out my letter of introduction from our Peace Corps country director and gave it to the chief. The letter had the United States seal on it and it was praised by all the men who had slipped into the room and were now occupying the stools next to the wall. I took out the picture of my four children, paused a moment to let the homesickness pass, and put it on the bureau. When the Chief saw that I had finished unpacking, he asked me if I would like to take a walk around the village - at least -I think that's what he said.

The village was fairly large, and the smell of wood smoke filled the air. Abu took me to meet the blacksmith, a short, stocky man with a pleasant smile. When I looked at the huge muscles on his arms, I was awed. He nodded briefly and went back to his work, operating a bellows over a fire surrounded by pieces of metal, wood, and an audience of dozens of village people. I watched and asked permission to learn the bellows, he shook his head no. After Abu asked him in Crioulo, the blacksmith handed me the bellows and showed me how to use them. Sweat began pouring down my forehead and the salt stung my eyes, but I was determined not to stop. Finally the fire was hot enough and he handed me a huge hammer. He put a piece of metal into my other hand and then showed me quietly how to hit it. Now I knew why his muscles had muscles. The reverberation went through both my arms. After what seemed to be hours, most likely five minutes, the blacksmith took the hammer and the thin piece of metal and smiled. He nodded to me to follow him to the edge of the jungle that surrounded the clearing. The blacksmith grabbed a limb from a branch and started whittling, then gave me his knife and motioned for me to continue. The whittling almost finished me, but I hung in there until he told me by body language that it was done. He strode back into the clearing, I limped. He put the stick into the hole of the metal I had banged the hell out of and there it was: a real hand hoe. John Deere could not have done a better job. All the children smiled, Abu smiled, and I shook hands with the blacksmith who had given me my first metal-work class.

Abu saw how tired I was and took me back to his home for a short nap. Later, after a long walk through several villages, a wonderful dinner, and great conversations about my life in the United States (which, with the help of miming and body language, they seemed to understand), Abu motioned for me to follow him out to the field. I went with him with complete trust, for he had sort of adopted me and treated me like a sister. It was now midnight and the stars were so brilliant they took my breath away. In my mind, I reviewed the day as Abu sat quietly next to me. I was remembering the day when a wild rainstorm burst upon us and we were forced to duck into a hollowed out tree to shelter ourselves from the downpour. I thought of the brand new baby, only hours old, that had been given to me to hold for good luck, of the small Muslim temple where I was asked to write my name on the tablet, and of the lady who ran after me to give me her best ripe banana, of the animals constantly surrounding us, and of the earth, productive and worn out at the same time. It was now midnight, I looked up towards the full moon. Abu smiled at me and began talking in Crioulo, about the stars. He gave their names and I listened in fascination. I then told him the English names and stories I had been taught by my parents. The simplicity of the night and our comfortable conversation made me realize how fortunate they all were to have a Chief like Abu. An hour went by, he took my arm and we walked back to our homes. I barely remember the process of getting into bed.

The light of dawn reflecting from the orange clay bricks awakened me, and I could hear children's muffled cries, pots being filled with water, women cajoling babies, men coughing, all telling me that life and the day were beginning again in Africa. As I swung my legs out over the large bed, I felt something touch my feet under the sheet. I saw a huge banana leaf tied with a vine at the bottom of the bed. Picking it up gingerly, I untied the leaf and there was the hoe, the very hoe I had made the previous day with the blacksmith. He had come in the night with his present and I never heard a sound.

Diane and Chief Abu - Guinea Bissau June 1990

Francisco Martins Silva – Assistant Director, Peace Corps

During our training, there were a few incidents that will remain in my memory, some traumatic, some fey, all just this side of absurd.

Mail was very important. We learned always to be in the middle of a letter/post card with U.S. stamps affixed - there was always someone who was going stateside and always at the last minute so we learned to write out the last line quickly and put it into the hand of the departing American.

I figured out another way to beat the system. Wrote a letter to one person and inside their envelope, four other one page letters were enclosed, all addressed. The person who received that letter then had to put the other letters into envelopes and stamp and mail them. It worked like a charm and it seemed that everyone touched base with other friends and family as well. Film is very difficult to process in Africa. I would send one roll to a friend, they got to see the pictures, made two copies and sent one to my son Bill (for my scrapbook) and one to me. I gave my copies to those photographed and they were pleased. I owed a big debt to my family and friends.

Another way I connected with Americans was through visits to the American Embassy, located in the capital city of Bissau. It is a filthy city: open sewer trenches on both sides of the one main road with garbage, vegetable and human, accumulating in the heat of the sun. Flies covered all and then covered us. We gave this part of town a wide berth. Dozens of languages filled the air. All Africans know at least four languages: the language of their village, the official language of their government, French and a smattering of English. I cringed when I thought of how narrow minded Americans are about learning another language. Taxis careened madly and accidents occurred at a frequent rate. The Embassy was across the road from a huge Sheraton Hotel and had lovely plantings in front. A Marine smiled and waved us in. The next minute I was in a huge pool, doing laps. The jungle dirt, the anxious fretting over the language, the strangeness of training disappeared in the swimming. Later PCV Rebecca and I strolled to the Sheraton that had real rugs, electricity, and my God, a dining room. We looked at each other, counted our pennies and walked in rather shyly. Shrimp cocktail, white wine, and a tiny but heavenly chocolate mousse. We shot our entire $22 monthly allowance, but felt grand.

Back at the Embassy, we heard about a war - how could they have a war without us? We had a sense of isolation that got stronger. Curtis and Winifred, an African American couple who worked for Afro-Care joined us at the pool and after hearing their tales of foreign affairs, one step forward, half a step back, Curtis leaned over and said, "enjoy Cape Verde and oh yes, it is okay to have a foreign affair." I laughed and thought that would never happen and that was not why I was here, older PCVs did not do that. Little did I know something like that would happen.

After that visit to the embassy, back to training and grim reality. David Bellama was the Peace Corps Director, one of those common sense type people who just got things done and always with a smile. I told him of my language fear and frustration, he invited me to his home for a cup of grog. It was made from sugar cane wine and gave me a slight buzz. His wife Nancy joined us and also allayed my fears. I meandered back to my room, slightly high and watched a praying mantis do her mating dance. Mating done, the male turned to go but, she grabbed him and devoured him - not nice. On the weekends we were freed from classes. One brutally hot day we were volunteered by one of our trainers to assist a peanut farmer. Our trainer, from Cape Verde, sat under the cool shade of a huge tree, while we toiled in the fields. I remarked about the situation and was told that the trainer/chief never sleeps - he was just resting his eyes and thinking of activities for his students.

After hours of backbreaking digging, we were invited back to the farmer's home. My brother Richard had given me the lucky brown bandana he had in Vietnam and it was now soaked. I was given some cool water with a fresh lemon and was refreshed. The farmer showed us how he grafted fruit trees. The fruits were luscious and exotic, a bit of lemon, a bit of orange, a bit of lime, all in one fruit. How many lessons I would learn, and another one was about to begin.

This is how I learned the parts of the body in Portuguese. The next weekend we were driven back to Bissau again, and booked into the Hotel September 24, the day of the revolution from Portuguese rule. Arlene, Rebecca and I took one room, after that we hit the dance clubs. I was asked how I learned to dance like an African; I smiled and did not respond. There are only two places I do not argue with a man, the dance floor and a sailboat - one has to be a leader and the other a follower and men were trained to do those activities. I wondered if there would ever be a time women would enter the America's Cup Race and prove me wrong. An African man whom I knew asked me if I liked to swim and I nodded my head yes. He murmured "piscina at 3:00 AM." The dance continued in the club where the tables were under a thatched roof, the dance floor was under the stars. We danced for hours. Back at the hotel, I told my roommates I needed to cool off and hit the pool. As I was doing laps, a long legged, dark chocolate brown body arched over my head in a perfect dive and hit the water silently. Until the dawn told us to hustle back to our different rooms, he taught me all the parts of the body in Portuguese. Hands on instruction wins every time.

Then there are some not so terrific memories of training, like when we ended up in a prison. Once again we were in a dance club and as Arlene and I exited with two Cape Verdean men, I noticed some police near the door. One of the men stopped Arlene and I thought she was flirting with them and paid no attention, and strolled down the road cooling off. The next thing I knew Arlene was yelling to me, "Deana, they want us to get in their van and go for questioning." I ignored her, what would they want from us, and was about to take another step when a not so friendly hand grabbed my arm and I found myself tossed in the back of a police van. Arlene explained that since we did not have our passports (they were back in the security of the PC office) they wanted to question us.

The prison was way out of town and I tried to catch glimpses of landmarks so when we were dumped, wherever that might be, we could find our way back to town. We were roughly hauled out of the van and shoved into a filthy office. The interrogations started with Arlene being patient and polite, I started to get New York aggressive and began to quote John F. Kennedy and his dream of peace and understanding in the world. The more they harassed us, the more quiet and logical Arlene got and the more I got closer to hitting high C. We saw a brown woman being hauled off to another area and then heard her cries as she was being hurt. We were ushered into another office, a little cleaner but still falling apart. This official was a tad nicer, Arlene told me to stop with the JFK number. Pictures of Fidel Castro were all over, next office, next official, now I was getting bone tired. We had been there for four hours. The next official had a very clean office and white hair and looked like the chief. I moved in for some heavy lobbying, and attempted to speak in my dreadful Portuguese. Arlene rolled her eyes and this man listened with a hint of interest. I told him he and I were about the same age and I was sure we could find a solution. Arlene explained one more time. We were then released. The chief escorted us out and I said we needed a ride. He and I were becoming friends by then and he gestured for a man to bring a car around. A grimy piece of junk was brought to us, I haughtily said, "No, not this one, I want that one" and pointed to a white Mercedes. The chief smiled and said that was his car and I said fine, that would be appropriate for us after what we had been through for the last four hours. He bowed, we bowed, and were driven to the PC flop house (all Peace Corps offices have a place designated for guest volunteers to sleep in, to "flop in) in the chief's white Mercedes.

Unbeknownst to Arlene, the Chief had asked me if he could take me out to dinner the next night; I said yes. It could be interesting to hear his

23

philosophy and I would share the Peace Corps philosophy with him. I thanked Arlene for being cool and diplomatic and fell onto a bare mattress and slept the sleep of the dead. The next night a former prisoner (me) and the Chief of Police (he) had dinner together; very interesting. I called my daughter Maura from the Sheraton and told her of our adventure. She laughed but I hung up with a lump in my throat for the rest of the day. I vowed not to call again: too much of a wrench. I decided not to call my other three children; it would be too sad.

Back at our camp, I acquired something I thought I would not have in Africa... a cat. The Director's wife could not keep a kitten after she discovered her three children were allergic to it, so it was brought to our camp and somehow ended up on my bed. My brother Richard had given me Skin So Soft to keep the mosquitoes away. He had used it in Vietnam; of course, the label was taken off when issued to the fighting Marines. Never let it be said Marines had Skin So Soft! I put it on me and the kitty. I missed my cat Chin-Chin who had been given to my goddaughter Kathleen. One night, Frances jumped out of bed and said "the kitten is in trouble and I have no night gown on." Rebecca and I tore out of the dorm and, with flashlight in hand, finally found it – it had been pinned down by a piece of barbed wire. Rebecca held the light, I untangled it and then the damn cat bit me. Carrying It back to the dorm I told Rebecca that I had to wash out my wound, she nonchalantly took the light and went to the bathroom. I screamed "Rebecca, the cat ate a bat today and then bit me, I have to wash the wound" but she was out of sight. So, I washed the wound in the dark. The next day one of the trainers, Hugo, noticed the redness on my hand and took me to the local medicine woman. She made a potion, applied it, it healed. To this day, when I look at a small scar on my left hand, I think of the night the cat ate a bat and then bit me.

When things got dull, we all played a game called "what don't we hear in Africa": a car alarm, a TV, a telephone ringing, a train, a subway's roar, the metal zipper of a ski jacket in a dryer, and someone saying let's go catch some rays. We laughed and then we played what we did hear: morning roosters, pigs rutting, rain storms, yellow birds outside our trees and drumming, always drumming with the local gossip, the activities of the day or maybe just playing the drums for the sheer love of it.

As the weeks zoomed by, I got a sinus infection. Hugo, again to the rescue, gave me Chinese balm and my Vicks was immediately replaced. We were taught how to cut and bend and play with rebar. I brought my Waltz tapes to the lessons and taught some of the young trainees how to dip. Many weeks later at a dance, Doug, trainee, said he was ready to try the dip, I cautioned him, "not a problem" he told me and promptly dropped me on my head. "Not a problem", I exclaimed and when the language lessons finally started to sink in, they said it was because I was bit by a cat that ate a bat and also that I was dropped on my head. Hugo began to help me when I would study the damn irregular verbs in the library at night, sometimes I filled up with tears and Hugo just waited and when it passed, patiently began the lessons again. Peace Corps is very insistent on the volunteers learning the language of the country where they will serve. One day I developed a bright red rash on the inside of my upper arm. Kristin, the nurse said, "Oh good, now I can give a tumba fly lecture." Kristin put Vaseline on the swollen part, told me to wrap a bandana round it and get to bed and sleep. I looked it up in a medical book and realized a tumba fly had deposited larva in me, was she kidding, go to sleep? The kitty and I tossed and turned and the nightmares visited. The next morning in class, Kristin wrapped a pencil around the now emerging worm who had been suffocated during the night and he/she/it came out. Can't hurry this process or it will break off, she told us. We watched in horror as Kristin droned out the lecture. "You can't dry your clothes on the ground, that is when the tumba fly drops her larvae in the elastic of your blouses and then you put it on and thus a host is created." I gagged and got green and then finally it was over. The clothes were then Ironed with hot rocks to prevent this from happening again. Lesson #102.

Garrett Greg, the first trainee who decided to leave, said that Peace Corps was not for him. This was exactly the purpose of training, for PC to test us and for us to test ourselves. He said he was going home to the west coast and I asked him to call my two San Francisco daughters. He did and Claire and Katherine asked him if I was all right and had I gotten into any trouble. He laughed and said yes, as a matter of fact, I had gone to prison the Saturday before. Katherine and Claire called their east coast siblings with the news and were told that their father had gone to a Maine jail that very Saturday because he had been caught by a trooper with his expired driver's license. Our children had a laugh on their criminal mom and dad.

THE BUSH TAXI DANCE
LAST PART OF TRAINING IN MORES, GUINEA BISSAU, WEST AFRICA

I never thought I would make it all the way to the end of the journey, but did. There are many ways to travel, one of the most unusual and exciting ways is the famous - or infamous - bush taxi of Africa. It challenges all your preconceived notions of traveling.

While still a trainee, I took a huge bus type vehicle from the city back to our interior training camp in Mores. It was a bus type because that is exactly what it was, a type, one of a kind. The vehicle started service as a normal bus to transport people, but over the years, extras or additions were "put on", such as the tarp that was haphazardly strung over the top in order to keep the unrelenting rains from permanently damaging the passengers and their worldly goods. There must once have been a limit to the number of people allowed to ride, but over the years, extra benches were added, places for people to hang over the edge were added, 'til it was hard to see the bus for the people. I sat near the outside back door, only there was no longer a back door but an open cavity that had the remnants of a tail gate thereby making it easier for passengers to help the new riders aboard.

The night I took the bush taxi, we stopped for a young woman and her four children. The older one, all of about four years old, darted back into the dark interior carrying the second youngest in her little arms. The next child was handed back like a Chinese fire drill, all the passengers seemed to know what their part was in this procedure. The mother quickly handed me a tiny baby and disappeared into the crowd just as the bus lurched into motion. Only then did I realize what had happened; I had the baby; it was crying and I didn't know what to do. I held it to my breast and it started rooting around. Nothing there any more, baby. The baby fell asleep and, I began to nod off also when oh, oh - I felt a warm sensation. Ah, motherhood, I thought and smiled - nope, pee. So I did what I saw the

26

African women do, pulled my cotton skirt up over my knees and let the baby pee on the wooden floor boards. That done, my skirt back in place, we all went to sleep. The live chickens clucked, the baby goats bleated and the rain pelted on the tarp. In all, it was comforting and we hunkered in together in a rocking and rolling bush taxi knowing we were safe. Approximately four hours later, the bus screeched to a stop and the young mother came from the depths of the bus, three children in tow, nodded and without a word took her/my baby back and disappeared - one more experience etched into my memory.

During the three months of training there were many visits to other places, all to teach us about sustainable development. The Dutch had sponsored a leather factory, where the smell of the tanning fluids overwhelmed us. There was a make shift store attached to the factory where I bought a back pack, the first one I had ever owned. The smell was dreadful so I doused it with baby powder for days and finally the stench left - much to my relief. The leather factory was an example of good sustainable development, for the Bissau nationals were running the factory and the Dutch had left.

I wondered if any of the projects I would become involved in would become sustainable. To guide us toward this goal, we were told a fascinating tale. It seemed the Minister of Agriculture in Guinea Bissau decided it would be a good thing for the people in a certain village to grow a kind of starchy vegetable. They managed to receive seedlings from a donating country and told the people in the village to come and get the seedlings and plant them. No one came; finally the Minister decided to give them a reward if they planted them. The villagers were told that if they planted the seedlings, they would receive a cash bonus for each one planted. The chief and the people said fine and came to the agriculture center to pick up the vegetable plants. Six months went by and the Minister decided to visit the village to see the success of "his project." He went to the chief and asked if he and his people had planted the seedlings, "yes" was the reply. "Good, I would like to see them." He was taken to a field that had been cleared for the planting and saw a sight that dumfounded him. There were all of the seedlings that had been planted carefully, as agreed upon, row by neat row, only they were planted upside down. The lesson we learned was: when working in development, one should go to the people and to find what THEY need, not what was perceived was needed. The villagers had kept their part of the bargain; the Minister learned a hard lesson.

After our three months of intense training here, we began to say our goodbyes; twelve of us would go to Cape Verde for our final two weeks, twenty eight of the original group stayed in Guinea Bissau, the rest went to Sao Tome and Principe.

The final farewell celebration included killing and roasting a pig. Some of the children gleefully pulled the pig's tail while it gasped its last breaths. I watched in fascination and revulsion as the cook retrieved the vividly bright blood for use later for the ceremonial blood pudding. As I walked back to my bunk, I was told I was a lovely shade of green. But I didn't make it to my bunk, just to the bushes where I vomited.

At the farewell party that evening, there was a beautiful moon and an air of anticipation for the dancing, the eating, and the sharing for the very last time. The musicians arrived early and the village children gathered around to watch them tune up and play little ditties just for them. As the dancing swung into action, I was surprised when our head cook who had become my friend during the training, asked me to dance. Never having danced with a woman before, I felt awkward but one of the trainers nodded yes and so – out onto the dance floor. Ten steps into the dance I realized I had met my match; she was indeed the best dancer in the village and that was including all the men in training. We broke loose and danced as though there was no tomorrow and indeed there would be no tomorrow or occasion for all of us to be together again like this. Hating to leave the celebration and the dancing but filled with its happy beat, I retired for a few hours of sleep before the dreaded language test in the morning.

 My teacher Sabu, a kind and gentle man, began the test in a quiet part of the library, by asking me about my family in a most kind manner. At first I faltered with the strange Portuguese language, but soon begin to hit my pace and the right words started to come. What seemed forever, was most likely only thirty minutes, he told me I had done well, and said "congratulations." I was stunned that I passed, and knew I had just barely made the grade, but he smiled and so did I. When I left the library, I noticed some movement near the trees in front of the library, and then saw a small woman who I could not recognize at first, but as she moved closer, I knew who she was. This is how I met this old woman.

When I had been walked around by my evening tutor one night, he took me to a small table on the outskirts of the village. There sat an old woman, hardly a tooth in her head, one eye was definitely wall-eyed, and a body that had seen many wars. She sold grog, she and my tutor talked, she nodded to me (he must have explained who I was and that I needed to have some "relaxing liquid"). She poured three tiny – we are talking teeny-glass cups of a clear liquid. The tutor downed it with one swallow and the seller did the same so I thought I could handle what they were handling. After all, I was a single malt girl, Oban being my chosen poison. Well, as soon as the liquid hit my throat, all air escaped my lungs, my eyes dilated, my sinus cavities were on fire, tears came streaming down my face and I almost could not catch my breath. They looked at me, smiled and had another one, I waved weakly no, thank you. That was my first lesson in straight grog. After that night, I would go to the woman's stand without my tutor and buy a teeny cup and slowly sip, she would smile, and we would "talk". I mimed, I had 4 children, she had round about 20 or so, husbands, yes, and so a friendship began. She taught me words that my tutor would never have tried; she did not know I was the language class dunce. Now, after my language test was finished, she was standing in front of me saying "Si Deana o nao?" Yes or no, I smiled and nodded "si"; she pulled out a teeny glass bottle from her pano (her cotton wrap) and handed it to me. It was grog, the liquid dynamite. I hugged her, she hugged back and then she was gone, no dialogue. How she knew I was having the test that morning, I will never know. She just did.

It was sad when the first group of trainees left for their final destinations, for we had become close, and even as I told them I was sure we would meet again, I knew in my heart it was very unlikely. But life goes on and the first order of the day was breakfast. Even though I knew we had none, I decided I wanted eggs. Finding a bike and with the help of two village boys, I teeter tottered out of camp. I hadn't been on a bike for about twenty five years, so my riding left something to be desired and prompted my young friends to laugh and observe that I was "mulher forte", a strong woman. I remembered saying at the beginning of this beastly training that I was a "mulher velha" (old woman) but they now said, "mulher forte!" that was better. It was hot and I was slow but we arrived at the first village where they left me to rest saying they would return. Resting under a nice shady tree, I noticed a woman of the village pounding maize. She smiled at my offer of help and shook her head no. I asked again and, since she was younger than I and age must be respected in Africa, she handed me the pestle. Trying to imitate her, I wound up and came crashing down, producing a teeny bleep sound and laughs from the other women who had now assembled to see the old white woman make a fool of herself. I tried again, a big wind up and again, a teeny bleep sound. I laughed again at

29

myself and gladly allowed the young woman to take the pestle from me and as before, she easily made a huge thump, thump sound. African women must have been born with the knowledge of how to crush the maize, and thus make that resounding sound. My two bicycle companions screeched back into the village with four eggs, and with these plus the two given to me by the women pounding the maize, we pumped back to our village for breakfast. On the way they tested me, by pointing to colors, I sang them out in Portuguese. They pointed to people on the road, I sang out descriptions and everyone laughed. We left our jungle fortress amidst warm goodbyes from the ladies of the kitchen, the trainers who had done their best and the two children, who went bike riding with me. Warmest goodbyes went to the old woman who sold me grog, taught me how to savor it and gave me the realization that this was the living experience I would always cherish.

GUINEA BISSAU TO DAKAR, SENEGAL TO CAPE VERDE
"THERE IS ALWAYS SOMETHING NEW COMING OUT OF AFRICA"

PLINY

Dakar, the capital city of Senegal, West Africa, was our next stop. Its feeling is what Paris 100 years ago must have been like... tall, elegant women with their graceful, arrogant walk and the very handsome men, who also moved well. Our little group of Cape Verde destined Peace Corps trainees were booked into a small hotel, and immediately went in search of food. Our first stop was a Vietnamese restaurant where the food was quite good, the currency very large and the coins were really lovely. Next we went to the market where I bought a huge boubou for Win, an old friend, where I discovered that Africans like and expect to bargain, which to me came naturally. That night at a little dance club the rhythm and pulse of African music again propelled me up and on to the dance floor with one of the waiters. He was most polite and when I told him I was with the Peace Corps, he said he knew that for we have been in his country for more than twenty five years and they had great respect for the work the Peace Corps had done. I was glad to hear him as tomorrow I would be entering the country that for the next two and a half years would be my home where I would do work that had been planned by both Cape Verde and the PC.

Once again the airport shuffle, and in two short hours, we were 380 miles off the mainland of Africa in the middle of the Atlantic Ocean headed to The Republic of Cape Verde. It was very hot when we landed but not unpleasant, for as John, the Peace Corps Director who met us, pointed out, there was no humidity. John was young, enthusiastic, and a returned volunteer from The Central African Republic. Our hotel was called La Anjos, "the angel", a misnomer at best. All the rooms faced an inner court yard, but when we looked up, the top was covered and sealed in a quite bizarre way which gave me claustrophobia. After breakfast in a pleasant room, we

31

walked over the cobblestone streets to the American Embassy, hearing music blaring from every door along the way. We were given a series of lectures, and then various functionaries welcomed us with the perfunctory smile and bow. This, and my New York blood told me there was no sense of urgency so I put my reactions on hold. We were invited to the Directors' very comfortable home where we were shown "Volunteer" a humorous movie about the Corps during which, I must say, the popcorn and chocolate chip cookies baked by his gracious wife Kathryn, were most welcome. The next day we went with the Director to the local beach, where the huge surf was perfect for diving through, relieving tension and having a good time. At night we fell asleep to hearing "The Girl is Mine" which came from a room in the hotel.

The next morning we were sworn in by Ambassador Terry McNamara on the patio of the Director's home, with the sound of the ocean in the background, and the Cape Verdean sun completing the picture. After repeating an oath to uphold the Constitution of the United States, we were bussed to the interior of the island to an ancient part of the city that was the capitol. That evening the moon and ocean behind us created the perfect setting for our leisurely swim and dinner. In Cape Verde I became very aware of the sky, the moon and the stars, which I paid little attention to when I lived in the States.

Later there was a reception for us in the home of the Ambassador and Mrs. McNamara, who put all of us at ease. When introduced to my new Cape Verdean boss, Senhor Gabriel Evora, we bowed and received all of the expected niceties. At this point Arlene Nunes, a fellow volunteer, came over to say hello. She spoke to him in her fluent Portuguese and his reply caused her to smile stiffly and crisply bid him goodbye. I had a feeling that all was not well with this conversation and it was confirmed when, as we were strolling over to the bar, Arlene said, "you must watch out for that man. I told him that you were looking forward to working with him and he corrected me by saying you would be working for him." My roller coaster ride had begun.

That next morning, we three, Arlene, Frances and I, now designated "volunteers", boarded a tiny prop plane and were off to our new home. An hour later we landed on a tiny brown island; it looked like a lunar landscape - there was no grass, no trees, no flowers, no bushes, just a lot of sand. The hills surrounding the landing strip were like silent sentinels. John, the PC Director for Cape Verde, had accompanied us, introduced us to a local merchant and Cape Verdean, Pedro Almeida who spoke perfect English and had lived in the United States. He told us that his wife Maryann was in the States visiting her family but we would meet upon her return. I was taken to my new home - a cement apartment on a cobblestone road next to the ocean. It had one room on the first floor, stairs leading to my sleeping room, and then, the best part, the roof. As I looked out over the harbor town of Mindelo on the island of Sao Vicente I somehow felt good about the roof tops, about the children's laughter in the street and the brilliant blue sky. Dinner time found John, Arlene, Frances and me in a nearby tiny restaurant where the sea food was so fresh, the sauce so spicy, the beer so cold and all so different. The owner had greeted us warmly - a good sign for a good beginning and with it all, I smiled at last.

SETTING UP HOUSE IN THE BUSH ..
ONLY IT IS NOT THE BUSH, IT IS A HARBOR TOWN...

I awoke in the morning not to a rooster but to the sea which was across from my home and to the sounds of women going to market along the road outside my windows. It was a Friday, which in Portuguese is Sexta Feira. Frances and I had decided that Friday would be the day to go to City Hall to meet our bosses. A fifteen minute walk brought us to the building which was the hub of the town. Large, graceful and Portuguese, it stood alone in the main square. Frances found her boss first and he smiled. When I found my boss, he just looked at me and did not say one word. It was as though we had never met the prior week. I remembered Arlene's warning, "be careful of this man." At our office there did not seem to be much to do, not much direction, so we decided to go shopping for necessities, like towels, sheets, which were expensive, but my Scottish frugality and my haggling came to the fore. A young boy went through the streets selling wire hangers with homemade yarn wrapped neatly around the form made in the interior. I bought five, not a lot of clothing had I and thought of the hangers at Saks, Neiman's, Nordstrom's. Ah, but these had a charm those did not have.

On Sabado, Saturday, Arlene and Frances came to my house and we went shopping. Arlene was fluent in Portuguese, Frances was fluent in Spanish, and I was fluent in ... New York City street. During a coffee break in one of the cafes, the two young pretties were invited to a party by two local men they had met before; I was included, I felt like a duenna – a chaperone entrusted to protect a young lady's virtue. The two men drove us to the mountains where it was lush because only the very tops of the mountains received precious moisture, not real rain, just moisture. Guitars came out, dancing began, food appeared and a typical Cape Verdean party began. The unspoken rule that we learned that night was a party does not end until dawn, so we danced, sang and laughed till first light came over the

34

mountain top. When I was dropped off at my new home at dawn, I looked up at the mountain and noticed it was shaped in the form of an old man lying down on his back. Then I realized that was why they called it Mount Carra. "Carra" is Portuguese for "face".

On my first Sunday in the harbor town of Mindelo, I decided to go to evening Mass. This Mass was a whole new experience. It was two and a half hours long, I was used to a quickie 30 minutes, and the people sang a lot. I smiled and hummed, maybe I would get through this experience by humming. Glad to escape back to my home for dinner and bed and to think of the work week ahead, for after all, I had come to work.

The next day I walked to my new office and was introduced to Ulla, a blonde Swede who had a kind and lovely smile and her colleague Jonathan with bright blue eyes. Eleven of us were crammed into one rather small room. They both spoke English and I said a silent "Thank you, God". Engineer Pedro, architect Miranda, clerk Guga, driver Josa, various clerks to take care of the vast paper work were all introduced. The first order of business was, of course, to retire to the Cafe Royal for coffee. When I ordered tea I was told they didn't have that so I learned to drink coffee. Jonathan started my education by telling me never to put mail in the red post boxes as they are from the Portuguese days - it was an in joke. Noon time came and everyone madly dashed home for lunch and the two hour nap. The afternoon was all business and at the end of the day, I limped home, weak from listening and trying to talk Portuguese.

During the following weeks, I listened and watched. I was told I would be working for the Minister of Housing and he was responsible for 573 families who lived in tin shacks on the outskirts of town. The name of our project was PACIM. My job was to figure out how to help these people in whatever way I could. I was given a tour of the tin shack towns and was told that Luxembourg sends money, Sweden sends people. I pondered what America sent, and then I laughed when I realized they sent me. I grew quiet with that thought. News from the States told me Leonard Bernstein and Art Blakey died and Michael Gorbachev won the Nobel Peace prize. I felt out of touch and thanked my friends silently for their gift of the short wave radio. Voice of America was good, B.B.C. was far superior. I was also studying books like Sanford Ungar's book, Africa, which informed me that Africa has 11,635,000 square miles, the second largest land mass in the world with 500 million people with 50 nations. I read about the 1860 Berlin Conference when European nations decided to divide the African continent. Not one African was invited to this conference: colonialism at its very worst.

Keeping in touch with my old world was through letters and care packages. I was so grateful when I received either, that I delayed the opening for hours. Another wonderful look at my former home town, New York City, was through Jonathan. I discovered he used to work for Bill Zeckendorf in New York City at the same time I worked for Papert, Koenig, Lois advertising agency. We all went to a party one evening and I decided to leave early. I took off, bravely at first and then realized I was hopelessly lost. Round and round, trying to find the ocean, I ran into a street party where there was a young man from our project and he said "Deana PACIM?" He came over and led me home. From that day on, my name was Deana PACIM. The next day I was teased about being lost the night before; this was a lesson about living in a gold fish bowl, everyone knew all about you.

When I realized I needed to learn Portuguese better, I hired a tutor, Yvonne. Sweet and so patient, she came to my home and we giggled at my mistakes and applauded when I finally got an irregular verb conjugated correctly which was not very often. I decided to talk in three tenses only (not the 12 they had in Portuguese): agora (present), passado (past), or futuro (future). Many people kept saying to me, "why aren't you like Lisa, she spoke perfect Portuguese." Lisa was the volunteer I replaced and I tried not to dislike her without ever having met her. She had called me in Boston right before I left to encourage me and told me the Cape Verdeans were wonderful people, I would love them and they would love me. She was right on all counts.

Talk about Cape Verdeans being nice, here is an example of the first time I gave a party in Mindelo. During the first week at the office I was told by my colleague Josa, "festa" -party /"Sabado"- Saturday/" oito hora"- 8pm / "seu casa." I understood the first three parts but thought that seu casa meant at the house of Seu and thought I had not met her yet. Josa kept repeating to make sure I understood and I nodded yes wondering why he kept repeating himself. The day of the party Ulla asked me if I was ready for the party, I replied that I was and she said she was looking forward to seeing my home." Wait," I exclaimed, "My home, what do you mean, the party is at the house of seu" she laughed and explained that seu meant you, the party was going to be at my house that very night. I almost choked and Ulla reassured me that Josa and the rest of the young men from our office would do all that had to be done. I had one of the best roofs in town and it was perfect for a party. It worked but I did not get over my shaking till the party was in full swing and I had enough grog to dull the fear.

INTRODUCTION TO AMELIA AND PAULINO
"IT TAKES A WHOLE VILLAGE TO RAISE ONE CHILD"

African Proverb

When I met Amelia during my first autumn in Mindelo, she was sitting inside of her tin shack at Ilha de Madeira, which means island of wood, an ironic name for a neighborhood seeing as how there was absolutely no wood anywhere. She had the face of a starved person. Her cigarette smoking had left her with bad lungs. Having no nutritious food had left her frail. Her little son Paulino clung to her and never said a word. This family became a favorite cause of mine because their plight was so desperate. As far as I could read in the town records, there was no other family, just the two of them.

One day when I went to visit them; Amelia was so desperately sick I took her to the hospital where we did the dance of the poor. People who have no money received cards which entitled them to receive medicine and medical examinations for very little money. The lines were always long, the heat was intense but no one waiting seemed to mind. I fussed and fretted. I learned that she had given her two older daughters to other people to live with and bring up, as she could not afford to keep them. In return for the boarding and feeding of the two girls, the family used them as servants. Amelia's youngest baby, her fourth, died immediately after childbirth, the little baby had no strength to survive.

Paulino, Amelia's son, chose me, I did not choose him. He grabbed the hem of my skirt one day as I walked through the Sahel sand that drifted across the Atlantic Ocean from the continent of Africa. The little hand that touched my skirt was not tentative, the pull was insistent. I looked down and saw big, deep, brown eyes sunken into the huge head of a little boy about two years old with a tummy distended by worms. My head said, outta my way kid, I am here to do small business development. I can't stop for a hug, pat or even a smile. But a smile did come over my face for here I was, in a tin shack town of over 250 families jammed together by amateur construction and linked together by devastating poverty. Paulino was a part of that and I had come to help.

The next day it was the same walk, the same Sahel sand, and the same little hand clutched my skirt and still I said no. On the third day, it was a day of cloudless sky, and intense heat, a tug on the skirt. Well, one hug wouldn't hurt. As I bent down, he leapt into my arms. I said he could stay there for two minutes. Those two minutes lasted two years and was the beginning of our friendship. If he had lived in the States, instead of West Africa, he would have had a U.P.S. FRAGILE sign attached to him. My maternal response kicked in, I plunked him onto my right hip where he was content.

There he stayed, totally happy for the duration of the journey, at ease on the swaying hip of the white woman who had invaded his town in West Africa in the autumn of 1990. Throughout the next two and a half years, this little boy became an attachment to my right hip. His mother, Amelia, beautiful when young, was now a shadow of her youth. Time, poverty and dreams never completed had etched lines in her face that would never be erased.

Paulino in his tin shack home

Paulino Gomes Silva – 2 years old 1990

Paulino and Diane – 1990

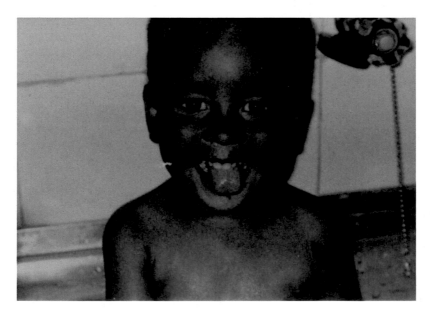

Paulino – Bath time

Paulino 2 years old, in Diane's apt with post cards from U.S. friends

Amelia and Paulino in tin shack room

Amelia and Paulino

Paulino in tin shack town

Tin shack bairro Campinho
No trees, no grass, no plants, no green, just Sahel sand that blows over the Atlantic from the continent to our little island – The Republic of Cape Verde.
Urine, shit, vomit and dinner – all in the same place

HER WRINKLES HAD WRINKLES

In Ilha d' Madeira an old woman sat on a wooden stool near the door of her one room shack. There are no windows in a tin shack so she had to catch the breeze coming through the door. Looking closely at her, I could see her wrinkles had wrinkles. Her eyes were dimmed from squinting in the sun, for without enough light in her tin shack, she had sat outside in the brilliant African sun which enveloped the land so fiercely that there were no shadows. All around us outside the exterior of the shack were sounds of crying babies, yelling children, mothers talking and laughing and scolding all at the same time.

Ulla had told me we had to try to find a way to make a very old woman, who lived by herself in the tin shack part of town, eligible for a real cement house. The shanty town hung by its thumb nails to the edge of the harbor town; too poor, too ragged, too devastated to be actually in the town. I stood awkwardly, trying to become smaller so as not to overwhelm the old woman as she sat silently on her stool. She did not rise as Ulla walked quietly over and spoke to her in Crioulo. She nodded and extended her worn hand to me. I walked over the sandy floor and as I held her hand for a brief moment, I was surprised to feel how cold her skin was on that blistering hot African day. Listening to the quiet talking of the two women, one questioning, one answering, not one word did I actually recognize, but I understood the meaning. As the women spoke, I looked around and saw a row of tin cans standing neatly against the wall. Each can had a precious bit of water in it, and a green, yes, a bright green piece of ivy the color I had not seen since arriving in this town of Mindelo a few weeks before. This island had not had any rain for seventeen years so the colors of the island were light brown, dark brown and soon to become brown. Ivy vines struggled for water in the cans, not much really, but to me it was a beautiful sight.

44

I looked at the woman and saw her eyes when they glanced away. Not a word was spoken, not a signal given or received. There were just three women, sitting inside a shack in the middle of a tin shack town, trying to get information that would allow this old woman to move into a cement house. My eyes were drawn to the ivy but then went back to golden haired Ulla, so kind, so gentle in her probing, so tuned in to what was needed. Ulla stood. The interview was over. The woman stayed seated, so I went over and stood in front of her; then, as she looked intently at me, the wrinkles moved ever so slightly into a small smile. I smiled back and felt a strange bond with this old woman alone in the middle of a hot, confusing community. I took one more furtive glance at the tin cans with their bright greenery and left.

Later that day dusk told me it was time to leave my office and go to my home. The route was via the cobblestone road among a row of many houses. I had been given a calico kitten by a Cape Verdean man, which he named Tarek, play thing in Portuguese. Tarek met me at the door where I picked him up, buried my freckles in his fur, and proceeded to share with him my dinner of rice, and, because I was feeling flush, a banana. On impulse, I tucked the kitten under my arm, walked the 21 cement steps up to my roof to watch the faithful stars - silver dots blinking in the pitch black sky - and the moon, a thumb nail, rolling between the clouds. When we descended the stairs and while I was closing the wooden door against the night air, Tarek ran ahead of me and pounced on something. I thought It might be one of the mice that inhabited every home or that he was tackling a rat from one of the ships in the harbor. When the object did not move, I came closer and saw that it was a package wrapped in a piece of the local newspaper. Sitting in the sand in front of my door, I un-wrapped it and found that it was a vine, a bright little green ivy vine, with water still sticking to its small roots. I spotted Valentina, my next door neighbor, watching and asked her who had left it. She smiled, shrugged and pointed to the road leading to the tin shack town. The old woman had walked the entire long way, over three miles, in the dark, by herself, for she had seen and understood my desire to have a piece of green in my cement house.

Maybe success and understanding would be mine after all in this new job in this so different place - maybe the old women of the town of Mindelo would help pull me through as the old woman had shown me how to make a new friend. Maybe.....Maybe....

THE MAN

The knock on my wooden door was not tentative. It was one of those knocks that had a mission. I opened the door with all the trust in the world, not like you would open a door in New York City. That thought stayed with me as I stared at the two gentlemen smiling at me. Looking past them, I thought, where in the world was Arlene? I was still getting used to the "Bon Dia" to start the day off, "Boa Tarde" for the afternoon greeting and then slipping ever so smoothly into "Boa Noite". "Boa Noite", I said a bit weakly, "Boa Noite", they both answered. Then came the pause, the pause, that during the next two and a half years, I would become so familiar with. The pause in which to think - what in the world do I say now? Will they understand my dreadful Portuguese? They stared, I stared. Then my mother's good manners lesson came to the fore and I ventured "Ummm, a, ah, entre" and they did.

The younger man walked in first. I recognized him as the young man Arlene had been out with at dance clubs. The older man had shaggy hair, a floppy mustache, and to my discomfort he started smoking the minute he got inside. He barely smiled but his eyes caught everything in the room. The young man was dapper Dan, the ladies' man; pressed slacks, nice shirt, trim. The older man was just the opposite - plaid shirt and a pair of print slacks that had not recently seen an iron. There was something very attractive about this older man, but the visit flustered me and I could not concentrate on my thoughts of him.

They came quietly into the room and sat down on my newly purchased wooden stools. If I had had a clock, its ticking would have been deafening. Mother's manners came to the fore again and I thought I must give them something to drink. I had no food to offer, how do I say "would you like?" and what are the names of the various drinks I have; beer, grog and water.

I made the international gesture of bending the arm to my mouth, smiling and gulping. They got it. How polite they were, watching me sweat bullets and trying so hard to be the gracious hostess. They pointed to the grog. They drank, I drank - again, the non-existent African clock tick tock, tick tock.

What the hell do I do now? Oh, I know, bring out the pictures of my children, say their names and ages. Out came the pictures of daughters Maura, Katherine and Claire taken at Amy Buckley's wedding long ago. I pointed, said their names and then put fingers up to get the ages across. Thank goodness I did not have a 70 year old child; it was tough enough with Maura at twenty eight. Then I got the frame with the picture of my son Bill and me at my fiftieth birthday party in Boston. Could that person in the elegant pink evening gown and feather boa really be me? Now I was in bare feet, very comfortable, in my loose fitting cotton skirt and blouse, my hair in a ponytail, the makeup kit still in my duffle bag.

I thought I'll give them a tour of my home. That will use up some time. I stood up, they stood up, I motioned to the stairs and said "Mindelo aqui" (Portuguese for "Mindelo is here"). I thought it would be nice to show them the view from my roof. As we went up the steps, I pointed to my room where I slept and did the gesture of my hand under my left ear and closing my eyes. Could I remember "dormir" was the verb for sleep? Not on your life. I pointed to the church and then to the sky and said "Deus", the word for church was not in my mind but the word for God certainly was. Then I pointed to the ocean, roaring and swirling in the night and said "mar." Hey, I was on a roll. That was a word that was exactly right.

They both smiled and then I pointed to my watch, yawned and they got the idea. I had run out of activities; words and energy were leaving. We walked down the cement stairs and they went out into the night after saying thank you. I leaned against the door, mindful of the perspiration which drenched my light cotton blouse. Never again, I hope, never again. I tore upstairs to study my irregular verbs and more nouns - must get those verbs - and instead fell into an exhausted sleep.

Five nights later there was another knock on the door. I wondered who it was this time. When I opened the door, I saw Elisio, the same young man who was here before and another older man. This older gentleman had no mustache, his hair was cut neatly, and he did not smoke as much as the first older man and his clothes had indeed seen an iron. This time I knew the words for the beverages. As we sipped, I dragged the pictures of my children out, not much of a variety here, and said the names and this time I had the ages down pat. Then the tour of the roof, the places of interest, and again, I pointed to my watch, yawned and off they went. The next day I saw Arlene and said "please tell Elisio not to bring any other gentlemen around, I know what they are doing and I do not need a gentleman friend for the next two years. I am here to work." She looked blank and said she did not know that I was talking about.

Five nights later, there was, once again, a knock on my door. This was too much. I was going to tell them off in their own language. I threw open the door and there was only one man looking at me and smiling one of the most brilliant smiles I had ever seen. The brown hue on his face set off the white smile with such intensity it took my breath away. "Uh, ah, a, entre," and he did. We sat on the wooden stools, looking at each other. There was an intensity about this new man that dazzled me. This third man was very focused, he watched me closely when I spoke and made much more of an attempt to understand me. There was a little aura of each of the previous gentlemen, but there was also something very different. He smiled and said "beber," which I now knew was to drink; I jumped up, got the grog and sat back down.

For some strange reason I did not break out in a sweat. I was more composed, so was this man. We started to talk, hesitantly, slowly, with many pauses. When we did not understand the other, one would wait while the other struggled on. I said something to the effect that he was my third gentleman visitor in the past two weeks. There was a silence. He smiled and said quietly, "no, you have had three visits from the same man, my name is Vitorino and I would like to be your friend." Then as he was about to leave, he lifted his finger, kissed it and touched it to my lips. The tingle of that touch never left my body the entire night and it lasted for the next two and a half years.

Vitorino Santos

Vitorino

Vitorino

Elisio and Arlene, Diane and Vitorino

Vitorino

Diane and Vitorino under small wild gazelle skin Diane was given as a gift in Guinea Bissau

CAMA VS CALMA
OR
MAKE SURE YOU KNOW THE DIFFERENCE BETWEEN A NOUN AND A VERB

With all of the problems and anxieties that the Peace Corps had presented to me, the farthest thing from my mind was a relationship with a man. He was a kind and considerate gentleman, which appealed to me. He was also exotic, different, spoke another language and did not understand one word of mine but most importantly, he was there and this is how it all happened.

We had been dating, not in the traditional American style with long stem red roses, fancy dinners at the Ritz, trips to Paris, and all that "stuff." We had simply been seeing each other; in my small apartment or taking a ride around the town late at night after hours of talking. One night, about three months after we first met, after a ride to the ocean to see the moon make love to the waves, he drove me home as usual, but as I started to get out of his car and turn to say good night, he was not there. He had come around to my side of the car and, with a slightly odd smile, stood at my front door. I got out slowly and with a questioning look, put the key in my lock expecting him to get back in the car, but he was right on my heels. This was not like him for he usually drove away after a hug in the car. He shut my house door behind us and took me into his impressively strong arms for a most passionate kiss. I did not resist but, when his hands started to move in other directions, I stood back and said with all the strength I could muster (having given up most of it to the kiss), "CAMA!". He moved back and said "Que?" (Portuguese for what) and I said it again, this time with great emphasis, "CAMA"!!!!! I thought that was the word for calm down, get a grip on yourself. A large and somewhat knowing smile came over his face and he repeated what I had said, "Cama?" I smiled, bobbed my head yes and thought "wow, I am really making myself understood even in situations where my head might not be working so swiftly." He then said "aqui?" again I nodded yes. Just to make sure I understood he said agora,

"Now? I nodded yes. He then picked me up in his arms and I found myself being carried up the stairs to the second level towards my sleeping room.

Wait, this is not what I was yelling about, I was trying to tell him to calm down, nothing was going happen. I grabbed at the crumbling cement wall on the staircase and again yelled "CAMA!!" He set me down with a puzzled look on his face. "Deana, (he said in Portuguese) "you told me what you wanted and that is what I am trying to do."

Whoops, there is a problem here. I took a deep breath, for emotions were pounding in my whole body, feelings I had not had for a very long time, and in Portuguese I said, "I asked you to calm down." He lifted his head and laughed. "My dearest Deana, you have mixed up two words. The word for calm is calma, and the word for bed is cama. What you were saying to me was, bed, bed, here and yes, now. I was taking you upstairs to your bedroom. I was being a gentleman and doing what you asked me to do."

When I realized how I had confused the two words, I smiled, looked at him and the two of us laughed so hard, we nearly fell down the stairs. After a moment, he looked at me, put my hand into his and in silence we sat there on my stairs, holding hands. The moon had made its nightly trip around to peep into my wooden shutters and its beams played along our legs. We sat very still, both of us thinking about what had happened. Then he slowly took my other hand and together we climbed the twenty steps to my bedroom in a calm and knowing silence.

MEET, GREET AND DANCE

Now that I had my new home, I had to decorate it. I hung my one animal skin that had been given to me by Abu, the Chief from Guinea Bissau. I bought two wooden stools from the local market. Then I put my wood hoe with the metal piece in my window reminding me of my training in the village of the blacksmith. This new nest would be mine for the next two and half years, not exactly New York City or even Brookline, but it had a charm that made me comfortable.

I was ready to invite guests into my home. Arlene and Frances had been out scouting the young men in town and brought one of them over to meet me. His name was Adam; tall, lithe and very handsome. He was 27, the exact age as my son. He invited us all out to dance, he was excellent and I realized I had a young dancing partner for the duration of my stay. There were two dance clubs in Mindelo: Pimm's and J'Taime. J'Taime was outside of the town, had a dance floor under the stars, the tables were under a thatched roof, just like Guinea Bissau. Pimm's was in our town and it reminded me of a New York City disco; fancy dance floor, a real bar and very expensive. After a while, the bouncer/ticket taker at Pimm's got to know me for the work I was doing in Project PACIM and would say, "Ah, Deana, entra" and I did with no cover charge. Arlene and Frances were constantly networking with the young men and I was always graciously included. A Latvian fishing vessel came into our deep harbor and of course the two of them wangled an invitation for lunch on board. It was most pleasant until the captain took me to his control room where he explained why they were there. A computer was turned on and I looked in fascination as little fishes came into view, then many more came and the captain pushed a button and a gigantic net went down and scooped up all of *our* fish. I was infuriated and told him so and he tried to assuage me with some vodka. His ploy didn't work and I left furious and frustrated. Cape Verdeans used oars in tiny row boats to catch fish. Talk about unfair, and there was nothing I could do about it.

During the weekends, I would take off on long bike rides with Gatorade, sweet cookies, my lucky brown bandana my brother Richard had given me and my Swiss Army knife tucked into my Bissau leather back pack I had bought only months before. An old Portuguese fort was high on a hill near the harbor, goats wandered in and out. The sun dried my sweat and the harbor scene played out for me. Large sailboats, small sailboats, and the ubiquitous wooden row boats of the islanders with their bright yellow, green and blue colors toasted in the sun and bobbed in the water. I would race down the hill and swim in the huge waves. The mountains behind me were like Japanese cut outs or velvet paintings, not a hint of green anywhere. One day I brought my camera with me and asked an older woman to watch my bike and bag. I lied and told her I just had groceries in it. When I got home that night, my camera was gone. A letter was quickly written to my camera buff friend and photographer Kay. She bought me one in the States, got the money from my accountant and it was delivered two weeks before Christmas. My neighbor said she was sorry my camera had been stolen, nao faz mal — "it does not matter" which was said on all occasions for all reasons.

The door to our office opened one bright morning and a pretty woman with a Christmas Eve smile walked over to me, "Hi, I'm Maryann Almeida, my husband Pedro told me you had arrived." From that moment on, Maryann and I were like sisters. When dusk came to City Hall, and our office closed, I would amble over to her hardware store, compare the gossip of the day and began a friendship that would see me through the good and the not so good times in Cape Verde. She was born in Massachusetts, worked at the Boston Herald newspaper and then fell in love with Pedro; handsome, tall and friendly to all. They were a very happy couple and I was lucky to have them in my life.

Maryann and Pedro Almeida

PCVs Amy, Diane, Gary

PCVs Leslie, Melanie, Miles and Diane

My days were spent working, sharing stories with Maryann and being with Paulino. On Fridays I would walk to Ilha d' Madeira and pick up Paulino, bring him back to my apartment. I would scrub the bejesus out of him, the lice, the scabies, the crabs and general dirt disappeared in the small plastic tub I used in my kitchen sink for this ceremony. Singing all the songs I sang to my children during the very same activities back in the States made the missing of my children lessen. We played soap games with bubbles, the first time he had ever seen bubbles and now smiles came frequently. Sunday night was the difficult time; he had to put back on his rags and would carefully hide the new T shirt and shorts my daughter Maura had sent to him in my apartment. He knew that they would be stolen in a flash in his part of town. When I took him back to town, I always heard, "Billie, Billie", I thought how many children can be named Billie. Later found out that "billie" meant come here in Crioulo, lesson #37.

There was always activity in my apartment. Volunteers from the island across our channel came to visit: lovely and sweet teacher Amy (who had indeed returned after her cancer scare in Atlanta), Ross the agriculture worker with a grand laugh and Jim, the quiet and effective small business development worker. They usually stayed at my place and we traded war stories. I told them about the Nazarene minister and his gracious wife Paula Trotman, who told me about the origin of Cape Verde. This is the story. After God made the world, he shook his hands and the mud, the dirt and the rocks that fell off his hands became Cape Verde. Cape Verdeans were special, maybe because of the way God made them. Paulino was certainly special.

Every time I would visit Paulino, he would look weaker and weaker. I would ask Amelia if she took him to the Swedish clinic to get Pablum and powdered milk for him to use the rest of the week. She nodded yes, but I knew she never did. Three days a week I would carry him over the sand hills to the clinic to be weighed, fed and given food for the week. He gained no weight because he had worms and when I would give her the worm medicine, it would disappear. The nurses at the clinic were so kind and so sad when Paulino would stay the same weight for months at a time. Soon there was to be an election and the hope was that the new government would bring money into Cape Verde to help the very large number of desperately poor people. But Thanksgiving was on the calendar, my U.S. calendar, not the Cape Verde calendar, and I would learn that quickly.

HOW NOT TO CELEBRATE A HOLIDAY IN AFRICA:
THANKSGIVING

Thanksgiving was coming on Thursday. I had never met real American missionaries, these folks were honest to goodness ones serving and living in Africa. They were both big people, Cape Verdeans are not tall so Paula and Philip Trotman towered over their congregation, by height, not attitude. I had been biking and decided to take them up on their invitation given at the post office to visit. One Sunday afternoon I knocked on their sturdy wooden door. Paula opened the door, took one look at my sweat stained clothes and face and ushered me into their cool living room, giving me a glass of iced tea. We chatted, they were warm, pleasant and their two sons were delights. I had forgotten, in three short months, how American children played, very different from Cape Verdean children with books, chess pieces, and scrabble sets. Cape Verdean children played with rocks and old pieces of card board. The Trotman's asked me what I had planned for the Thanksgiving holiday and when I confessed to no plans, they invited me for dinner and said their parents had sent them cranberry sauce. Paula said she would stuff a chicken, serve biscuits. I was salivating. Then I remembered my two attachments, Arlene and Frances so I asked if they could be included; yes was the quick response. I told Arlene and Frances,- they were thrilled.

On the Monday morning before Thanksgiving Thursday, Senhor Evora came in to our office and told us we would be leaving for the island across from us, Santa Antao, on Wednesday to work on Thursday, Friday and return on Saturday. My face flushed. He said "Deana, problem?" "No" said I. I told my two friends, they went to the Trotmans and I went to the ferry boat. Wednesday morning we trooped down to the dock, where the ferry was being piled high with produce, live animals and anything the other island, Santa Antao, needed. The ferry chugged over a calm sea, passage perfect to Porto Novo, that being the first port. This town had trees and moisture and my dry skin could feel it. We had lunch at a nice restaurant: rice and fresh fish, and Ceris beer. Rice was now my staple and I vowed I would never eat it upon return to the U.S. A deserted cement factory was seen, we learned that the tin shack people would not use that cement; they wanted the best from Portugal. We stopped by a community, well, kind of a community. Caves clustered together ringing the bottom of a light brown mountain. We spread out in all different directions. I was pulled in one direction by seeing a slight woman with five little children moving their possessions from one cave to another. Fearful eyes met my eyes when I walked over to them. I did not put out my hand, that gesture seemed too aggressive, but rather went into a crouch position and used my halting Portuguese to offer my help. The mother, sand sticking to her sweat soaked ragged dress, did not respond. Her headscarf moved ever so slightly in the unremitting wind racing over the terrain, her sweat had made the scarf heavy.

While I waited, the children began to come near me. One of the older children was dragging sacks from one cave to another, so I lifted one and went into the cave with the child. Inside the walls were ivory colored. No person had left marks inside it as yet. The mother pointed to the left hand corner, so I put the sack there. We all went back to the old cave; and then I knew why they were changing caves. The old cave was filled with smoke smells from cooking fires and a stench reeking from another corner. We dragged more sacks to the new cave until it was piled with possessions.

The mother looked at me, hesitantly and picked up a spoon. The light was beginning to fade and she knew what she had to do and perhaps she sensed this tall white woman did not have any idea of what the next move should be. She walked to the back of the shallow cave and started to carve out the soft sandstone to make the cave deeper. Clan of the Cave Bear came to my mind, thank you Jean M. Auel. I grabbed another spoon and hunkered down next to her, carving out the sandstone so she and her children would be protected from the elements. I thought of my hoe from Guinea Bissau and how useful that would have been. It was in my home so this spoon would have to do. My spoon was bent and had seen a lot of carving; it was weak but did the job. Thank God the stone was soft and frail and fell as soon as the spoons hit it. The younger children, 2 and 3 at the most, were huddled in a corner, watching with huge brown eyes. The older ones were racing and laughing outside.

My arms were aching when after an hour or so, she smiled at me, and put her spoon down. Dusk was beginning to creep up the land and she had accomplished what she needed to do. She touched my hand. Not one word had been spoken since we began digging and her touch said thank you. I smiled, did sign language telling her that I had four children and understood motherhood. The three outside children now were inside children as dark made them come into their new home. Voices were yelling "Deanna" which made me get up and answer. I nodded to the mother, touched her arm, felt the dried sweat and ached for her and her children. She nodded in return, small smile and I left. That is how I spent my first Thanksgiving in Cape Verde. It had been perfect.

That night we took a wild and chilling ride to the north side of the island. The roads wound round and round, the night enclosed all on the road. We arrived in Riberia Grand and met Amy and Gary. We were invited to the rooftop of Amy's new friends, the married couple Alexandra and Joaquim. She was American, worked for an NGO; Joaquim was Cape Verdean and worked for the Minister of Agriculture. There was a huge banana tree in the courtyard and stars formed a roof among all of the rooms of Amy's house. She took the sofa and honored me by giving me her bed where sleep came swiftly. The boat trip back to our island of Sao Vicente was rough and many people were sick, but not me.

In Mindelo water was precious. Poor people had to buy it from water sellers in the two villages. The rest of us paid to have it delivered one day a week to reservoirs that were on the top of our roofs. As a frugal Scot, I would bathe in the ocean and rub off the salt. My hair no longer got daily washings, but only when it was too stiff to comb. The Cape Verdeans had learned to live with this scarcity of water. I was constantly impressed by their tolerance of what life had dealt them; their courage was outrageous.

The political election activity was heating up and I decided to hear the candidates from the political party MPD. Aristides Pereira, the President of Cape Verde, had fought with the great Amailcal Cabral and had been elected, in the first free election in 1975. He was the 12th son of a Catholic priest. I knew as PCVs we were not allowed to participate in any political activity, but I decided to sneak to a speech. In my black tee shirt, black slacks, hat over my sun bleached hair I snuck into a dark corner of the huge plaza where all the speeches were being made. The next week's paper showed that my hiding did not work. There was my picture, on the front page saying I was attending a political rally. When a messenger told me I had a phone call from the Mayor's office, I knew what was coming. Our PC

Director chewed me out, asking what kind of example was I setting by disregarding the PC rule.

After that excitement, the usual events continued. Frances came to my home, to visit, then Arlene. I thought I had left my four children at home, but it seemed as though I got two new ones. I watched my favorite new animal, a pink lizard. He had been rooming with me for about a week and I loved to watch his dance. Frances spied him and put him up to her ears saying she used to wear them as earrings in Puerto Rico. The next day, his withered body lay in a corner, perhaps he died of fright at being an earring. The other animals in the house were flies; they were everywhere so when I got a cut, I put a band aid right over it. Cuts took forever to heal and my Swiss Army knife was getting dull so I cut myself a lot. My health was good, stomach cramps from time to time for no apparent reason; after a time, I ignored them.

Work continued at City Hall. We had one computer (no email) and so we all took turns using the only one there. I had to input all the names of the various families I was working with for relocation, which was hard to do, but after a while, with the help of the Swedes, I got the rhythm. Peace Corps does give assistance to any volunteer, but the volunteers have to know what kind of questions to ask. When visiting staff PC administrators would visit, I would always have a list at the ready to ask for their assistance. If they did not have the answer, they had resources to turn to, and always got the help I needed.

One of the interesting aspects of not having a phone was that people came over any time. One dark December night a knock on the door announced Hugo from Guinea Bissau who was one of our trainers. I invited him in as he had been so kind and sympathetic to me during my horrid language training and he listened carefully now. After I talked in Portuguese for about 10 minutes, he told me in Portuguese that I was speaking much better. "Let us meet tonight and I will buy you a drink." This time I did bite the bullet and took a real shower with my bucket that meant 10 minutes of throwing water all around.

Walking in alone, I felt awkward and could not see for the darkness. Then a hand wrapped around my waist, and Hugo smiled at me. The Piano Bar was tiny, but the spirit made it huge. A young man got up and sang. Hugo brought the singer over to our table to meet me and Manocos Matoes walked into my life. He would become a close friend, never a beau, and a magnificent dance partner. When Manocos asked if I danced, I nodded yes and off to Pimm's we three went. As we danced, Manocos whispered into my ear. "You move very well, Deana, I have wanted to dance with you ever since I saw you arrive months ago." Then I realized he was speaking in English. What a welcome sound. I hugged him like a sister and said thank you.

The parties of the evenings were forgotten in the harsh reality of the day and the physical work that had to be done as part of my job. Swedish Jonathan invited me to my first "covering". That's what it is called when the residents of tin shacks put a roof on their new cement homes. He picked me up at 8 AM. I wondered why so early, but soon found out. All the men had gathered around a pile of small rocks, a pile of sand, and bags of cement imported from Portugal. The responsibility of the women was to provide food and drink and to serve until the mission was accomplished. The covering really had started at 7 AM, but Jonathan though he would ease me into this, thus the 8 am pick up. All the workers wished to avoid the blistering sun - they knew their land. The women were the ones who carried the metal buckets full of wet cement on their heads to the front of the house. There was a platform constructed the night before, and the most handsome young man was standing on it six feet in the air. The women with buckets stood in front of him; he bent down and lifted the bucket over his head to the waiting men on the roof, and they spread the wet cement on the rooftop.

When I said I would like to help, the old man looked at me and filled my bucket half full. I told him I was as strong as any other woman. He shrugged, and filled the bucket to the brim. One woman came over to me, said "wait", took a wet towel, and coiled it and put it on top of my head. Thanking her, I crouched as the man put the bucket on my head. It was the heaviest bucket I had ever felt, and my knees almost buckled. The woman yelled "Deana PACIM" as I wobbled over towards the new house. The young man looked surprised as I stood there praying to God for him to take the heavy load off my pounding head. He bent down, grabbed it effortlessly, and lifted it over his head without breaking a sweat. Then I was handed a tin cup. I did not even pause, but slugged it down. Then gagged and coughed as I realized that it was the alcohol grog which went immediately to my head. I went back to the cement mixing pile with a little wiggle to my walk and a smile on my face.

It went like this: another bucket, another line, another sip of grog, another spin. It was a Congo line and I was in it having a grand time. The grog helped me skim along, the music they played on a boom box made us all move with the rhythm of the beat. Hours went by and then a piece of the owner's clothing, usually a scarf, was hoisted on top of the now completed roof. We all cheered, hugged each other, of course had a congratulatory last sip of grog and I walked off into the noon day sun hoping my door would miraculously appear. Valentina, my next door neighbor, smiled and said "couberta hoja, Deana?" "Si", I smiled weakly and spent the rest of the day in bed, only getting up to make a cup of tea at dusk, and then went back to bed.

When I awoke the next morning, I had a very strange pain. It was as though my neck and collar bone had been fused and my teeth and jaw ached. Jonathan came by to check on me and asked how I was doing. When I told him he said that everyone was impressed that I had stayed till the end. During the next two years, when invited to a covering, I made sure my cement bucket was not full to the top.

One night the Cape Verdean Adam took me to a new dance club, Katem, which means "I have". The young owner, Jean Pierre, was a different kind of Cape Verdean than I had met in the tin shack towns. He did not smoke or drink alcohol, had one wife, educated his children, and ran a good business. He made a tape for me of traditional Cape Verdean music and through him I discovered Cesaria Evora. Born in Mindelo, she was a bigger than life lady who sang like a dream. There are two kinds of Cape Verdean music: the sad, melancholy "Morna" a lament of the nostalgic, slow song form expressing love and longing and the "coladaras," the fast dance music. Cesaria Evora is a master of both and I played her music on the boom box Ellen & Hank gave me on my first floor and on the boom box Winthrop gave me on my second floor (no speakers here). Music surrounded me and I fell in love with her sound. When I complained to Vitorino that my batteries did not last very long, he taught me how to make batteries for my boom boxes and flashlights last longer - put them in a frying pan, over a low heat on my Bunsen burner and heat them up, careful not to have them get too hot and fly through the air.

My next challenge: teaching English. Arlene got sick and I was chosen to take over teaching her English as a second language class. Thursday was her busiest day. Her first class started at 7:30 AM and the last class started at 6 PM. The students were from the middle class of Mindelo, none of the children from the tin shack towns would ever have made it here. Most of Arlene's students seemed not to want to learn. I was polite and slightly hesitant about how tough to be during the first class. When we were in training, Cape Verdeans taught us about their culture which was rich and full and very different from the American culture. I had to be careful and not over step the boundaries.

When the class ended, I went to the teacher's lounge, had coffee and thought about my teaching days at Humphey Center Madison Park High School in the inner city of Boston. Then it hit me, these students are just like those students, you have to get tough and push them to learn. The 9:30 class got the message. Anyone that talked out of turn was made to stand at the front of the class. Pretty soon, I had more students in the front of the class than in the back of the class. I could not put them in the hall, they would have run away. I came down hard on them and tolerated no bad behavior.

I was exhausted by the time the 10:30 class began, but something was different with this group. The word must have gotten out, this woman is tough. I noticed their posture was poor, always a pet peeve of mine, so I had them stand, move around, and recite. When the class ended, I limped home, exhausted, made my standard rice dish, took my standard two hour nap, and went back to my office to work till 4:30 when I returned to the school for the two remaining classes.

Clearly word had really gotten around. After all I was the only white woman there and I was different. Arlene was young, pretty, would ask for discipline but was not the Marine drill sergeant I was becoming. This class listened, we laughed, and maybe I got a little more relaxed. The 6pm class was even better, and though some of them had invented reasons to leave early, not one of them did. I went over to Arlene's sick bed and regaled her with the stories and told her I would teach any day but Thursday.

Diane teaching business English to employees of Shell Oil - gratas

My American calendar told me it was Pearl Harbor Day, December 7, Peace Corps sent all volunteers a copy of Newsweek, only by the time it arrived, it was stale news, so we called it News - month. My dear friend Nedda Casei from New York City had given me a present of the New York Times Sunday edition. I literally raced home with it from the post office and took a full seven days to digest every single page. I bought inexpensive gifts for my children and a few close friends, boxed them up and sent them to Maura/Bill in Boston to distribute to the east coast and to Katherine/Claire to distribute to the west coast. I was starting to get pangs about the upcoming holidays but the increasing work load gave me little free time to mull and feel sorry for myself. The pressure was on to relocate the tin shack families in a timely manner. The Minister of Finance was squeezing me about asking for more funds for my daily work so I had to be careful of my budget.

My little ivy plant started to sprout a few new leaves. I was thrilled and so grateful, and vowed I would never take a living green plant for granted again. One weekend, I was biking around and noticed that the road to the airport had aloe plants on the side of the road. I didn't recognize them at first because they were brown because ... no rain. One night I took my handy bike, rigged up a basket of sorts on the handles and peddled the three miles out. Not many cars in sight, no night planes ever came in. I dug up four plants, felt like a scavenger and thief and peddled furiously back to my apartment. Ulla had told me where to buy pots, so I saved up and bought four for my front entrance, inside my wooden door. After much watering, they miraculously turned to green. My Cape Verdean friends exclaimed how pretty they were and wondered where in the world they came from. They said it was not possible they were the same plants from the airport road. When I got a sun burn (frequently) I would break off one leaf and put the soothing goo on my burnt skin.

Swedish Jonathan continued with his tutorials. He gave me Saint Augustine's quote; "give me humility, poverty and celibacy, but the latter not quite yet." Saint Augustine is a North African saint. Jonathan also told me that Portuguese was the most pure of all the Latin languages and was the closest to Latin. Maybe that was why the language was beginning to kick in, all those damn Latin classes from high school. He was a font of information and I wrote down all of his teachings to re-read them at night. I got used to the pleasantness of the candles, their kind and gentle light and the shadows they cast on the one animal skin on my wall from Guinea Bissau. But there were always situations that came along that needed attention.

One morning I awoke with a tooth ache. I called the Peace Corps office from the City Hall and they gave me the name of a dentist in Mindelo. Dr. Anabel had been trained in Portugal and spoke English. "You have a lot of money in your mouth, those teeth will last you till you are 100, and I can tell you will live until you are 100." "Massage your gums three times a day, take some grog before you go to bed and you will feel fine." I left his office where he did a dozen extractions every day. Cape Verdeans had no money for false teeth. My God, he was right, that tooth never bothered me again.

HOW NOT TO CELEBRATE A HOLIDAY IN AFRICA:
CHRISTMAS

Christmas presents started to arrive. Joanie sent me a teeny, fake Christmas tree which I immediately put on top of one of my two stools, with the Scottish runner Kay sent me under it. Figured I had best buy one more stool for the upcoming holidays so saved money from my $200 a month salary and purchased one. Pauline sent me Richard Burton's "A Christmas Story" and I read it over and over. Maura sent me tapes from her friend Iggy. Mylo and Miles sent me two small brandy glasses and some cognac, Dr. Bach Rescue Salve Remedy. Katherine sent me Safari perfume.

Christmas was now ten days away when Yvonne invited me to her church Christmas pageant. The choir was in perfect tune, all costumes that had been handmade were perfect, and we all felt good as we walked home after the show. The next day I was very blue and could not for the life of me figure out why. Went to my friend Pedro when I could not find his wife Maryann and asked him where she was. I did not look at him because I knew I would fill up with tears. Still, I did not get why I was so sad but Pedro knew. He invited me for lunch at noon but I told him we did not get out of work till 12:30. He said come at noon and I could have a gin and tonic with Maryann. I explained that I didn't drink during the day, went back to the office, but ended up on his door step at noon. Maryann made me the very best gin and tonic and I began to cry. They comforted me and explained I was sad because I missed my family and this was the first Christmas I was not with my children. I told them last Christmas I was swimming with my brother Richard in Los Angeles and eating Christmas dinner at the home of my brother Terry and his wife Kathi in Thousand Oaks, California, with all four of my children, Peg my step mom and Robbie my step dad. After the gin and tonic and their kindness, I went home feeling much better.

At home, there was a small package from my neighbor, Adelia, who lived on the same road. In it was a lovely pearl necklace. I was touched by her remembering. Then the kind missionaries invited Arlene, Frances and me to a dinner and gave us presents, wrapped in Christmas paper. They played a video, "Christmas Carol" with George C. Scott, there was not a dry eye in the house.

On the day before Christmas, visiting volunteers Amy, Gary and Ross came by. Maryann and Pedro invited us for Christmas dinner, we all accepted in a flash. Her table was set with linen and china and crystal and it was sheer heaven. At this dinner I met Suzanne, a very pregnant American and her Cape Verdean husband and knew we would become great friends. They played the famous and much loved tune, Glenn Miller's "In the Mood" and we all danced happily. I had made eggnog for them and when we finished that holiday dinner, we PCVs went back to my home and finished all of my delicious extra eggnog. The Cape Verdean young man I had met a while ago, Adam, and I had gone food shopping during the week for all the various ingredients for chakupa, the traditional Cape Verdean dish. Adam did absolutely all of the cooking, I watched him fascinated and learned a great deal. Frances gave me a large blue and white water-color poster with lovely calligraphy, saying "The hand that rocks the cradle is the hand that rules the world," (William Ross Wallace.) Arlene gave me two ceramic candle holders; Adam gave me a lovely fan. Our PC Christmas dinner had seven guests; Arlene blew some of the soap bubbles I had received as a gift, Adam played his guitar, Amy laughed, then we all cooked, swam, ate, and toasted each other with "Feliz Natal."

Peace Corps is very demanding about job reports and the administrators check on the volunteers on a regular basis. I did not want to leave Mindelo but we were commanded to go to Praia for language classes and to submit our job reports. After we landed in the capital town of Praia on the island of Santiago and checked into the same dreadful hotel, we met all the other volunteers from the other islands, twelve in all. We learned a new expression, "Prospero Ano Novo," Happy New Year. Classes during the day were dreadful, but dinner at the home of the Ambassador and his gracious wife, was terrific. She served an eight course dinner: turkey, potatoes, vegetables, freshly baked delicious bread and not a glimpse of the dreaded rice. We met their two young sons home from boarding school in England: quiet, reserved and proper.

The next day, was filled with classes and then soul searching among the volunteers, about our success, frustration, stone walls. I heard about a health conference in Mali, West Africa. Rebecca and I volunteered to attend. We would have to pay our own way and use our vacation time: John (Director) was a stickler for playing everything by the book. I visited a new friend, Bernice Powell, Counsel at the Embassy, in her elegant home. She was tall, red haired and wired for fun, and had her mother visiting for the holidays. I watched in envy when they talked together. My Mom died in 1952, how was it possible I still missed her. The next day we were treated to a sail in the Ambassador's boat all along the coast and I remembered my sails in Annapolis with Bill and our children. Flying fish accompanied us and we swam off the boat watching porpoises flying.

December 31st dawned and I became one year older. When I was a little girl, my New York City parents always went out on New Year's Eve, in tux and long gown with boa. They said when I got older they would give me a party but it never happened. College days - no New Year's Eve party for me, married, no party, so when I turned 50 in Boston I threw a large bash, my very first birthday party. This year Peggy, secretary to the ambassador, invited me to a lovely and elegant dinner, much different from Mindelo style entertaining. Then Dale and John from the Embassy invited me to their home and I trotted over to have a grand Scotch, my first in six months. The volunteers were having a party too so I walked by myself with the full moon lighting my way to Jill's home - there was a surprise birthday party for me – the first ever given for me. Amy and I talked about where we had been for last New Year's Eve and where would we be for the next one.

"DIE KNOWING SOMETHING, YOU ARE NOT HERE LONG."

Walker Evans

Anyone who thinks being in the Peace Corps is a slice of Club Med with a little action among the locals can guess again. When I was handed my job description exactly one year prior, I thought to myself, me, a platoon of Marines, and ten years could maybe do this job. It seemed so overwhelming, so exhausting, so demanding of skills I was not sure I could offer. At the end of my first year, a three month work plan for my Peace Corps Director was due soon. The cement houses, the sewing association, perhaps a children's library, AIDS lectures to teenagers and their parents, and teaching English as a second language. When friends from home wrote to say how noble I was, a smile slid across my face as I thought of the kind women water sellers who were my bosom friends, the children who would hug me when I entered their tin shacks, and the dancers who would spin me until I lost my breath. No, I was not noble; the Cape Verdeans who lived in Mindelo were the noble ones.

One of my projects that really did heat up was the English classes. I loved teaching and I certainly loved having no one telling me what and how to teach. The night before the class, I would copy poems, scenes from plays written to be acted and stories from the New York Times. The class would struggle to read the words in English. I knew I was getting through to the students when they stayed after class asking more and more questions until my head danced with their eagerness. They were bright, fun loving and despite the fact that we had all put in a grueling day of work, in a temperature that knew no air conditioning relief, we enjoyed the learning. Quotes in English that made jokes were fun to use, like Peter Mayle "God, they say, was embarrassed after he created France, it was too beautiful. So he created the French people to even it up." After I explained the thinking behind that quote, I had them write quotes about their country in

Portuguese and then translate into English. We all learned from each other.

My new friends Maryann and Pedro were also my constant teachers. One night they invited me out to a dance at the Club Nautico, an old fashioned members only men's sailing club. Later, when they began to walk me home, I realized I did not have the key to my apartment. It must have dropped out of my pocket during the dancing. They offered me their guest room, which I gladly accepted. It was cozy and warm and I never imagined I would be tucked into this very same room many years later on a very different mission. Generosity was another gift I learned about from Maryann and Pedro and the people of Mindelo.

The next morning, soft, white curtains were making a slight rustling sound and the sounds of people going to work awakened me and I realized this was the first time I had slept in another bed in Mindelo for all the time I had lived there. Maryann said there was someone at her door for me. A stranger asked me if I was Deana PACIM, I nodded, and he put my house keys in my hand. "I found them on the dance floor when I was cleaning up this morning. I saw you dance last night, you are very good." He bowed, and left before I had a chance to thank him or ask his name, yet another kindness from a Mindelense.

The time came to write a proposal for a sewing association. The PC office on the island of Santiago called my office and told me to fly there ASAP: a grant might be available but I had to work on it from their office. When I ran to the airline office, no seats were available, but as I turned to leave, I saw my friend who lived on the same road as I did and worked for the airline. She gave me a nod towards the plane, nodded in the direction of my home and then another nod to the plane. No word were spoken, just the canny look of a woman who knew how to solve a problem.

I ran home, grabbed the overnight bag, which was always at the ready, toothpaste, brush, underwear, a rolled up skirt and blouse and my ever present Portuguese dictionary. I had been given three; one was always in my office, one always in my home and one always in my travel bag. I went to the road and stood for only about five minutes before I got a ride from the first truck that passed. By now people knew that I was working for the poor of the tin shack towns and everyone had empathy for my work. One plane was revving up, the propellers were starting to turn, and I was told "no room." There was another plane, one I had not seen before and I was told it was a cargo plane going to Santiago. I walked over to the pilot and explained my problem: the possibility of money in Santiago for a sewing association and that I was with the Peace Corps and needed his help. He replied in perfect English "jump in, Deana PACIM, but do not tell anyone." He opened the cargo door, gave me a hand up, closed the door and we were off. There were huge boxes, furniture, all sorts of bags jammed into the storage area. Then, of all things, a rocking chair was there. I jumped into it and did not move. The belly of the plane was totally dark. One of the more spooky rides I had ever taken.

When we landed one hour later and the baggage handler opened the cargo door, he was surprised to see me. I said "Bon dia" we shook hands and off I went to the PC office. When I arrived at the office, the Director frowned and said he had been told there were no more seats. How in the world did I get to Praia? I told him I had used my creativity to get another kind of seat. I never told the truth because I didn't want the pilot to get into trouble. After working on my proposal at the office, I went to Bernice's home and got caught up with the latest gossip. When we went for a swim the next day she gave me protective salve for my hair but we looked at each other and laughed, saying at the same time - "it's too late, our hair is fried!!" From the beach we watched the dusk of Africa sneak up in front of us engulfing the bright and bringing in the dim.

PCV Arlene was going to be 23, and I had volunteered (getting to be a bad habit) my roof for the party. This time I knew the ropes, got the musicians lined up first, got the huge metal barrels to store the cold beer in and then put the word out. No invitations to be purchased, written or posted, but word of mouth was the method. It was not the message of the drums used in villages of Africa that I had heard in training. This was the message of the conversation being passed around. Arlene was radiant and so thrilled when many of her students came to pay their respects along with their parents.

We started dancing early and continued throughout the entire evening until "madrugada" (dawn in Portuguese). Arlene had dated a few gentlemen and of course every single one came by to claim her "friendship". The challenge for that party was to keep all of her gentlemen on their best behavior. My next door neighbor Valentina came over and she and I danced. I knew how to dance with a woman since my dance with the head cook in Guinea Bissau. Valentina was a good dancer and we wheeled and reeled round the roof like two young girls, she leading strongly and I following. Vitorino came too and even though Arlene used to tease me saying that Vitorino was just being polite and saying he understood me, pictures I later saw told me he understood everything I said. When we danced together for the first time in public, I was nervous, but he put his arm around my waist, held my right hand, and I forgot my worries.

I thought about a story I read about Lady Isabel Burton, wife of the famous Sir Richard Burton, as Vitorino gently guided me around the roof. When Isabel first met Richard at a dance, he took her waist into his arms and she felt light headed, exactly how I was feeling then. Later Isabel took the glove and waistband that he had touched and pressed and saved both, never to be worn again. The blouse I wore that night, a light, off white cotton blouse, went into the closet and was never worn again. Vitorino asked me what I was thinking as I smiled to myself so I told him I was thinking how I would always remember that night when we were apart in the future. He whispered into my ear, "You may not always live in my country, but we will never be apart." Even though I was happy that night, a small part of me felt a twinge of sadness at the thought of having to leave a man who was so gentle, so empathetic and so loving.

Arlene finally came to us and saying it was time for the cake and the spell was broken. But our eyes kept finding each other and secret silences were shared for the rest of that night. Madragada came and all the musicians serenaded us from the road. As I climbed up my cement stairs, fading moonlight peeped into my shutters telling me a magical night was over.

The next party was given for Ulla and her husband Janna. It seemed such a short time ago when we three had first met and now they were leaving. Ulla's replacement had arrived and the changing of the guard was about to begin. The wonderful singer Cesaria who was becoming my good friend came with the Swedish engineer Rolf and honored our party with some of her fine songs. She was called the "cantar sem sapatos" - the singer without shoes. She explained that she did not wear shoes because she always wanted to feel her roots beneath her feet - thus no shoes ever. After hearing her sing, I saved up and bought a tape of hers. Now I totally understood the devotion that Cape Verdeans had for their music and she, the Queen of their music.

When the farewell party was in full swing on my spacious roof, it was time to give one gift and for Jonathan to give the farewell speech. Ulla was the personification of everything that was good about people working in development work and the love that everyone felt for her was evident that night. Ulla set a high standard not many would reach.

The day after Ulla and Janna's party, the dreaded truck came to drive us all to the airport. When Ulla and I hugged each other, I realized my throat had closed and I could not say one word. She had the same reaction. A part of me was going with her. She would be so very, very missed.

GETTING THE HANG OF IT ALL

One day we were told there would be a staff meeting the next morning. I walked into the meeting room noting the chief, Senhor Evora, was not there. The Swedes were in place (promptness was one of their attributes); the Cape Verdeans came in a little late and no one moved, no one talked. Then the great man, Senhor Evora strode in; he never just entered, he strode in. We all nodded with respect for he was, after all, and lest anyone ever forget it, the chief.

I had done some homework, grabbed a PACIM booklet and learned the history. The housing project had been started by the Swedes five years before and was under the umbrella of the Ministry of Housing and Urban Planning. Our mission was to eliminate all of the tin shacks constructed illegally by poor people who had nowhere else to go, in two areas of town. One was right up the road from my house, called Campinho and the other was Ilha de Madeira, way outside of town. Our job was to assist the people to make the necessary income to buy cement to build houses. Then we were to destroy every single tin shack. I had asked Jonathan one day at the Cafe Royal, our daily gossip mill, where they kept the bulldozers to raze the tin shack houses. He laughed and said one day a young boy was riding his bicycle through one of the uneven lanes in the tin shack town and as he was about to make a sharp turn, missed and ploughed right into a tin shack. Boom, the entire shack went down like so many match sticks - the old woman resident was hauled out and looking stunned but unhurt. She held her cup of grog up and said, "I did not spill much": so much for bulldozers.

My role was to help the villagers make money to buy the cement for the project. To get myself knowledgeable about Cape Verde, I read Basil Davidson's most scholarly book, Fortunate Isles. Portuguese explorers had discovered the small group of nine islands huddled in the Atlantic Ocean,

382 miles off the coast of Senegal, West Africa in 1460. There were magnificent green mountains and lush vegetation thus the name - green cape - Cape Verde. Pure water wells, balmy and pleasant weather with no humidity and deep harbors were ideal for settling. The Portuguese sent settlers and they adapted. Then the slaving trade brought ships, full to the brim with slaves, to take on water and fresh fruits and vegetables. The stronger and more courageous slaves jumped ship and ran for the mountains. Since there were so many slaves on board, the ships' captains did not go after them. So a mixed race came about: Portuguese features mixed with the strongest Africans and a magnificent and most lovely race emerged. The Portuguese began to take the tall and strong trees off of the islands to build their sailing ships, but reforestation was not in vogue then so nothing was replaced. An inadequate education system was put into place and the Cape Verdeans learned not to do anything unless Lisbon said they could, an example of colonialism at its worst. Once when President Salazar of Portugal was questioned about his colonies, he said: "I don't have any colonies, there are just outside territories."

Then during the early 1920's and 1930's, the English came to Cape Verde to build coaling stations for their freighters. Once again, another strain came in and mixed with the already mixed races and blonds and brunettes and blue and green eyed children were born on all of the islands. When the poor people had nowhere to go in the 70's, they came to the island of Sao Vicente, and since they had no money, they went out of town, stole tin drums from the ships in the harbors and made shacks out of them. This diverse history made Cape Verdeans both strong and vulnerable at the same time.

The housing meeting droned on and I began a habit that would stay with me during the next two years. When the language got too difficult to understand, I just tuned out and began to daydream. It saved my sanity. I looked at Senhor Evora. He was a small man, had the eyes of a weasel, never looked directly into your eyes and was always shifting - papers, his feet, his hands, his agenda. He was Cape Verdean born, had been a member of the ruling party PAICV that took over when Cape Verde got their independence in 1975, and had risen in the ranks, not because of talent but because he was devious, dishonest and knew where the power was and how to make sure he stayed on top. Evora was not one I wanted to teach me, but one did not always get the outstanding leaders one wanted either. During the two years I worked at PACIM, I saw him build an extraordinary home on the hill facing the harbor. It was ugly; he was a lousy architect. It jutted out in all directions, had no subtle gentle lines, faced the harbor but had no windows on the harbor side to watch the sunsets. The house was typical of a man with no sense of beauty or imagination. He only took; he did not give back to the land of his birth. On the weekends and sometimes even on the weekdays as well, he used PACIM trucks and laborers - never asking permission from anyone. His brother was a lawyer and held high office, in a high place, a sister was in the National Assembly; he had no worries.

At this meeting Senhor Evora asked me to do a report, a survey and analysis. It was very difficult to obtain the information because the people in the tin shack towns kept moving around, to detect discovery, to flee from the law, to get around the rules any way they could. My job was to hunt all of them down, write up my findings and submit it to Senhor Evora. If Jonathan had not helped me considerably, I never would have completed it. It took months of analyzing, documenting and living with my Portuguese dictionary. When I went out to check on the number in a family it would have changed because homeless Aunt Joanna would have come from another island and had plunked down in her niece's shack. Or men came and went but the women stayed and took care of the children of the men who had come in the night.

When I submitted the report to him, he said "I want more, go and dig more." Months of my hard work and sweat produced a fine 79 page paper. About six months later he went to an important conference in Geneva taking my report. I was told later he put his own name on the report where my name had been and never gave me a note of reference as though he had produced the report himself. A week later he returned and asked me if I had an extra copy of my report. I said it was not in my office and that was the truth. I had taken my copy to my home. The next day all of my papers were disturbed in and on my desk at the office, as though someone had been looking for something. He was wild and I was smug. I discovered the reason he wanted my extra copy was that his very elegant brief case had been stolen in Geneva with my report in it.

A GHANAIAN SAYING:
IF YOU WANT TO CLIMB A TREE, YOU HAD BETTER START AT THE
BOTTOM

The first day of the New Year 1991 dawned clear, on the island of Santiago. It was bright and very, very warm. Last year I had run a five-mile race in Los Altos, California visiting my friends Pauline and John. This year, PCV Amy and I took a bus to the interior. Huge mountains jutted up at all sorts of odd places - shades of Atlantis - once again. Of course the bus ran out of gas so we coasted downhill until we cruised into a gas station - a pump by the side of the road where the bus driver knew the brother of the owner - that is the way things work in Africa.

We visited PCV Melanie who lived in Terrafel, a small town snuggled next to the ocean and lo and behold, a chocolate birthday cake was waiting for me. I was touched by her thoughtfulness. We swam from her magnificent beach and enjoyed ourselves thoroughly. Then back to the bus and the city to continue the hated language class. I did learn two types of past tenses, and hoped I would retain them.

There were benefits to being in the capital city. Shelia, who worked at the Embassy, invited me over to her home for dinner. Her home was a total surprise - a Victorian in the middle of West Africa with high ceilings, wood paneling and huge rooms, very different from the other homes. She explained that her parents had built this home at the turn of the century before the devastating droughts, when there had been money for building such beautiful homes. We had a tasty dinner with traditional Cape Verdean food of chacupka, a mixture of rice, fish or chicken, peas and lots of spices. I told her that day, January 5th, was my son Bill's birthday and I was feeling slightly melancholy so we toasted Bill and her son and all of our children. Images of my children came into my head, made me sad.

Flying back to Mindelo made me realize how much I had missed it. Meeting and getting to know the merchants in town was great fun. A sweet lady who owned the bakery across from the Catholic Church would sometimes slip me a free roll when I bought a loaf of her fresh baked bread. My shoe repair man had a gleaming smile and I thought always undercharged me. The film lady took special care of my film and the grocery lady and I compared irregular verbs and laughed at my miserable pronunciations. One night I came home late from work and saw the shoe repair man closing up his shop and realized then that the reason he never stood when I entered his tiny shop was that he had only one leg. He smiled and I walked home thinking how a one legged man would be working in an occupation that made two shoes for everyone except him.

The country was about to have its first two party election and political activity was heating up. Not a night went by that one or the other of the two parties drove a car by with a bellowing bull horn. The two parties were PAICV, the party in power now for the last 15 years, and MPD, a new party, full of hope and promises. Local vendors would set up stands in the streets to sell Stempra, the local drink, in anticipation of the crowds that would gather around to hear the results. We went out to the streets just to watch the celebrations. Around midnight MPD was declared the winner and all hell broke loose. It seemed to be the party of the young people, for they were the only ones doing the celebrating. In contrast to the news about this election, my radio told me that there was a gathering storm about Iraq invading Kuwait. Listening to the U.S. and France debating who should send in troops, it seemed, once again, that the U.S. was going to be the saber rattler, the world's policeman. Wednesday, January 16th, war was declared and Saddam, the monster, said "this is the mother of all battles." My short wave radio stayed on and people from the street who didn't have a radio came into my little apartment to hear news stories which we learned were being censored.

Despite the rumblings of war, packages from home continued to arrive. Son Bill sent a Japanese lantern which immediately went up in my room to hide the naked bulb that never had electricity. I received Wet Ones, a godsend in this waterless world, a Nutcracker tape and six thin bracelets, lovely and pleasing since I had not worn jewelry for so long. Julie, my friend and fashion editor from the Boston Globe who most likely did not want me to disgrace myself (fashionably that is) sent a lovely purple silk scarf and a cream colored Russian shawl with bright flowers. I put the shawl on while listening to the war news - strange juxtaposition. Jack, from Duxbury, faithful to his word, sent his monthly package of sponges and kitchen equipment. I shared the goodies with friends who shared their care packages with me. Antonia, tall and elegant with a wide smile, brought her two daughters with her to hear the war news. The girls, both in junior high, had become like my daughters. Sandra and Sonya bought gifts for New Year's, an egg and a loaf of bread; I gave them each a t- shirt, a scarf and a book in English. Antonia adored Elvis so I wrote home and two months later presented her with the prize of prizes, her own Elvis poster.

As a social person, I decided to have a high tea for my new friends in Mindelo who had been kind to me. I invited Jonathan who advised me not to invite the different groups: many of the women who lived in the tin shacks, women who lived on our road and Ministers. He said they would not mix. I think it was the only time I found Jonathan to be wrong. The night before, I swept the room, got everything ready, borrowed cups, and after all the preparations were complete, boiled myself a dinner of two hot dogs which I had bought in a tin that came from Holland. About two hours later, I felt as though I was going to die; vomiting, sharp stomach cramps, dizziness, all came down on me and the whole night was spent retching. The hot dogs were spoiled and I had food poisoning. First light told me it was the day of my first tea and I was out of it. With no telephone to call Arlene and Frances, I could only hope they would come over early, but, of course, they did not. Adelia was my first guest, a very elegant woman who lived three doors away. I smiled, bowed, poured the tea and then without a word, raced upstairs to my bathroom where I did the following: had the dry heaves, put powder all over myself, fluffed up my damp hair and descended with a smile. Cuia, from the tin shack town of Campinho, arrived next and talked to Adelia. Poured the tea, smiled, ran up the stairs, same activity, descended to find Cuia opening the door for others - they really did not need me at all. The guests rolled in, I rolled up the stairs, and no one seemed to notice as all were too busy enjoying each other. Arlene & Frances finally arrived, took one look at my face and asked what in the world was wrong with me. I explained, they thought it was very funny. The Swedish contingent arrived and Jonathan, who predicted disaster, was surprised that everyone mixed so well. Even Baptista, the artist, came. He wore pressed clothes, his eyes were clear, and soon he became the hit of the party with all the old women asking him to paint, draw, and do a picture of them. They knew talent when they saw it.

Of the many interesting people I met during the two years, the artist Baptista was one of the most memorable. He was Cape Verdean born and had amazing talent. His drawings, his water colors and his oils took your breath away. When I met him first in Cafe Royal he was dirty, unkempt, and rude but had a quality about him that intrigued me. I discovered he went to the States to live but was deported back to Cape Verde because of his drug use. He would come over to the Cafe and we would talk. I told him I would love to see some of his work but he had to be clean, off drugs and sober to come to my house. I told him I had books in English that he could borrow. He came, one time clean and I would give him a book, one time wasted, and the book would be taken away. He was like a child and I worried about him constantly. One night he received a lot of money from the sale of one of his pictures and went on a drinking spree. The next morning he was found bleeding and unconscious in a dark alley. He was taken to the island hospital and stayed in a coma for a week, I visited him every night and would try to get him to tell me who had hit him, and he would just shake his head and squeeze my hand so tight that it hurt. A young boy from the hospital came to my office two mornings later and told me Baptista had given up the fight. The boy handed me a scrap of paper - it had Baptista's handwriting on it. I read it and wept. He had told me he had written a poem for me, but never gave it to me. It must have been in his small sack of possessions he always carried with him. He had written it in English, knowing how poor my Portuguese was, a kind, last gesture.

"I ONCE KNEW A WOMAN WHO HAD A HEART OF IRON,
AND THEN ONE DAY SHE DISCOVERED A GOLD MINE.
NOW SHE PREFERS A HEART OF GOLD,
THAT'S WHY SHE'S A GOLDEN WOMAN.
To Diane; my dear, sensitive friend. Baptista 1991 "

He was an extraordinary person. I have that sheet of paper in my home to remind me of the kindness of the artist Baptista.

At the tea, after what seemed to be 10 hours, but was really only 3, my guests finally began leaving. Now in the States, I would have said, no, have another cup of tea, another cookie, this time I walked them to the door, thanked them for coming and wished them a lovely evening. As I was blowing out the candles and was about to go upstairs for the rest of my life, there was a knock at my door. I didn't move, the latecomers knocked again, and then finally went away. Thank God. It took me another entire day to get back on my pins, and I never ate a Dutch hot dog again.

Parties were one of the frequent activities of the country. When an invitation came from Santao Antao, the island across our channel, to go to a Brazilian man's home, Arlene, Frances and I went with great anticipation. I had become friends with the ferry boat captain and he invited me up to his deck. He pointed out a huge hammer head shark and from that moment on, I swam with a tad of unease. Upon landing, we went to Amy's house and got all gussied up for the big bash. I wore Julie's elegant Russian scarf with my Fred Rogers skirt and sweater. This party was very different from a PC party. Waiters passed around a tray for drinks, a tray of fancy food, a tray of just about anything you would want, all with the utmost graciousness. Plenio was our host and his wine flowed frequently. One of the Brazilian guests said he was glad to meet someone who was not in the PC, he could tell by my dress. It pleased me to tell him indeed I was a PCV and that his perception of PCVs was erroneous, we were not all pony tails and Birkenstock's. Plenio was a cooperante – which meant he was an employee of Brazil and was paid very well by his country to do the type of work that PCVs did. PCVs lived on the local level, which made us quite credible in the eyes of the locals as we were not in country to make money. After the party, the PCVs walked to the closest town, danced and always remembered how kindly we were treated by the Brazilians.

That next week we three were invited to dinner at Chez Lucia's, a Senegalese restaurant, where Elisio, Arlene's beau, treated us. He toasted us and thanked us for our hard work in Cape Verde. The owner, a woman my age, came over to us as we were leaving and gave me a very ornate doll with a Senegalese gown on, one I could never have afforded. I thanked her and put it on my window sill so I would see it every morning when the sun rose and I opened my shutters.

My home land friends were getting very creative about the care packages. Kay sent me the Time magazine that had news of 1990 in review and I wept when I read that Pearl Bailey, Sarah Vaughan, and Mary Martin had died. Nedda sent me lovely clothing, bottles of shampoo, magazines and a bottle of Lavoris and a bottle of Listerine. I thought the mouthwash was nice however on the label she had put a skull and bones which said "Happy Birthday, Beware of Mouthwash." Love, Nedda." I set the bottles aside and dove into the book and magazines - who needed mouthwash? I didn't open them for a few weeks; the other treasures sent were too enticing. Then I needed the box for storage and upon cleaning it out noticed a note tucked inside saying that I should rinse my mouth out immediately upon receipt. I had not seen that note when unpacked so decided to use the Lavoris that night. My cat Tarek watched me gargle, complete with all the gargling sounds and then I screamed - stopped - took another swig - it was NOT Lavoris - it was Pear William. Damn clever that lady. I thought the other bottle was the real mouth wash so did not use for a few weeks. When I took a swig, again I scared my cat and let out a holler yea - Scotch, real Scotch! Oh My God! I treasured my two "mouth washes" like gold and thanked Nedda over and over and over again. Dennis sent me a blue tea pot, with a sign "open very carefully and slowly", did, and there was another sign - "New York City contaminated air."

Life in Mindelo continued and so did the lessons. Jonathan continued his tutorials, using poetry. "Twas hand to hand we fought them, all in the blazing sun, stripped to the pants we did advance, at the Battle of Bull Run." He also told me about the Nestle baby food scandal. The company launched a campaign to sell powdered milk to new mothers in East Africa. The women bought the product and their babies died by the hundreds for there was no way to refrigerate the liquid formula once made. He said that cemeteries for the babies had the Nestle cans over the fresh mounds. He explained that ARO, the organization that sent him, was left wing, socialist, against the World Bank and the International Monetary Fund. I sensed he had the same philosophy.

The other Swedes, Ulla and Janna were gems. It was always a pleasure to be invited to their home. They explained that Thursday was the traditional night to make Swedish pancakes. One night, just as we were finishing a delicious dinner, there was a bright flash in the sky. We ran to the window and saw lightening and clouds over the mountain. They looked full of water, but a bare sprinkling was all we got; the drought continued. When we weren't eating pancakes with the Swedes, we went out to restaurants when our rice dishes got too boring. One restaurant, Calypso, owned by Ophalia, featured our friend Cesaria Evora. Her mournful songs made us think how much we would miss Mindelo. I wished she would be heard outside of the island of her birth; suspected that would never happen.

One night Vitorino took me out to a dinner in a restaurant on the ocean and I asked him to explain how the desalinization plant worked. He was the chief engineer of all the machines. When he received a part from another country (never requested - just arrived) he would not be able to read the directions (always in a language other than Portuguese.) People from other countries who knew how poor Cape Verde was had sent all their extra equipment to the head of the desalinization plant. I asked how he knew what to do with the machine parts. "I just figure out what the piece should do, attach it to another machine and see what works." The Director of the plant asked Vitorino to draw a new design for a certain function. When Vitorino did, the Director took it to an international competition and it won a prize. What he did not tell me, what one of his many sons told me – was the Director put his own name on it so he got the credit - not Vitorino. I was furious, told Vitorino that I would address that scum (in typical, huffy N.Y.C. manner.) Vitorino hugged me and thanked me for my loyalty and said it did not matter. Vitorino could have taught classes at M.I.T. if only, if, if, if. However, he was a big man on the island, respected by all for his abilities and that satisfied him. One evening he asked me what color I would tell my family he was and when I quickly said "my color," he laughed. He held my hand, kissed his finger and put it on my right wrist. To this day there is one lonely, very dark freckle there reminding me of Vitorino. I remembered that I had been told freckles were drops of chocolate holy water, now there was a new one. When I asked him why his hair was not curly and wiry, he said his grandmother was Portuguese and she had coloring like mine.

Evenings we went driving in his old car, telling each other stories, sharing feelings, sometimes arguing, but the making up was always worth the fight. He never spoke a word of English and when I got angry and started to babble in English, he would sit back, chortle and smile. Our friendship had many levels and he helped me so many ways. He was not free to be mine so we could not be seen together in the town. When I went dancing, he sometimes would wait for my return and we would dance alone in my apartment. My daughter Maura sent a tape of Nat King Cole and his daughter Natalie called "Unforgettable". Vitorino thought it very weird that one was dead, one was alive and they sang together. I had to explain dubbing in Portuguese, not an easy feat.

CREATIVE SOLUTIONS FOR SERIOUS PROJECTS

It seemed that there were new problems all the time that needed action. One was a health issue. Often at dance clubs I would see young people in romantic dances and wondered if they were using protection and if they knew about AIDS - SIDA as it is called in Portuguese. I went to the Red Cross person in our town and he claimed there really was not a problem in Cape Verde with AIDS. His attitude made my blood boil. He hastened to explain when he saw I was getting upset that he was waiting for the capitol to send a book they were working on. There was that old Salazar thing - don't move until Lisbon tells you what to do. It would take a long time for the citizens of Cape Verde to get over this conditioning - the young would have that responsibility - the old could not relearn. When I asked the young adults about AIDS, they said they were not worried as there was no AIDS in their country and then the kicker - if they had any cases of AIDS, they would simply ask the U.S. to send the medicine and everything would be all right. Holy mother of God! They really believed it. I explained that no drug had yet been found that could cure, must less stop, the terrible march of this

85

disease. The Director of the hospital had the same mind set. I decided I would have to get going, create story boards, get audiences lined up and force feed AIDS education to the population, no matter what they thought.

I made story boards in Portuguese and in Crioulo (not easy) and advertised my lectures. No one came. I shared my frustration with Vitorino. He smiled and said he would help me. He came to my home and asked for a condom - in Portuguese is called Camisa da Venus - blouse of love and a pitcher of water. "Now, pour the water into this condom as I hold it." I told him that if one drop spilled, I would be very angry, he smiled and I poured. The water filled up 1/3, more water and then more water. By now the damn condom was almost touching the floor - "See, Deana, these camisas are very strong and will get very big for everyone to have protection. Use this demonstration in your lectures and you will surely get the young people to come and listen." Next class, a few brave souls came. I picked the prettiest young girl and the most handsome young man - this was not hard as Cape Verdean youth are beautiful young people. They looked apprehensively at me when I told one to hold the condom and one to pour but did as told because I was the old lady. I played that age card every time I could. The demonstration worked and from then on, my lectures had standing room only.

Now I needed more condoms so went to the Swedish clinic and asked for 10 for the weekend. The next Friday, I asked for 20 - my classes were growing - next weekend - 25. The head nurse said that the Director wanted to see me before I got my next supply. "Deana, why are you using so many condoms, do you have many boyfriends?" When I could stop laughing, I explained about the lectures and then the Director laughed. That would be a story to tell my children. After many weeks of carrying the Swedish condoms around (they were the strongest - the U.S. ones really did not hold the water as well) I went to the dance clubs and handed them out to young people - discreetly of course. After a few weeks of this activity, I gained a new nickname - "Rainha de camisa de Venus" - the Queen of the Condoms. So, it was "Deana PACIM" for my day life, "Rainha de camisa" for my night life.

Diane teaching AIDS prevention using condoms and water – lots of water

Diane teaching AIDS prevention - Mindelo

Weeks before I had written a letter to Father Timothy Healy, the new President of The New York Public Library. My letter said, "you and I have six commonalities: we are both Irish, Catholic, New York City born, dedicated to education through reading, love jazz and most important, love single malt Scotch." His letter of response said that if I could get someone to come to the library, pack the books, send them to me, he would donate books to the children of Campinho. I had asked Father Healey how his new job was and he said he felt like Sisyphus. I asked him who Sisyphus was and he responded, "Your lack of classical training shows, dear." He also responded to my invitation for a fine Scotch at the Plaza and set the date for winter 1993. I was thrilled with his offer of books and now had to find a way to get them to our island. When I wrote a letter to Ellen Davidson Baer, a schoolmate from high school, and told her about the books, she said she would get the books and she and her husband Hank, would pay for the cost of sending them. It was a miracle, indeed.

About three months later, the first box of books arrived. <u>Heidi</u>, <u>Tom Sawyer</u>, <u>The Rand Mc Nally Atlas</u>, <u>Winnie the Pooh</u>, <u>Little Women</u>, <u>Lassie</u>, all spilled out of the box. Each night after work or dancing, I would select one book to dive into and reveled in the stories of my youth. I wrote a letter to my first grade classmate, Saranell, a librarian, asking her how to start a library. None of my friends were safe from my requests and every single one came through with flying colors. The books were treated like gold; no books in English had ever before been seen in this tin shack town. I sent letters to friends telling them to rob their attics, basements, go to yard sales and send books and boxes began to arrive. Then every single plane that landed in Sao Vicente had boxes labeled "Deana Pacim" - all that was necessary for delivery to me. Dennis, my New York City friend of the blue tea pot with NYC polluted air, sent his collection of Hardy boys and Nancy Drew books.

As I was receiving all these books, yet another miracle occurred. Shelia, my Boston friend from Fidelity Investments days, received a copy of my plea letter from our mutual friend Kay. Shelia was a member of the Sweet Adelines of Arlington, MA and their director's mother was a Cape Verdean who had just died. The chorus wanted to dedicate a living memorial to her - my project to build a children's library for the children of Campinho sounded just perfect. I sent her a letter explaining our need for books and a library to house them went back to her in a flash. The project was accepted by the Sweet Adelines of Arlington. Another miracle!

Diane's front hall of home – ivy growing – books donated by friends

Saranell's explicit instructions came and I had to figure out how to create library cards for the children, remembering Maya Angelou said the very best gift her mother ever gave her was a library card. Again, it was another miracle. Jay wrote to me saying that since I wrote her that nothing was ever wasted in Africa, would I like a huge box of hundreds and hundreds of post cards that she had made of a water color she had done of a Mexican scene long ago. I accepted, received the cards safely and stored them for the day the library opened. As the books started to arrive and stack up in my little room, I began to worry about where in the world I was going to house the books. One day I was walking to Campinho to meet with the water sellers and noticed some digging going on in the middle of a bare spot. They told me it was going to be an elementary school for poor children. I could not believe my ears. I had to hunt around for the correct person to talk to about the potential library - which in Cape Verde or any developing country takes weeks and months of digging, negotiating, knocking on lots of wrong doors before the right door is found. Finally I found the man who had the authority and told him what I had for the school. He said he was very sorry but he would not be able to accept the books as they did not have money to pay for such a large purchase. When told these were a gift from America, he hesitated and said to come back the next week.

One day I had to bring the PACIM truck to the post office to pick up three huge U. S. Postal bags with books jammed to the top, the women there said, "Deana, only a German dentist many years ago received more packages than you and that was because he received dental equipment." The word got out and when I received one box at the post office, I would sneak behind closed doors, a book here and a book there for the women who worked there. You could tell by the smiles and the odd bulges under blouses which women received a book that day.

Then the Mayor, Onesimo, an honest, forthright and clever man who had been elected Mayor during the recent election, said he would like to have some books to start a library at City Hall. He explained that when Cape Verde got its independence from Portugal in 1975, books were burned in protest to the Lisbon rule. I said the books were for the children and he smiled and returned two minutes later to show me sophisticated adult books. Surprised, I asked how he got them since they were all in boxes addressed to me. He smiled and said he had a friend who worked for Customs. Every single box had to be opened so that no guns would be smuggled in, a hangover rule from the Portuguese days. I told my friends to list the contents of the box, in English, on the inside top flap of the box. Most of the time, there was at least one piece missing, but as the customs men got to know me, less and less disappeared.

Onesimo Silveira – excellent Mayor of Mindelo (l)

Catholic Church – no rain - drought for 29 years

When I asked Onesimo who would be responsible for the books, he asked me to write a proposal. The difference between the Mayor and my boss, Senhor Evora, was that the Mayor was doing this project for the good of the people. My boss did nothing for the poor unless he could make a profit. The Mayor also spoke English and said, kindly, I could do the proposal in English, thank God! It was on his desk the next day. He appointed a woman he had given a cabinet post to, Maria, to work with me on the library project. Maria was to be the librarian, and Saranell's instructions about how to start a library were used. A huge room on the first floor that was never used was transformed into the City Hall Library. Maria and I sorted through the piles of books to select age appropriate books for Mindelo's first public library.

As a PCV, one receives a primary job description and that is the one focused upon, but the wonderful aspect of working with people is listening to their needs and wants and helping them figure out a way to get other projects going. I was working with the women in the towns figuring out a way to help them make money, working to create a brand new library, best of all responding to a request from the women saying they wanted books in English for their children.

91

In between cataloging the books and working with the women in the sewing association, I was invited to dinner with new friends. Suzette and Carlos were most gracious hosts and since they had electricity, she would use a waffle iron. Her pregnancy was wearing on her, she missed her family and we were both flummoxed by learning Portuguese. We decided to take classes and would sweat new assignments together. Carlos was a Baptist minister and most kind and the three of us developed a close friendship.

There were many other people who became kind and valued friends. The Director of the Swedish clinic, Harriet, had the brightest smile and was the ultimate in knowing how to work in developing countries. She never told the women she worked with what to do; she watched how they did it and then suggested ways that might be better. She told me the women of Il de Madeira were most difficult to work with; Campinho was a more friendly population. She was right: I had to fight every time I went to Il de Madeira for whatever I needed to do; Campinho women came forward to help me help them.

The Association for Social Work on the island was an interesting study. Ulla and I would meet with them and try to figure out how we could assist a family and it always seemed to be the family they would stone wall. One step forward, two steps back. I found out that abortions were few and far between, for two reasons, the hold the Catholic Church had on the entire population and the expense for an abortion. Health was always a problem for the poor and yet they kept their courage for living. Another woman who became a good friend was Ana Filo Da Cruz. One day I was feeling lousy and our PC nurse was on another island so I cruised into the pharmacy where Ana worked. She smiled and said "How may I help you" in English!!! Yea and off I went in my language explaining the symptoms - "Oh, a sinus infection." Her medicine did the trick. She had studied at the University of Washington and was very aware of what medicines were available. She lived by herself, over the pharmacy. She longed to have a child but did not think it necessary to be married. About one year later, she became pregnant and had a beautiful son, supported herself and him on her salary - a new kind of Cape Verdean woman.

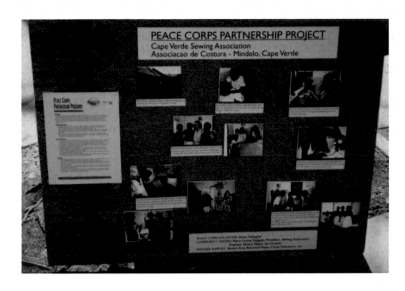

Sewing association

President, treasurer and secretary of the sewing association and friend Diane (not an officer!)

One of the ways Cape Verdeans were able to cope was to plan for the fun events. A big event was Carnaval, the beginning of Lent. I had never been to New Orleans, so I watched the CV parades and the partying with wonderment. Floats created out of nothing by the men, the women created fantastic costumes from nothing. There was a students' float with all of the young people who had done well at school. The tragedy was they would never get off the island to continue their schooling beyond high school; there was no college in all of Cape Verde and it was very hard to immigrate to other countries. Even the tin shack people had fabulous floats and the dancing on the streets lasted for a full 24 hours. Went to church the next morning and was confused when they put the ashes on the top of my head - not my forehead. When I asked why, they explained it was so God could see the ashes.

Valentine's Day came and I received three packages from an old beau Win. My friend Roberta in Boston gave a "party for Diane, bring a present, wrap it in my home, enjoy dinner, read some of her letters." Win came and took the boxes and paid the freight. Small bars of elegant soap, Crabtree and Evelyn hand lotions (which I must confess I did not share), expensive shampoo, and exotic perfume. The kindness of friends, distant and near, treasures all.

Diane painted and made up for Carnival

Another treasure was Vitorino. He picked me up one evening and we drove to his second home in the interior that was right on the ocean. On the way, he stopped to buy some freshly roasted chicken. Ranchero Carmel was run by Fernando; he was a delight and an excellent cook. While he waited for dinner, three musicians played wonderful and mellow Cape Verdean music. Vitorino had paid them to serenade me. With the brilliant moon and the stars abounding (no electric light this far out of town), the world looked and felt good. I swam in the ocean, he smoked the pipe I bought him,

94

watched me, dried me off and we talked and then tucked into each other and I got lost in his arms till just before dawn when he drove me back to my home in town and back to reality from cloud nine.

Letter writing became my best habit. Rose had sent me a clipping from NYT book review about reasons for not writing. E. B. White's was the best. "Please excuse me for not writing but a Christmas ornament got stuck in my pancreas and it kept winking and blinking on and off and it was much too distracting for me to write you a letter." In the same paper I read this quotation "You might say life is a game, you play with loaded dice, you're always losing, first you lose your childhood, then your youth, then you lose life itself, but what cannot be taken away from you is that you can laugh." Gilot Picasso, one of Pablo Picasso's wives said that. I put the quote over my mirror and it made me laugh every time I looked at myself which was not very often. The wrinkle brigade was forming and they were becoming deeply etched. I was, after all, 54, and had earned every single one of the lines. Vitorino visited and made me laugh and gave me a lecture on how not to care what I looked like, it was how I felt about myself that was important.

The more I learned from Ulla and Jonathan about Sweden, the more I was impressed with what they do for developing countries and all with no strings attached. Two huge boxes of clothing arrived and Ulla and I had distributed the contents to the poorest families in our project. Cuia in Campinho and Tonya in Maderia assisted us with the sorting. When there was a problem, the tin shack ladies would be the mediators. They had become my good friends and I relied on their honesty. In contrast, Senhor Evora told all of us not to send any reports to our individual directors, ARO or PC, he would do that. I quietly disregarded him and sent mine with PCVs going to the capital. His reports had no truth in them, ever. When he called meetings, many times he did not include the cooperantes or me. He kept us out of the loop and information locked in. We learned through the grapevine of a reception for a new government minister. Everyone went, including the drivers of the PACIM trucks, but not us. Vitorino counseled me not to get angry, to save my strength for the big fights; he was right.

Julianna, an old woman from Campinho, died one night and I went to console Cuia. Cuia was so sad; she saw death all the time at the Social Organization and ran the Casa De Idosos which was the home for the elderly. Cuia was in charge of fixing them their meals, making sure they took their medicines and was nearby if needed. She was paid a pittance, but never complained. "If I don't take care of them, others will come in and not do the correct thing for them." Cuia was a woman who kept her own counsel; she would take care of all in a fair manner, and then would take care of herself last.

Friend in Mindelo

Friend in Mindelo

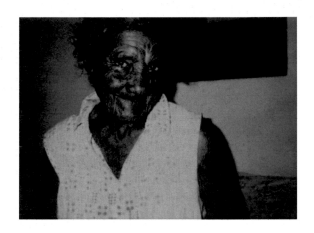

Friend in Mindelo

Friend Maria one leg

All of the women from the home for the aged went to the chapel behind the hospital where Julianna lay. The coffin was covered and we learned that the man who sold flags and stationery in town had paid for the coffin. The wailers were in full force, their piercing screams and sobs made the hair on the back of my neck stand up. Since we had no ability to preserve bodies, the day of your death was the day of your funeral.

Talk about funerals. I went to the right funeral for the wrong person. Manecos was sitting by himself in Cafe Royal, looking sad and I asked why. His friend, the old violin player, had just died. I was shocked, "You mean the man who plays at Calypso" "Yes, that one", "The one with the hump on his back?" Yes, that one," "The one who knew Broadway songs and I used to sing along with him", "Yes, that one". I was crushed, as I had never told him how much I loved his music, how his music transported me. I went to the church, which was filled up by all who loved his music, and walked to the cemetery with the rest of the mourners. Many times if the deceased was rich, the family would hire funeral musicians. This man was poor but all of his musician friends played for him because he was so loved. I cried and cried.

Father Bernardo gave a dedication about the man and his music, we said a prayer together and then a hush came over the huge crowd. A musician went to the top of the little hill and began to play his violin. As I was crying, I thought, how strange, that is exactly how the other violin player played and so I looked up to the hill to see my friend, the violin player I thought had died. He was THERE, standing, playing, and living. I lost it, got my handkerchief out, and started to choke so I would not laugh; Manoces took my arm and tried to comfort me. I could not let him know I was laughing and crying at the same time. I put my head down, and, when the playing was over, we all walked to our homes, accompanied by the music of the violin player I thought we had just buried. That very night I went to the Calypso restaurant and told my friend how much I appreciated his talent, his warmth, his playing and thanked him for being alive!

THEY GAVE A WAR AND DIDN'T INVITE ME!!!

The Gulf War news was coming fast and furious – reminding me of what Gertrude Stein's said "Everybody gets so much information all day long that they lose their common sense." I was having a hard time keeping up with the war. 20,000 Iraqis surrendered and American companies were being hired by the dozens to rebuild Kuwait.

When I came out of my door on the morning of the beginning of the war, there was a soldier standing at my door. I never had seen a soldier anywhere near our road before. He said "Bon Dia, Deana, dormir bem?" – "good morning, did you sleep well?" I sputtered an answer and went to my office wondering why he was there and how did he know my name. At the City Hall, there was yet another soldier and he gave me the same greeting. When the Mayor's secretary told me there was a telephone call for me from the capital city of Praia, I figured it was my boss. It was and he asked me if I noticed anything different, I told him about the soldiers and asked if he had requested them. He explained he had not and thought it must have been the President. He told me to keep a low profile, not discuss the war and be alert.

We noticed the price of gasoline went sky high - direct result of the war. I listened to my short wave radio early in the morning and late at night. My neighbors and friends became more protective, when I would walk down a street; I found there was always a friend or neighbor who just happened to be going in my direction. Friends came up and said they understood what the war was about – they were smarter than I - and that the United States would be the victors. When I heard a lot of noise in the street one morning, I knew something had happened. Pedro told me that the war was over. We also heard that many black troops refused to go into battle because the Kuwaiti still bought slaves. Jonathan told me this war was fought in the cradle of civilization between the Euphrates and the Tigris Rivers. It all

99

seemed so far away but it still made me so sad.

A few weeks later, a full moon ushered in the month of March. I brought waltz tapes to Vitorino's ocean home and we discovered we could do that dance quite well - a West African moon and ocean was a far cry from the war. He talked to me about tides and the full moon and why the moon was so important to the tides and the fishermen. As he continued his lectures, I would jump into the sea and play in the waves for a long time. I also brought a jar of soap bubble solution and we would laugh like three year olds as the bubbles flew around his house. He told me stories in Portuguese so that I would learn new words and practice speaking with him. He told me a story of how resourceful Cape Verdeans were. If they were given a gift of a truck they would cut it in half, hitch donkeys to the back end of the truck and use the front end of the truck with the motor all by itself. That was a lesson on using imagination to get two jobs done.

One day I was at the drug store buying medicine for Paulino and noticed a very old woman with the disfiguration of a person with Hansen's disease. I asked Ana Filomenia if leprosy existed in Cape Verde. She said they had in the past but no longer but still she wished a dermatologist could come to their island. Needless to say, I jumped on that suggestion and wrote to the former beloved in Bangor, Maine asking him if he would come, Ana volunteered to be his interpreter and said that he could stay in her apartment. Sadly I never did get a response. Ana told me about another aspect of Cape Verdean life. When wealthy women got pregnant they went to another country, mostly France or Sweden to have the baby there so the child would have dual citizenship. Dual citizenship would allow the child to travel from one country to another without much hassle. She was a font of information, such as the name of the tea that makes men impotent was Belgata. She also explained that the islands of Cape Verde had a history with different countries, Sao Vicente people went to Italy and Norway, Brava people went to the United States, Santa Antao people to Holland and Luxembourg and the people from Fogo went to Germany. There was always so much to learn. That is part of the Peace Corps magic, you learn more than you teach, that was for sure.

I remembered Charlie, my PC recruiter in Boston telling me not to go back to the United States but to visit the countries around me. I continued to save money for our Mali trip in August.

There were other trips in the offing. Denise Sugrue wrote and told me about a Shugrue family reunion to be held in Ireland, in June of 1992. About one week before I left the States in 1990, Denise had called me up and introduced herself as a member of the Shugrue clan. She had found my name in the telephone book, where I was listed as Diane Shugrue Gallagher. I did that listing so that people who knew me before my marriage would be able to find me. Gloria Steinem always said that when a woman married and took her husband's name she lost part of her identity. Denise was beginning to gather Shugrues/Sugrues/ from all over the States to explore their heritage and had invited me to a meeting in July of 1990. I told her I would be in Africa that July so could not go but invited her to my going away party at the Hampshire House in Boston. She came and I knew she would be in my life forever. She had been a Roman Catholic nun for 30 years, lived in Japan, left the order and moved to Massachusetts. Now I wrote back saying that money was an issue and I did not think I could make that trip. But, then when I told Vitorino he said, "talvez" – "maybe" in Portuguese. He counseled me - "you never know, Deana, you never know."

Senhor Evora managed to get our project kicked out of City Hall - and we were sent to another location, a deserted Army barracks building, high on a hill outside of town, overlooking the magnificent harbor, but next to nothing. I now walked forty-five minutes to get to work and the wind was always in my face. I said that I arrived at 8:30 and my hair would arrive ten minutes later. I thought that was hysterically funny, but no one else in the project thought so. We were too far out to go for coffee in my favorite place, the Cafe Royal, so had to settle for less than adequate coffee served in the barracks.

David Bellama, our country PC Director, came for a visit and told us John would be in charge of Cape Verde, as David had been asked to open Zimbabwe. We would miss David greatly: while David was an instinctively good director, John did it by the book. March 22 was the inauguration day for the new president, Antonio Mascarenhas Monteiro, a lawyer who then became a judge. There was hope that he would be a good leader. Because Peace Corps is very strict about getting involved in the politics of the country, I could only watch and not participate - that was hard for an old activist to swallow. I put my mind on other projects, like the home for the elderly.

Dona Juliette lived in the Casa De Idosos (the home for the elderly) in Campinho. She was so frail. The last time I saw her, she was in the hospital.

I went to visit Dona Cuia who was in charge of the Casa De Idosos to see how everyone was doing. Dona Cuia looked so sad and beaten down when I walked into her cement house, I knew it had to be Dona Juliette. Dona Cuia told me she had died the night before and the funeral would be in about four hours. Since Dona Juliette had no money, we had to wait for someone to donate a coffin. The flag seller man, once again, paid for a coffin. We all cried in Dona Juliette's now deserted room and went to the church and then took the long walk to the cemetery outside of town. I asked Dona Cuia who would be moving in there and she said the room would have to be painted first. Dona Cuia never asked me, I just got some paint, got Arlene and Frances to help and with the boom box at full blast, we three painted the room for the new occupant. To take a break, we visited blind Maria and she would feel our faces and see which one of us was standing in front of her. Then our visit to Dona Joanna left her laughing. She only had one leg and a finger that pointed to the ceiling - it had been broken as a child and never set. Then "Maria one foot" we called her would come in and laugh as we all danced together to the Cape Verdean music that blared over our boom box. These women had so little and yet they were content, so joyful with all of the little aspects of their life, so giving of anything they had, which was never much. I always felt better when I left the compound for the elderly.

Carmileta – Beat Diane's son Bill at the game of jacks

Little girls carry very, very heavy cement bricks on their heads - Mindelo

I was living in interesting times now as my real home was Mindelo. Even when visiting other nearby islands, "going home" meant returning to "my" island. In my new home I read American newspapers which kept me abreast of news of my former home and which, of course, I was eager to hear.

One day I read that Martha Graham, the dance legend, my old dance teacher, had died. The news took me back to the day at The Neighborhood Playhouse School of the Theatre in New York City when we students auditioned to be in her dance class. I had never taken a dance lesson in my life. She terrified all of us and when she asked us to walk across the floor, everyone became wobbly kneed. A magnificent looking young blonde woman stood in front of me and glided effortlessly across the floor like a perfect ballerina. I thought about imitating her but realized I would look like a fool so I walked across the floor as best I could. The beautiful blonde and I were both accepted and I was dumbfounded. When Miss Graham was asked later why she chose us, she replied, "By the time I un- teach many of you, the ones who have never danced before will be equal to the ones who have been previously trained." I smiled to myself and thanked her for giving me the confidence I was sorely lacking. Now she was gone.

My current world was very different from my N.Y.C. world. Next door to me to the right was Dona Valentina, her husband Pedro and son Pedro, an engineer in Project PACIM. She sensed when I was down and bought me a bowl of chicken soup, which prompted me to tell her about the Jewish philosophy of healing with chicken soup. When I told her about Miss Graham's death, chicken soup came my way.

I always had to work hard to translate a story for a philosophy into Portuguese. The chicken soup translation reminded me that many things got lost in the translation. One evening Vitorino, whom I had not seen for a long time, came to visit. As he entered my apartment, I used Mae West's famous line, "Is that a gun in your pocket or are you just glad to see me." He looked surprised and asked me to translate. I did but it was not the same, and what's more, I blushed in the translating.

One day a young boy named Hamilton, stunningly handsome at 10 years, came into my life. His street age was about 25; he had seen it all living in Campinho with his mother and five brothers. The father had deserted the family and lived in Boston. The mother sold fish at the harbor and always looked exhausted. For some reason, he and I struck up a friendship. When there was an extra piece of fish left over, he put his hand behind his back and gave it into my hand behind my back. Knowing that he would never have the privilege of going to a school because his mother did not have money to pay for books and supplies, I tried to interest him in reading. He would sit in my room and look at the pictures over and over again. How I wished I could pay for him to have the simple gift of going to school but all I could do was give him picture books. One was always tucked into his pocket as he left to go back to his tin shack home.

So many different people on our island came into our lives. Frances, another volunteer, received free tickets (she was a member of the "in" crowd of young-ins) to a dance for the "Mindelo Stars Dance Company" to celebrate their fifth anniversary. When we walked into the large dance hall in an old hotel on the outskirts of town, I could sense the party was going to be a dancing party, even the older people were out on the floor having a grand time. Frances was asked, as usual, to dance, and I, as usual, was not, the Cape Verdean men preferred the pretty young women to me, the old wrinkled one. I watched for quite a while and then told Frances that I wanted to dance with a certain young man. He looked slightly disappointed when she pointed to me, but because older people receive respect in Cape Verde, he came over, bowed and we were off. He did not look at me, surely he was thinking about the beautiful Frances, but then he made a tricky move and I followed him perfectly. He looked at me, did not say anything and did another fancy step, backwards. He said, "Do you dance?" and I shrugged my shoulders a little and nodded yes. He then swung me out to the middle of the floor and for every move he made, I was there on the beat. He was a professional dancer, the lead in the company and I had chosen him because of his grace. I did not realize his power until I was in his arms, he was about the age of my son and whirled me around and around until there were times I lost my breath. The crowd stopped dancing and watched us and clapped and then I knew I would have to finish the set. The set was finally over and my partner bowed and said he was proud to dance with a "mulher velha" (old woman) who moved like a young woman. Frances smiled and we both limped home in time to see the sunrise over our sleepy harbor.

The next morning I was about to swing my legs over the side of my narrow bed, but discovered they did not swing. My legs felt like two cement blocks, when I gingerly put them on the floor and rose to go to the bathroom. My rib cage began to ache and then my back had such pain, I had to sit back down on the side of my bed. When I realized that dance had totally abused my old body, I started to laugh, but that hurt too, so I held my side and quietly laughed while the pain shot all around my body. I stayed in bed the entire day, one or two pee runs and that was it. I kept falling asleep until at twilight, I heard Vitorino's car. I had always been at the door to greet him, this time I crawled to my second floor window and threw down my keys. He came bounding up stairs with a funny expression on his face. He said he had heard I had danced with Fernando, the lead dancer, and had been quite good, then he looked at me in bed, not able to move and he realized I had done myself in. He laughed. I did not. I grimaced when he came to hug me. He said not to move, he would be right back. About a half hour later, he came back and gave me some grog, holding me up in bed so I could drink it, and then rubbed Arguila all over my body. Arguilla is radioactive sand from the mountains near Salamanca in the interior and he caked me with it. After two grogs, I must have fallen asleep because I awoke many hours later to find him sleeping next to my bed. I did not go to work the next day either.

Word got around town. When I finally ventured my aching body out of my home three days later, I was greeted with "Deana PACIM, ahletismo and boa dancar", Diane the athlete and good dancer. I heard the young dancer went to France soon after the party with his company. My body was glad, it might not have lasted another go round.

But back to work which continued to occupy most of my time. I noticed a huge tower on one of my walks to the harbor. It was in terrible shape, cement falling, large cracks, no one could use it. I asked Pedro about the tower. He explained that it was a replica of the Tower of Belera in Lisbon,

Portugal, and was used to assist the mariners when they entered the harbor of Lisbon. I also found out that the Cape Verdeans let it fall apart for two reasons: they still had a bad feeling about the Portuguese who had used and abused their country, and they had no trained masons to repair it. I went to Senhor Evora and asked if I could get it repaired. Maybe we could use it as a tourist bureau, for the many ships that came into the harbor, both small sail boats and large cruise ships, and we could have them visit this lovely tower. He grumbled and said write a proposal. I did and added a training section for the young girls and boys of Campinho, who would have uniforms, would learn English and would be proud representatives of Mindelo. The proposal got shelved and though I brought it up from time to time, it never became top priority.

I noticed that my life was becoming simpler and simpler: how Thoreau would have loved it. I used candlelight all of the time; I bathed in the ocean, the wind dried my hair. I sharpened my Swiss Army knife the way Vitorino taught me on a rough piece of cement he had given me, and my cotton clothing just got more and more comfortable. Makeup was a thing of the past and my body was getting taut, my freckles might just band together to give me a tan here in West Africa. But then little things bothered me in Mindelo that never caused me a thought in the States: when my deodorant dried up and died, when my fingers and toes developed cracks and bled because of the intense heat, when my hair looked like Alfalfa from the Little Rascals and I had only have two pairs of shoes from which to choose. But, I was still so happy here, doing what I could do to help that minor inconveniences did not really make a big difference. I had no television, no radio, no car, no computer, no rugs, no microwave, no stove; I had everything.

Then there were the sad events that took a toll on me. When I went to the post office one day in April to pick up my mail, a worn out telegram was put into my hand. I swallowed hard as I took it to the informal park area outside of the post office and sat down. From my son Bill, "Mom died April 9th, have taken care of everything, she was peaceful at the end." Mom? Mom? I kept saying that name, I was not dead, my mother had died when I was 14 years old, my mother-in-law had died five years before, and who was he talking about. Then I realized whom he meant. Western Union had screwed up. My son said "Mill had died", they put "Mom" instead of Mill. It was my beloved Aunt Millie, my mother's sister, who lived in Boston. I put my head into my hands and cried. She had been so brave when I told her I was going to live in West Africa for two years, and now she was gone.

I walked past my City Hall office and went straight home. There was a small dish of food with a cover over it on my stoop. I picked it up and ten minutes later a knock on my door bought another dish, this time from Hamilton's mother. The afternoon went on with various knocks, various dishes, and various offerings of sympathy. Maryann brought fresh tuna, Valentina brought her faithful chicken soup, Cuia brought special rice. No obit ever appeared in the local paper, no telephone call went around saying that I was in trouble and sad and cried for the first time in public, but there was the grapevine. Someone had seen me in the park, knew something terrible had happened and the word went out. The people did not have much to give, but they gave me what they could.

"I TRAVEL NOT TO GO ANYWHERE, BUT TO GO. I TRAVEL FOR TRAVEL'S
SAKE; THE GREAT AFFAIR IS TO MOVE."

R. L. Stephens

Some times on the weekend mornings when I didn't have to pole vault to work, I just sat in my bed and watched the early morning clouds spin on into nothingness. The light grew brighter and back lit the clouds and magic was painted. I never tired of this activity. In the beginning when I discovered the clouds running across the sky as I opened my wooden shutters with no glass to distort the view, I thought how this new activity would never hold my attention in my little apartment in Brookline. Here in Mindelo, I was satisfied with the dawn colors, the sounds of the children awakening next door and a small bustling sound on the road that meant people were going to our outdoor market to buy the vegetables and beans and rice for the evening's dinner. I also was totally in tune with the moon and could tell exactly what phase the moon was in: on the wane, on the wax, a thumbnail - which path it was using at this particular time of the year, things I never thought of at home.

Two thin, emaciated trees grew on our road and they gasped daily for the rain they were never granted. They were acacia trees, specialists in living off a land with no moisture. The people of Cape Verde seemed to have learned their lesson from the trees too, as they never complained about the lack of rain. I secretly vowed to myself when I returned to the States, I would never, never, ever walk in the rain with an umbrella. I longed to feel rain, moisture, dampness on my face, and remembered what an old Irish woman told me when I visited that green, green country in 1982 with daughter Claire, my friend Roberta and her son Teddy. When I told the old woman it was raining, she smiled and said quietly "No, t' is a fine soft day." Well, the poor people of Mindelo hardly ever felt the fine soft days and a

108

mist caressing their cheeks, but ah, they could dream, for the poor dream more.

I vowed that I would keep a list of men vs. women letter writers, but after the first few weeks the score told me that the women outshone the men eleven to one. I noticed that my women friends wrote me and gave counsel about my health and sent articles about how to stay in good shape. I had lost about twenty five pounds and felt good except when there were times I would feel lousy with a sinus headache. One of these "bad sinus days" I was sitting in the Cafe Royal and my friend Manacoes asked me why I looked so dreary. I explained about the sinus headache and he whisked me into his car for, as he said through his smile "the ultimo cure." He took me to his family's bakery on the edge of town. He went to a huge tree in the front court yard and pulled hard, and four huge leaves fell to the ground. He picked them up, took them into the bakery and washed off the sand. Then he took me to my apartment, put me on my bed and told me to sleep for four hours with them over my eyes. I smiled politely. Who was he kidding? I had Tylenol, Actifed, and all the modern wonders. I awoke about four hours later, pain gone, lesson learned.

The next night I felt so good I decided to take myself out to a dinner and went to the Pic-A-Pau Restaurant and had their famous dish, marisceo, a fresh fish dish with tasty rice. I could only finish half so decided to ask if I could take the other half home with me. The "take home tactic" had not yet come to Mindelo. I had to explain that If he gave me his dish with my food in it, I would eat the food the very next day and then bring the dish back so he could use again. Now, remember, this was all in Portuguese, not an easy feat. But after I told him the same description many times, the owner, who was also the chef, who was also the waiter, gave me a dish that he covered with a cloth. The next night I brought back his dish and explained I had eaten his food for lunch and thanked him very much. From then on it was easy for him to say, "Deana, you want 'took out.' He never got the correct tense but he did get the concept.

Weekends were relatively quiet at this point but weekdays brought many visitors to our island and one charming young American man named Jay Cooper showed up at our office one day. He was a trainer for PC and said he would help me with some business ideas. PC did make sure that we had access to people who could give us advice, could help us with a project we were having difficulty with, and teach us new methods. I took him around on the tour of the two tin shack towns that our project PACIM was responsible for and saw the look of utter dejection that came across his face when he saw the abject poverty. He was entranced with Paulino and took pictures of the two of us on a stretch of land between the tin shack area and the harbor town of Mindelo. He said it was one of the most depressing pictures he had ever taken.

PC always had each volunteer on their radar. No PCV was allowed to slide by on their job description and we were always accountable for where we were in the project, what was hindering us from completion and when we needed help, they were right there to give council, give advice, make it work. If you did not work hard and did not do was expected of you, you were called on the carpet. PC was not shy in telling a PCV to shape up and get the job done. We had to be on target, we had time lines, had mandates from both the CV government and the PC. In fact, many times, I thought, this *is* the toughest job there is ... bar none.

As life went on between the tin shack towns I worked in and the town hall I sat in, the Peace Corps was always there, to assist, train, support. We traveled frequently and the first of June was designated as the next flight to the capital city of Praia where the country Peace Corps office was located. I had applied to be a trainer for the new batch of dewy eyed young trainees who were coming in the middle of July. All of the volunteers from the other islands came in and we had a grand reunion. Lectures during the days with reports, and reports and yet more reports, (another term was "bureaucracy"), meetings with functionaries who wanted to know just why the Peace Corps was successful in our assignments. At NGO meetings, they were sometimes people very full of themselves and our young director John tried his best to keep the 12 of us in line, not an easy task. More language classes again, and, no surprise to me, I was at the lowest rung of the ladder and came out of the classes wringing wet with the effort of learning this most difficult language. Finally the moment we were all waiting for came - our assignments for the training. I was thrilled when they told me I was to give the cross culture lectures.

Settling back into my apartment after five days in Praia, a quiet took over and the surf, which was always my constant companion, lulled me as I watched the stars choosing their territory to shine in and the moon doing her dance of movement. A huge fly was caught in my Japanese lantern on my ceiling and I listened to its banging against the sides, tricking myself into thinking it was Fred Astaire dancing his famous upside down dance in the upside down room. Now this was theatre at its best. I remembered Martha

110

Graham saying that theatre was a verb before it was a noun - this was sheer theatre. Vitorino came over in the early evening and sensed that I was still jingling from the hustle bustle of the Praia meetings. He would hold me in his arms, saying nothing and then stroking my hair. The hair stroking led to his combing my hair with his hands and that took all the frayed nerve ends away. He would lean over and whisper "Tenho sonhos cordoa rosa," "I wish you pink dreams," which is what lovers say to each other before they go to sleep. Then he quietly took his leave and I would dream pink dreams.

As the weeks went by, I noticed that my hearing was becoming more acute. One night I was walking home from City Hall and heard, of all things, the wailing of the trumpet of Miles Davis, nobody could fool me on that one. No, couldn't be. I ducked into a bar right by the ocean's side and felt immediately like I was in a Greenwich Village coffee house, a San Francisco pub, a French cafe. People were playing chess and a man in a corner was oil painting. Then Ella Fitzgerald scatted out on his cassette player and then Louis Armstrong's trumpet blared forth. What a treat to my ears. I sat down and ordered one grog com laite, a grog cut with coconut milk and watched the scene. A tall, American Indian looking man came over and introduced himself. "So you are Vitorino's woman, he has good taste." I smiled, bowed my head a bit shyly and realized on a small island there were no secrets. He said his name was O'Chalie and he was very glad I had come to his bar. His wife came over and her young beauty took my breath away. He showed me his father's worn wooden board with niches, polished by hundreds of hands in the playing of bisque. It was a mathematical game played with seeds and now I knew what the men played under the sun, day after day, under the stars, or whenever two Cape Verdean men got together. I asked Vitorino about it and asked if he would explain it so I could play. He shrugged and said it was for men only so I let it drop. If that remark had been made to me in the States, I would have challenged him, but here I had to be "culturally sensitive".

There were times that I acted completely like a Cape Verdean and then there were times I reverted to being a plain ole American. Jay Cooper had mentioned that his birthday was going to be the following Wednesday and he would be on the other island. I decided to throw an American birthday party and surprise him. I invited all of the people he had met during his three weeks of training and assessing the Peace Corps activities in Mindelo. I told them to come at 7, not a minute later. Cape Verdeans have a very different sense of time. America is ruled by time; Cape Verde pays time no mind. I knew this fact and told them 7 pm even though I wanted them there at 8. Had to use psychology, don't you know. Maryann and Pedro would bring food, Virginia, the woman from the bank would bring desserts, Yvonne, my Portuguese tutor, would bring pastiches, (tasty fish pieces fried in a great batter) and the men were to bring the beer, the booze and the grog. I asked Arlene and Frances to go to the ferry that Jay would be on and tell him I was sick and they could come by and say hi to me and then the three of them would go out to dinner without me.

At about 7:45 the Cape Verdeans arrived, about twenty five in all. We blew out all the candles and got very quiet as we heard Jay, Arlene and Frances coming up my road. When he entered, we lit all the candles and sang happy birthday and he was floored and got very emotional. Frances, who was a very talented artist, had made him a huge poster with happy birthday on it in many different languages and we all signed the poster. Everyone brought presents, some made and some purchased. Manacoes had brought four guitarists as his present and the singing, the playing, the dancing began. The rule is, the party is not over till madragada (dawn) so we took the party to the interior. We all jumped into trucks and went to Riberia Julio as they were having a night in honor of Saint John. Gambling tables were set up in tin shacks, dancing floors were laid down and the musicians would take turns playing. We all "fested" till the early morning hours. Jay went back to the hotel tired, a year older, but with presents and memories of Cape Verdeans giving a "festa" for him to be remembered.

Presents were given with great thought in Mindelo. I had dropped into a funeral store to buy some material for one of the women in Campinho to make a shirt for her daughter and the owner was very sweet to me. We talked, me in my halting Portuguese, she as smooth as silk. I then met her again at a school that was having an open house to show the works of the students. Sewing, crewel, stitchery, embroidery, lace- making were all disciplines taught to the young girls. I saw a particularly lovely cloth and did not know what it was to be used for. As I held it, my friend from the funeral store came over and explained what the stitchery meant and then she handed it to me. "This is my present to you because you are so simpatico with the people of Cape Verde and we all love you for that." I was deeply touched and used the cloth that had "fruita esse" on it for the rest of the time I lived in Mindelo. I told Vitorino about it and how touched I was with her saying "simpatico." He told me that that word was a Portuguese word. English speakers had taken to using it as if the word belonged to their language.

112

Death was always with us. An old lady named Joanna died in the Casa de Idosos (the old age house) in Campinho. When a vacancy occurred, the fighting began. The group in charge, the Social Association, was composed of politicians of the first order. I had one candidate, they had another, someone else had another and so the struggle went. When my candidate finally was approved, meaning she could live there and not have to pay, we were told that all the rooms had to be painted before she could be moved in. I went around and got some volunteers, Arlene and Frances of course, and some of the young boys I had become friends with at both of the tin shack towns. Got the paint, not easy to get the Social Association to part with the money, with my boom box in hand, began the chore of painting six filthy rooms, dusting the huge cockroaches away. One by one, the volunteers slipped away, except faithful Frances and Arlene.

That day I met Chiquinaha's nephew, Augustino, with whom I had danced at the local dance clubs. Chiquinaha was a very old lady who lived about ten doors away from my door and we said good morning to each other as I left for work. She sold bread and always gave me a small extra piece saying "You need to add more flesh to your body. Cape Verdean men do not like skinny women." We laughed and I always felt better after seeing her first thing in the morning. I was moaning one morning that I had run out of volunteers for the painting job and she volunteered her nephew. The same afternoon as my boom box blared out Glen Miller, Augustino walked in with two friends, all tall (good for the ceiling work.) The job was completed in jig time, between rounds of dancing that we just had to do as we turned a corner, finished a ceiling, or completed a room. Dancing was part of their heritage and took the edge off the poverty, the sense of isolation, the

113

sense of futility that we all felt from time to time. We continued to have no rain and when I heard my cassette player do "Rain drops keep falling on my head" from "Butch Cassidy & Sundance Kid", I would quickly change it to the next cut.

Here is one funny, well, maybe not so, funny story. We were doing the room of another resident named Joanna A., who I had wheeled out into the small courtyard so the fumes would not bother her. Four of us were inside, laughing, telling stories and of course dancing with the music going full blast so I didn't hear Joanna A. calling my name. Suddenly a little girl came in and pulled on my shirt and pointed to Joanna. She had fallen asleep in the wheel chair, only now she was not in the cool shade where I had first put her; she was in the hot, blazing sun. I ran out and woke her up and apologized over and over again and felt so bad. From then on she would kid me saying it was lucky she was not a white woman the day I forgot to move her out of the sun or she would have been burned to a crisp.

Another funny story about the painting: Cuia, the water seller of Campinho and fast becoming my good friend, was also the manager of the home for the aged. Cuia said that I had done a good job on all six rooms but that Maria was not satisfied with her room. With my typical New York defense mechanism jumping in, I walked to her room, ready to defend our job. I started to babble to Maria and all of the old ladies started to howl with laughter, for I was talking to the blind Maria, not the sighted Maria. They got me on that. I put those stories down in my cross culture lectures, now filling up one huge folder, to take to Praia.

Talk about cultural sensitivity - sometimes I went a tad overboard and was not very nice with my Irish temper. One night I gave a baby shower for my friend Suzette Da Cruz, in my apartment. As we sat there, two young boys snuck in my open door and took 2 of my jackets off the hooks and ran. We ran after them but lost them in the streets. I put the word out on the street, I wanted them. The next day a boy came to me and told me they were in the plaza trying to sell my jackets. I sped up there, grabbed the two, dragged them to police station, reported them, then took them into a room and shook them till their teeth rattled. I did not hurt them but I was enraged. I hoped they would never steal again.

The time had come to go to the training in Praia. I said my goodbyes and realized it was hard to say goodbye to the old ladies, to Paulino, to Vitorino. How would I ever say good bye in one year's time when it was time for me to go forever? I put that thought out of my mind, hugged Paulino and asked the old ladies of his area to please take him to the Swedish clinic so he would not fall behind in his weight gaining. Saying goodbye to Vitorino on my roof in the moonlight was too difficult to record. I would be gone for a total of three months, two to train and one to go to the West African country of Senegal to give a lecture about the AIDS presentations I had devised. Vitorino warned me about falling in love with the blue veiled warriors of Mali, the famous Tuaregs. I quietly said to myself that his love was all that I would ever need, but could not say it out loud to him. He said something softly in Crioulo and we both got quiet in the sadness of parting.

The next morning our plane made Mindelo's lunar landscape fall away and the ocean took over. One hour later we arrived on the northern island of Santiago and went to the city of Praia. Ambassador Terry McNamara and his gracious wife had a delicious dinner for a large group. Mrs. McNamara and I chatted about women's rights, a subject I had stayed away from in Mindelo - at least overtly, and after a delicious dinner, cigars were passed around. All the men took one and Mrs. McNamara said, "Terry, I am sure Diane would like one as well." Whoops, so I said a quiet thank you, took one, one of their young sons taught me how to cut the end off properly and light it and I puffed away. Bernice, the Consul at the Embassy, smiled and nodded at me and I knew we would laugh at this later on.

Praia held more international people than Mindelo, connected with different government embassies, but the best dancers were still the Cape Verdeans. The next morning we were trucked to the training site at Sao Jorge. Huge mountains, full of tall trees, foliage, and green everywhere made me miss our very different island of Sao Vicente. The training site was situated next to an agricultural teaching station and flowers were everywhere. The Director of training, Cecilia Oterio, met us and she and I immediately hit it off. All of the other trainers gathered, were assigned beds and introduced. Jay Cooper, the birthday boy, was there, and Ricardo, the Portuguese professor from Georgetown University, who knew my friend Father Timothy Healy who had been the President of Georgetown University before he became President of the NYPL (small world department.) Carol, TEFL trainer whom I knew from Guinea Bissau, Lee, agriculture trainer, Sabu, from Guinea Bissau who had been so gentle with me when he gave me my final Portuguese test and passed me more out of kindness than for my fluency of the language. He and I laughed and talked in Portuguese and he said he was very proud of my ability to speak - still being so kind.

After a staff meeting and a lovely dinner served in a local restaurant, I took a walk into the moonlight that hid behind the mountains and then would spring out at me. The roses, the hibiscus, the bougainvillea, and the eucalyptus scents all combined to make me dizzy with the aromas. I was still in Cape Verde, but a very different Cape Verde. The next day was July 5th, which is the day Cape Verde celebrated getting their independence from Portugal so - guess what - no work. It is the tradition that everyone takes off work and goes to the local beaches so all of the 18 staff members went to the nearest one at Terrafel. The ocean had huge waves and we rocked and rolled all day, ate a picnic dinner and then went swimming at night. The moon followed us home. It reminded me of my home in Mindelo and of course, Vitorino.

Back to the training business; Harry, PCV from Sao Tome, and I were in charge of cross culture training. We brain stormed and wrote our lesson plans. After dinner Jay and I wandered out to check out the stars and my astronomy lessons began. Big dipper, little dipper, half crown, belt of Hercules, three sisters, swan in flight, Vega which was wildly bright, and of course the Milky Way. He said that there are more stars than grains of sand and it took billions of years for us to see them. Jay made a computer map for me to take to Senegal and Mali so I would know what I was seeing at different locations. As I came back to my room, a gigantic spider met me. I immediately wrote "An ode to a spider" - you stay there, I'll stay here, and we both will have a nice long life."

At the same time I was getting our lectures ready for the classes, Rebecca, a PCV from another island who was going with me to Senegal and Mali and I were racing into town to get our visas, our West African money and all that had to be done to take a trip off of Cape Verde. Peace Corps was not going to pay a nickel for our trip so I had sold many of my t shirts to pay for the plane ride to the continent. Rebecca and I also had to prepare our health lectures, double the pressure!

And then the new volunteers came! The bus was early, the copy machine broke down before we finished making all the copies, the binder was lost so we had to stuff the papers in loose leaf books - very loose, and they appeared! The new group tumbled off the bus like new born colts and fillies, awkward, shy, rambunctious, loud, quiet and all over the place. The quiet that we had enjoyed for the past four days was shattered, never to be found again. They were old, 74, they were single, they were couples, one was not quite 21, straight, gay, tall, short, they were all colors, but most of all, they were all enthusiastic about their arrival. The staff beamed, the trainees beamed, a mutual beaming occurred. We located all their beds, stashed their luggage, introductions were made and finally the last one was tucked in and a slight hush was heard, hushed relief from them that their journey had ended and hushed relief from us that they had arrived.

We posted class schedules, professors taught, the staff watched all. Cecilia asked me if I would keep an eye on the "older volunteers" so I invited them to my room. Discussions, apprehensions, fears and doubts came to the fore and I did my best to assuage them all. Because Rebecca and I were going to the continent we had to begin taking our malaria pills. Cape Verde does not have malaria so, after being off them for the past ten months, I had forgotten what wild dreams the pills gave one.

I decided to spice up the training a bit and do a play. I had asked my daughter Maura to send me two copies of a play I had seen in Boston and loved, "Love Letters" by A.H. Gurney. I gave it to Jay to read, "nah, can't do it," gave it to an older PCT (Peace Corps trainee as the students were now called) "nah, can't do it," and then gave it to David, a young trainee with a great voice. "Yup" was his answer and we rehearsed late at night for several nights. When we presented it a week later, we heard a giggle, and then a few sobs before the first act was finished, and we knew we had them. The end of the last act was received in silence and then the clapping and yells of approval came. The play did it, we were merely the messengers. I went to bed that night feeling most satisfied. Gave my last cross culture lecture, packed the bags and Rebecca and I were off to the next adventure, going to Senegal & Mali.

Winnie Luchie, the red haired wife of the chief of U.S.A.I.D. (United States Agency for International Development) in Cape Verde, met us as we arrived from the training camp back in the big city of Praia. She had heard about the production of "Love Letters" that we had just done and said when I came back from our trip her husband would love to do it for another audience in Praia. Yea! Bernice invited me to stay in her lovely home outside of Praia. She had made peanut butter cookies, one could do that when one had a real oven, and so we munched and chatted and laughed and compared notes on two red heads living in Cape Verde. That night the vivid dreams ushered me into the disorganization that always surrounded every trip in Africa. Rebecca and I called the airline to see if the plane was leaving on time. "Well, we are not sure, we will call you". Two hours later, we called, "oh, it is leaving in ½ hour." We wrangled a ride out to the airport and then did the "hurry up and wait" dance. If waiting was an Olympic sport, Africans would be the gold medal winners. Rebecca and I finally settled down, my NYC energy was running out, and began to delve into the ten books we had each brought with us - knowing ahead of time what it would be like to travel African style. We had arrived at 3 in the afternoon - the plane was to leave at 5pm. and we were told to go home at 10pm and come back in the morning at 5am. The flight crew took off in a van before we knew what was happening to go back to the town; we had to haggle with a taxi driver to get us back and managed to wake up Bridget, a PCV. She graciously let us go to sleep in her room and again the vivid dreams rocked us till dawn.

The next morning the plane was there; we got on, smiled and said "we're off." Not quite so fast, fifteen minutes into the flight, we turned around, back on the ground ... problems. The airline van took all of the very disgruntled passengers back to town; we had lunch on the airline at a restaurant we could never have afforded and went back to the airport in the late afternoon. And then, believe it or not, we actually did take off.

We arrived in Dakar, capital of Senegal, as dusk was settling. The whirl and the swirl of the big city caught us up and we immediately called the Peace Corps office. Maura Sene, gracious lady of the office, said "come on over", we haggled the taxi driver - we were now developing this into a fine art - and arrived to mosquito-netted beds at the ready. Jeff, a PCV from Guinea Bissau whom we trained with, took us out into the full moonlit city and shepherded us around. Hearing the call to prayer made us realize we were indeed in a very different culture. The tall, elegant women with disdain dripping from their very magnificent shoulders intimidated us, the tall and elegant slide and glide men made us feel inferior, the rush of life pounded us from all sides and it was all quite wonderful.

The next morning we began the visa dance. Mali's Embassy only issued visas every other fourth leap year, or so it seemed to us. We then went to the American Embassy and as we walked past the ramrod straight Marines, I whispered, "Happy Birthday, November 10th" and a barely noticeable smile briefly flickered across the Marine's face. We went to the cafeteria and had a BLT, and a milkshake. What a welcome change from rice, rice, rice! On the huge TV we saw Gorbachev fighting for his political life, a huge BCCI financial scandal and Iraq still under sanctions. The news all seemed so far removed from the life we were in at the moment, I quickly lost

118

interest. Tuckered out, we limped back to the Peace Corps Guest house and let the mosquito nets keep us from all bites of the night.

Bernice Powell, Maura Sene, Diane, Cecilia Otero (Director of Training)

Bernice Powell and Diane

"THERE IS A WORLD ELSEWHERE"

William Shakespeare

The next adventure was about to begin. The health conference that Rebecca and I had wrangled ourselves into was to be held in Mali, West Africa and as we had to get there as cheaply as possible, the train was the transit of choice. We hustled over to the "Le Gare" (train station in French) where everything was in chaos. We were finally seated in two seats. Well, you may call them seats, they had indeed been seats in the distant past, now they were skeletons of seats that had held many, many thousands of asses, black, brown, not many yellow, and white asses that had worn down the seats to a nubbin - to the thread bare cushion and the tough springs. As Alice Walker once said, "there was not enough room to curse a cat," but these were the seats we would occupy for the next 18 - 20 hours. Well, that is the time they said it would take to go from Senegal to Mali. The train was 45 minutes late in leaving, an omen of the time table to come for sure. As we lugged out of the station, smokers lit up, children began to howl and Africans began to enjoy this social excursion.

The booming metropolis of Dakar receded and the countryside took over. Towering modern skyscrapers were replaced by the baobab tree, the tree of mystery and intense devotion of Africa. Folklore says that God said to a gigantic baobab tree, "I do not wish you to grow there, I wish you to grow over there." The baobab tree responded, "I am the king of all the trees and I shall grow where I wish." So one night God took the arrogant tree, turned it upside down and placed it exactly where God wished it to grow. When one looks at a baobab tree today, it looks like the root system is up in the air and the top of the tree is firmly planted into the ground.

Our train sped by another train off on a siding, a hulk rusting in the sun. One African behind us yelled, "banditos!" and everyone joined in the laughter except Rebecca and me. Then the stops began. We began to slow down outside of a town and we could see the children and the women of the village running to be the first in line when the train stopped. When we stopped, there were women laden with mangoes, bananas, pears, fruits I had never seen before, Chinese toothpaste, fresh chickens, eggs, cookies, fresh baked muffins and breads, rice that had been cooked in pails and small plastic bags that bulged with water. Rebecca and I decided that one of us had to stay with the bags and one had to do the buying - so I volunteered and out I went. I walked behind a very authoritative looking woman and watched her very carefully. When she picked up a piece, she would start the haggling and the vendor did as well. They went back and forth, seemed like hours, settling on a price that I assumed was different from the price they began and coins were given. I then motioned that I wanted exactly what the woman had wanted at exactly the same price. The bargain hunting lady allowed me to follow her tracks and after the first few times when I screwed up, either when the product being sold the locals would try to substitute a less desirable piece or I would give too much or too little change, she would watched me with a hawk's eye to make sure I was doing all right. We sauntered back to the puffing train that seemed to threaten to depart without me. The first purchase was a muffin for each of us; it was delicious. And so it went, long stretches of sand, the ubiquitous baobab trees, market women, and then villages with their thatched tops looking like whirling dervish dancers in the swirling sand.

After looking out of the windows for hours, I began to look at our fellow passengers. The women had captured the layered look long before the fashion capitals of the world. Brightly colored cotton tops with varied patterns danced around the quite ample bodies of the women. Jangling bracelets, long, we are talking really long, silver and gold earrings all bedecked the women. The nails, both feet and hands, were painted with bright red polish and the bottoms of their feet and hands had a dark burgundy color. The men wore trousers of slightly toned down patterns and kept to themselves. The morning wore into the afternoon and the light reflecting off the land told us the day was coming to an end. Colors went from subtle mauves, oranges, yellows to come together to bring down the dark of the night.

As we were sitting quietly, our train stopped suddenly in the middle of nowhere and no selling women or laughing children came to us. Instead, soldiers got on and marched into the train. I watched what the others did and saw passports come out of many folds of clothing. We sat very still and waited. A soldier put his hand out towards us: I smiled, he did not. He thrust his hand closer to us, and said "passports" and after trying a somewhat hesitant dialogue which did not work at all, we gave our precious passports to the soldier. Everyone repositioned themselves in their seats, looked like this was business as usual, and some started to sleep. Rebecca nodded off; I stayed wide awake wondering what journey our passports were going on without us!

Then the train stopped, again in the middle of nowhere. Rebecca was now sound asleep. One member of each couple got up and moved to the doors of the train. I checked the crowd. My woman friend, the great haggler of pricing, was sound asleep, but the man with her got up and moved to the door, I was right behind him. His manner gave me a sense of security, what else did I have. His long and elegant dashiki flowed gracefully as he began to walk with a purpose into the pitch black night. I followed and somehow let him knew I was there. He glanced at me and continued his long legged strides. A gentle rain began and I lifted up my head and tasted the pure drops and then realized the man had come to a standstill and I had almost run into him. He motioned for me to stand where I was and the next minute he was gone. I stood in the dark, in the jungle with people milling round me, swallowing the rain and hoping my new found buddy would come back for me. Before I knew it, he was back in front of me, motioned me to follow and on we went about a mile before we came to a clearing. Torches lighted a large table and there were our beloved passports in haphazard fashion covering the table top. Soldiers with rifles, some had bayonets on the ends of them, stood at each end and then names were sung out and people came forth and grabbed their passports. There must have been hundreds of us, my ears were ringing with strange names and I was terrified I would miss our names. My elegant man got his, everyone parted when he walked through the crowd and he motioned for me to follow. After waiting for what seemed eternity, I heard my name and Rebecca's. I let out a yelp and ran up to get them and fell all over the caretakers thanking them. Everyone laughed and I turned around and said "merci beaucoup" to the crowd and many applauded and then we all trooped back to the train, which was puffing and about to leave. Rebecca slept through it all.

Dawn awakened us and the usual stop to buy came. This time we both took turns to get off: to pee was the thing. The bathroom on the train was a joke, a filthy joke as a matter of fact, and mothers had small pots for their children to use and then threw the contents out of the window. As I was leaving my jungle bathroom, I noticed a woman sitting on a little stool and knew I had to have it. Went over and started the bargaining, nope, not for sale, but the chickens are. Nope, don't want the chickens, want the stool. Back and forth, then I decided to buy the damn squawking chicken and get the stool. I heard the train whistle telling all to hustle and I continued to count out my small, unfamiliar French coins. The lady yelled, I yelled, Rebecca yelled at me to hurry and then the train actually started to move. I threw my coins at her, grabbed the chicken, tucked the stool under my other arm and ran. A man yelled, "chicken" so I threw it in the train, next I threw the stool, the train was increasing its speed and I was really scared. As I ran alongside screaming, four giant hands leaned down and grabbed both of my outstretched hands and pulled me ever so strongly into the train. Once again, the kindness of strangers saved me.

ARRIVAL IN MALI, WEST AFRICA

The man at the train station in Dakar, Senegal told us "the train ride will take about 18 to 20 hours". Thirty nine hours later we arrived in Bamako, the capital of Mali. We finally found a cab and went straight to the Peace Corps Guest House. This guest house was a serious guest house with more than 60 cots, all with individual mosquito nets, lined up in one huge room (with showers) which we fell into immediately. As grime on top of grime started to float down the drains, Rebecca said "Oh, My God, look what is on your bum." Since I could not see the back of my ass, I asked her to stop yelling, and tell me what she saw. She laughed and as I was about to punch her, I noticed there were other people looking at my ass and laughing. Rebecca finally said, "You have two perfect rings on each bun, with small rings inside the big rings from the springs of the seat in the train!"

We piled into a huge truck which ploughed through deep rain puddles. After showering and changing we arrived at the training center to begin our six day seminar. We were introduced, served dinner with rice and pieces of meat mixed in, and given treated drinking water. Finally we were shown our beds in our individual thatched huts with the comforting mosquito nets to stand guard as we slept.

At 7am, a huge bell rang, greeting the arrival of another day, another bucket shower and another class. In the huge hall we listened to volunteers from Mali, Ghana, Togo, Ivory Coast, and The Central African Republic. Different methods of teaching were presented, different stories were heard, but the one theme that was repeated over and over again was "The people have told us what they need. It is our job to assist them to meet those needs." The hot African air was always with us but the cool shade under the thatched hall made it seem as though we were air conditioned. An early evening rain came thundering down and while everyone else ran for cover, I walked out into it to become thoroughly soaked as I swallowed the fresh rain as fast as I could. When I returned to my hut to tuck in for the night, I noticed the construction of the room. The thatch went upwards to a huge cone and the air swirled round to make it cool for me under it, natural air conditioning. I had picked up a copy of <u>The Ugly American</u> by William Lederer in the Bamako PC flop house. As I fell asleep with the book on my tummy, I said goodnight to the huge spiders that were in all the corners: "Ok Charlottes, do your work." The next morning the fly population had been considerably reduced.

After three days of giving and hearing lectures, we all agreed it was time to have an outing. We visited a true Renaissance man, a farmer who had been trained in France and was a professor at the agriculture school in the district and a consultant to the country CARE office. Every single inch of his land was put to use. He had ponds for tadpoles and sold them when they became frogs, he had flowers planted that kept insects away, areas where he was doing grafting experiments. He had old broken pieces of discarded equipment made into pulleys to draw the water for his farm. His work ethic was fabulous. He explained that when one of his children was bad, he would not let them work in the fields but made them stay in the house all day. His 12 year old daughter had her own peanut field and showed it to us with great pride.

That night we were taken to a nearby village for a drumming session. We learned that the young boys were learning how to make the drums, how to make sure they were ready to be used and then were allowed to play before the elders and the rest of the village. In Africa the night comes down with a silent but thorough black curtain, it happens within the blink of the eye. We were walking down a dirt road towards a village when, all of a sudden, we could not see where we were walking. Then we heard the sounds of the drumming and we walked into a torch lit circle of about a hundred people who were quietly watching three older men. People shifted to make room for us to sit on huge tree branches that were lying on the ground. A silence and then the soft drumming resumed. The oldest drummer, white beard moving ever so slightly, had an amazing concentration - his head was cocked first one way, then another, then he would lean over and adjust the small piece of wood that held the skin in tightly over the top of the drum. This procedure was repeated time and time again, two other men were also tuning their drums. The younger men waited patiently and finally were allowed to sit next to the drums. They started to drum softly, the audience watching every move. An older woman got up and began to move and then another one. Pretty soon the circle was filled with dancing people. Some of the volunteers were asked to join the dancers which they did, I still watched the older men making adjustments to the drums. Then the oldest man came over and stood in front of me, bowed, took my hand and moved me to the middle of the circle. This man with the long beard moved ever so slightly, not touching me in an American way of dancing, but he was definitely dancing with just me. I mirrored his moves, long, slow graceful swirls, turns, and dips. This went on for about twenty minutes. My dance partner stopped, put his hand out towards me and I put my hand on his arm. We walked to a place where there were no people sitting and sat down. We could hear the drumming; he closed his eyes, I closed mine. We must have sat there for one hour. Then I felt a light touch on my shoulder, he was standing and helped me up. He led me back to the circle where people were dancing and we danced for another twenty minutes. By now the light was beginning to change and people were going home to their huts. He walked me back to where we were all living, touched me on the shoulder, smiled, turned and left. Not a word had been said.

The next morning, my Charlotte's web spiders looked fat and sassy and the flies that used to mate on my arm were gone. As I took my bucket shower, I noticed a huge, barn door red frog. He did not hop but crawled along with a big harrumph, harrumph. His sound was very different from the frogs I had heard when traveling in the jungle. The jungle was seething on all sides of us. The rain seemed to make everything bolder and louder. The birds were madly having a talking contest and all was noise and movement outside of my hut.

We took a group picture in front of the sign with the name of the training center on it, "The Maureen Reagan Center." We heard she had visited here when her father was the President. As we were leaving, one PCV from Guinea, Rachel, with whom I had become friends, said," do stay in touch" and we all went in different directions.

Rebecca and I went back to Bamako and visited the U.S. Embassy. Bernice from the Cape Verde embassy had asked me to deliver a present for her friend Rob so I left it with a note saying I was in town. We walked around and got a sense of the city. Colorful clothes on all the Malians, PCVs were very friendly and helpful. Ate dinner in a French restaurant; they sure did know how to do the fancy dishes. That night the swirling fans in the flop house lulled all 60 souls to a quiet sleep. Morning coffee smells awakened us and we were off to the Grand Marche, the selling place where bargaining is the name of the game and I bought a bead necklace for each daughter and a strip of mud cloth which was dyed brown with black patterns on it for me. Got into the haggling and had a grand time with the process.

After dinner we went to visit a PCV I had heard of, Don Lawler. Tall, quite elegant and 74 years old, he was a school teacher and you could tell all the villagers loved him. He and I talked about what it was like to be an older volunteer and agreed it certainly had its advantages as we would be respected without question. He was a delight to visit with and when I left, he said, "Do return." The next day the Mali PCVs took us outside of town to the American Community Center where we reveled in a real pool, a real cafeteria, real hamburgers and ice cream sodas. We glutted ourselves on American style food, and I did lap after lap in the pool till I was wrinkled like a prune.

We traveled next to Mopti, on the way to Timbuktu. The bus arrived a hour late, took off two hours later; the goats were put on the top of the roof, the chickens in the back of the bus. We also rode inside, now a group of four: Amy from Cape Verde had joined us for our expedition with Jeff from Guinea Bissau. The boom box next to me was blaring and I yelled asking them to turn it off but Amy said "no, that's Pink Floyd, we like that." I was out voted. We stopped for pee breaks but never went too far fearing the bus would lurch off when the driver thought all were back on, he never counted, just took off when he felt like leaving. Since every seat was taken and dozens of people were sitting in the aisle, there was no way for him to know how many passengers he had. It was a long, long ride, only took six hours but felt like ten.

We arrived in the town of Mopti, immediately went to find the PC flop house and of course, once found, flopped and slept like dead people. When we awoke, it was dusk so we four went out to find food, find out how to get to Timbuktu, and once again, get a sense of the town. The more we moved away from the big cities, the less we saw of people who looked like us and the more the Africans stared at us. We would smile, they would then smile: it was all in the manner of presentation. I taught myself, "Je suis Voluntier Corp de la Pays" which means I am a Peace Corps volunteer, and that always brought smiles. The Peace Corps had been in Mali more than twenty years so the Malians understood and valued our mission.

127

The swift running Niger River ran by Mopti and as we ate dinner in a restaurant near the shore, we watched men pull their fishing boats up, women washing their clothing and then men washing themselves. Bright colored boats with long, low hulls were rested on the shore, families living on them made the boats bee hives of activity. In the market, the merchants were not a bit aggressive. They showed us their wares: bright colored cloth, dried fish heads, batteries, fruit and cassettes, all mixed together. If we shook our heads no, they smiled, bowed and disappeared.

Young men raced around the crowded streets on mopeds, their dashikis flowing behind them in graceful swirls. The sunsets were brilliant, reflected in the racing waters that led to the north and Timbuktu. As I looked north, the colors got dimmer and grayer, almost ghost-like which only added to the mystique of Timbuktu. We discovered there were three ways to get to Timbuktu: river, road and air. The river gave us two choices: a small boat with no overhead protection and one guide doing the paddling, or the large river boat with guards on it. The problem was that the Tuaregs were shooting the guards, so if you were talking to a guard or next to a guard, you might not finish up the trip the way you started. We learned about the Tuaregs, a tribe of nomads who inhabit the northern part of Mali, where the country takes the shape of a butterfly in flight. They were called the Blue Veiled Devils of the desert and were strong and clever enough to push back Rommel's tanks during World War II. Tuaregs were angry because they were not represented in the National Assembly and so were making it very difficult for people to get to Timbuktu. Planes flew you there, at great expense, but could not guarantee when you would return. Land Rovers could take you there, but a group of German tourists had just come limping back into Mopti after their Rover had been hijacked and they had been robbed. They said the Tuaregs were very polite but very insistent about getting all their money and all their property. We decided we would go to a town at the edge of Timbuktu and play it by ear; that was a pastime everyone practiced in Africa. But first, we wanted to go the market to buy one of the famous Mopti blankets.

MOPTI TO ALMOST TIMBUKTU

The stalls in the market were fastened together by spit and a prayer. Men walked around with huge piles of neatly folded material on their heads, perfectly balanced. You bought them by the strip, called a panho, which could be used for a multitude of purposes: skirt, blouse, dress, headscarf, sheet, blanket, towel, container for items, to tie a baby on a mother's back, or use as a shield from the rain or sun. I bought a green and red patterned piece which I used constantly for the rest of the trip. Then I saw a "famous" Mopti blankets in piles. The Mopti blanket has a very distinct pattern, dark red wool diamonds on an ivory colored background. Some people hang them on their walls. They are unique and stunning. The merchant stood quietly as I approached his table. He was 6' if an inch, wore dark eye glasses, and behaved very differently from the hawkers in Dakar and Bamako. He gestured towards the blankets, I nodded, and he knew he had a buyer. The calculator came out from under his multi-folds and when I asked the price, he tapped in a price. I looked shocked and put in a price that was half his. He smiled, now here was a woman he could deal with. Back and forth went our fast fingers. In between he would shake his head, point to his small children and tell me that I was taking food from their mouths. I would point to my belly and say I had four children and therefore could not afford his high price. We warmed to the exercise. More back and forthing, I made a move to walk away, he came around and touched my arm, hung his head and said "last price." I put in a slightly lower price and he smiled, shrugged and said, "D'accord," which means okay in French. My magnificent Mopti blanket with its classic black/brown designs bordered by burgundy stripes went into my small red bag. He bowed, I bowed and we both felt as though we had both won. As I left the blanket seller, I noticed a man hand carving a pipe, went into my haggling mode, and walked away with a lovely pipe for Vitorino.

As I continued to walk through the market, I saw a very, very tall man wearing a very, very bright blue indigo veil and traditional robe ahead of me. He was a Tuareg, a member of a tribe of fierce warriors. I had read about them and learned they are a Berber nomadic pastoralist people who are the principal inhabitants of the Saharan interior of North Africa. I walked behind him. He casually walked through the aisles and as he would round a comer, I would see the back of his blue robe. I became fascinated by this man. He walked; I followed. As I came around a corner, he turned around suddenly and faced me. All I could see was his mesmerizing eyes; his lower face was completely covered by a blue veil. I took a quick breath, did not move and neither did he. I could feel my heart racing; the look lasted for 15 seconds. The Sahel wind moved his robe, my skirt clung to me, then his eyes changed, a slight lightness came into them, perhaps a smile was under the veil. He turned and vanished. I thought of Isabel Arundell when she first met Sir Richard Burton and how she felt after seeing his eyes, "I was about to swoon like a lady of quality," now I understood that feeling. Jeff came running up to me and said "are you all right, where did you go?" I shook my head and could not explain.

Jeff had managed to get us a ride to Bundgarda, the town next to Timbuktu. Amy, Jeff and I got into a falling apart station wagon and took off into a swirl of sand. The heat was oppressive, but when I looked for the window handles, there were none. When we got to Bundgarda, young English speaking guides said they would take us to Dogon country where people lived in caves carved out of the mountains. Jeff and Amy went, but I opted to stay to try to find a safe way to get to Timbuktu. In a park I saw a young boy with a sling shot hit a chicken at a distance of about 20 feet. The chicken was stunned; the boy went over and wrung its neck. I walked over and started to chat with him. His sling shot was a figure of a boy with intricate carvings on it and a piece of familiar Goodyear rubber stretched between the legs of the carving. I offered him some coins, he said "more," I gave more, no calculators here, and we finally agreed on a bunch of coins. I smiled, he smiled, done deal.

Back at PCV Julie's hut we were treated to a tea ceremony. Tea from pot to short glass to pot, to glass until a froth began to form. The tea was very tasty. Julie was most generous and let me stay the night in her hut. Her bamboo enclosure had a shower I reveled in. When I looked at my skin, I thought it has taken me 54 years to become a bronze beauty. Then the water came down, the Sahel sand went down the drain and with it went my tan. Julie told me to rest in her hammock and she would be back after doing some work. Snakes crawled around the ground, monkeys screamed in the trees and I slept through it all. Julie gently awakened me as the light began to fade. "My mother has invited you to come for dinner." She had been adopted by a Malian woman and the three of us had a delicious dinner of "toe", a dish with rice and meat served on a baobab leaf, and shared stories of bringing up children. I showed Julie the stool I had bought from the train trip and she said "you are very lucky, that is made from a baobab tree." Amy and Jeff came back from Dogon country and told all about the mysterious people who lived in caves.

That night I looked at Jay's computer map of the sky in this area - every single star was right where it should be. With Cassiopaeia and Regulus looking over us, I fell asleep with Julie's dog at my feet, the sling shot under my arm and visions of the Tuareg who had let me catch him. I tried the next day to get to Timbuktu to no avail; the Tuaregs had effectively sealed off the city. If they could not have representation in the assembly, no one would get into their capital city. I sympathized with their cause. Reminded me of a quote I learned long ago "taxation without representation is tyranny" which was a rallying cry back in the colonial days of the United States.

In Mopti we hoped to find a yogurt place Julie told us about, "go down this alley, go under an arch that is falling apart, then two lefts, you will find a fridge with the very best yogurt." We thanked her as we ate the best yogurt ever. As the sun set, we watched the well-known Bozo fishermen under their dark maroon sails go from the Niger River to the distant Bonnie River. Later Jeff, Amy, Rebecca and I took a bus back to Bamako.

I had promised Don I would return and visit so back to Bamako I went. One woman at his home was wearing a magnificent two piece outfit. When I admired it, Don said she would make one for me, if I bought the cotton material and came back in one hour. I bought a piece of yellow and black patterned material, with a most colorful and brilliant pattern and left it with her. She never measured me, at least not with a tape measure, and the next morning I returned to find an exquisite two piece outfit, perfect fit.

Later, as I walked back to the PC flop house, I began to have stomach cramps, barely made it to the toilet and had the runs and vomiting all day. I must have eaten something really bad and suffered the pangs of my body in revolt. Don heard about me from some PCVs (nothing is secret in PC) and came to visit. "Drink water constantly, and in 24 hours you will be up and dancing, I'll even come and pick you up." As I turned over into a fetal position, I never thought I would move again, much less dance. 24 hours later, I was, indeed, as right as rain and did dance that night.

The next morning I finally finished reading Bill Lederer's book, <u>The Ugly American</u>, and wrote him a letter saying friends had wanted us to meet many years ago, he had just divorced, as I had and they thought we would enjoy each other. I went into the PC, he went to his farm in Peacham, Vermont. Eugene Burdick was the co-author and to this day, that book is used as a teaching tool for people going to work in foreign countries. When the Peace Corps began in 1961, they gave each new volunteer a copy of this book. The book explained that when one lived in a foreign country, one had to learn the culture of the country. That is so important and I remembered the cross culture lessons that I was taught in our training in Guinea Bissau. Also told him, the situation that he described was, sad to say, still the same.

After being so sick, I wrote down a few observations about being in the Peace Corps. One loses control over: your housing, your food, your schedule, your vacations, your places to stay, your mode of transportation, your bowel movements, your medicine and your friends. But, there are so many good things about PC: working in a new environment, teaching those who have asked for help, meeting new people and learning, learning, learning. There are three missions of the PC: assisting and teaching those who have asked for help, learning about other cultures and then bringing the experience of the PC back home. My next invitation bore this out.

When you travel as a PCV, people always give you names of people to see, to call, to visit. Bernice had given me three contacts for Bamako; 1, Rob, 2, his wife Sandy and 3 Dennis. A message reached me at the flop house that Rob, of the U.S. embassy invited me over for dinner and if I would like, spend the night. Bye bye flop house with 50 others. Rob drove me to his lovely home with a guard, swimming pool, maid and nanny. Sandy, his lovely and gracious wife, showed me to my room and my shower and said the pool was available for a quick swim before dinner. I showered and was in my bathing suit in two shakes. Flowers grew all around the front yard and their scents filled the air with aromas. A house staff member served a sumptuous meal, my appetite came back slowly and we spent a lovely evening talking in their comfortable living room.

The conversation was lively, fun and I got a realistic picture of the politics of this mysterious country of Mali. Rob and Sandy had hired a Malian child sitter for their young son Matthew and we talked about the differences between raising children in the U.S. and raising them abroad. I told them of my child raising years and mentioned Dr. T. Berry Brazelton, our pediatrician. Sandy had heard that he was now taking the place of Dr. Spock as the leading child raising expert. Sandy had some questions about child rearing, so I offered to write them down and send them to Dr. Brazelton. After a Sesame Street bubble bath and on a firm, real mattress with clean sheets and the sound of rain hitting the roof, I tucked in.

After that fine night's sleep, I felt like a new woman. When I opened my eyes, there was a very large 12 inch pink chameleon staring at me. While we were having a staring contest to see who would blink first, young Matthew came bounding into my room, full of two - year old energy announcing breakfast. After delicious, freshly baked bran muffin and freshly squeezed orange juice, Sandy drove me to the National Museum to see an exhibit of Alfred Stieglitz' photographs. I thought of his companion, Georgia O'Keeffe, and wondered what she would have thought of the wild country of Mali. As we drove away from the museum, Sandy explained the roughly roped off area going right on in the middle of the city was for archeological excavations. The nationals were peeved that traffic had to be re-routed. She drove me back to the flop house and there was Dennis, my third Bamako contact, dapper Dan, ready to take me to lunch. I thanked Sandy for a grand visit and promised to get Dr. Brazelton's response back to her.

Dennis was the U.S.A.I.D Director and had his finger on the pulse of all that was happening. He was an elegant, gentle gentleman, but I sensed one tough man inside the Saville Row suit that could wheel and deal with the best of them. His daughter and son joined us for lunch and we had a delightful afternoon trading stories, my new person's impressions of Mali and his sense of the political situation. There were times he baited me about being a PCV. - it was almost as though he didn't believe one could be happy, work for no money and on top of that - make a difference. I gave him concrete examples of what had succeeded in Cape Verde and why, and he seemed to listen, but there was a slight air of cynicism. He graciously drove me back to the flop house and wished me bon voyage for the next leg of my trip.

COURAGE IS THE POWER TO LET GO OF THE FAMILIAR

The train ride back from Mali was different than the train ride to Mali with Rebecca. Two humongous ladies had set themselves next to the two doors at the end of the car. Huge wicker baskets sat next to them, groaning with fruit of every description. Then business began. At every stop, ladies from the fields bargained with the ladies from the train: one bracelet for this fruit, one necklace for these three branches with small fruits, a mask for a huge coconut, two chickens for ten fruits; money and trade went back and forth with amazing speed. As the train left each station, the two women put their turbaned heads together, clucking and sighing and chattering about the money they had taken in.

I watched in fascination and once the larger of the two slipped me a half of banana, smiling and bobbing her head. I bobbed my head in thanks and savored it. Jeff was sitting in a seat by the door and as we came to a stop a young, surly, filthy looking kid came rushing on to the train, grabbed a big suitcase from the overhead metal rack and jumped off the train as it began its departure. Jeff spotted him and tried to save the luggage but it was too late. The people on the train clapped for him and his efforts. Rebecca and I hung on to each of our small bags with new purpose. When the time came to give up our passport, we did with seasoned aplomb. About an hour later, I went off into the darkness to reclaim our valuable passports, only this time I did not have the chief to clear the path for me. I had learned how to do it. This time we were only ten hours late to Dakar. From the station we went off to the "flop house" where we began making plans for our last remaining days in Senegal before returning to Cape Verde. The "flop house" is the nickname the PC V's used for all guest houses that were in the capital cities where PC had offices. All volunteers were welcomed, some flop houses were elegant and small, other houses were large and filled to the brim. They all had one similar trait, they all welcomed any and all PC V's who needed a bed for the night, or nights.

While we were at the health training seminar in Bamako, a PCV named Cassie gave us the name of Harriet Boyce, an American woman who lived on the island of Gore, 2 miles out in the harbor of Dakar and said we must visit her. The next morning we took off in a small boat to Gore to meet this fascinating woman. Cassie had told us that during the slaving trade, Gore was the stop off spot for white slavers between Africa, Europe and the United States. We had our trusty guide book in hand and went to the prison where the slaves had been held. We noticed a small, cement block next to the sea at the entrance to the prison and were told by a guide that it was the place where the slavers weighed the slaves. If they made a certain weight, they were put inside the prison, if they were too frail and not strong enough, they were pushed off the block into the ocean where sharks were waiting. Even though it was a hot, blistering day, we were chilled by this terrible fate and stood silent for many minutes in this place of death.

We toured the prison that was being restored by the Dutch to its original condition. One particular room again gave us the chills. The sign over the door said "recalcitrants" and explained that slaves who were troublemakers were chained here and sea water was piped in so that it covered their bodies up to their necks. The recalcitrants soon were quieted by this means of torture. There were rooms where the small children were held, rooms for pregnant women, the young boys' room. The captives all were sorted and separated and families that had been captured together were separated, never to be united again.

Rebecca and I did not speak as we went around this house of unspeakable history. After many minutes, we sat down and realized we had to get away from this house of horror. We walked to the home of Harriet Boyce climbing up past tall steps and magnificent hanging flower vines until we finally found her lovely home. A young French girl answered the door and explained that Harriet had gone to the States, but we were welcomed into the house. On one wall a Mopti blanket hung with its traditional black, maroon striped and diamond pattern. I felt in my small bag for my recently purchased Mopti bag and felt very proud I had bought one to take home. African masks and wood sculptures filled every nook and cranny of this unique home. We received a cold glass of orange juice and sat and listened to the young woman talk about Gore and Harriet. She told us of a famous

French restaurant right on the water's edge, and as we left, we decided to pool our resources and blow it all on our last grand meal on the continent. For dinner we ate fresh baked French croissants, a fresh fish from the surrounding sea, a tossed green salad at the end and sweets to tempt our palates. We even managed to buy a fair bottle of wine. We toasted my daughter Katherine on her birthday, the 16 of August. I swallowed the lump in my throat that always came when I thought of one of my children.

After dark we returned to the city of Dakar by ferry and saw lights twinkling in anticipation of the night life about to begin. Rain was pouring down and got so bad I had mud caked between my toes in my sandals, a problem I never had in Cape Verde. But I was beginning to feel homesick for Cape Verde and was ready to return.

We got to the airport in plenty of time, without hassle which should have warned us, and off we went. The man who sat next to me asked me to dinner when we landed in Cape Verde. I said no thank you, some other time and went off to sleep. About an hour later, I was awakened by the same man saying he would like to take me to dinner in Dakar. I said, "No, we are going to be landing soon in Cape Verde" but he leaned over and said softly, "Wrong." I looked out the window and indeed, instead of the expected lunar landscape of Cape Verde, I was looking at Dakar. The pilot had turned back, no one made a fuss. We were taken to a motel next to the airport, complete with swimming pool and bar, and we were told we would leave on Monday.

All the passengers did what they were comfortable with, some went to the bar, some went shopping, Rebecca snoozed and I did laps in the pool. We did have dinner with the man who had invited me to dinner in Cape Verde. His friend joined us and the evening passed as we compared African travel stories. The men were Canadian on their way to Cape Verde to be coaches for a soccer team.

THE CONTINUING SAGA GETTING TO AND FROM THE CONTINENT

When one travels in developing countries, one expects everything and nothing, both at the same time. Rebecca and I had tried to get back to Cape Verde, only to be flummoxed by the flying machines. There was nothing to do but sit back, relax and go with the flow.

As we got used to the fact that we would not be spending that night in our home country, we decided to wear our fancy Malian dresses to dinner. We took a hot shower, fixed our hair in an elegant way, and pranced into the semi-elegant dining room. As we passed by the kitchen, the cooks and kitchen staff looked at us, smiled and then applauded. We looked at them and then we applauded them in thanks. They must have seen what wrecks we were when we came into the hotel and were pleased we had shaped up. The dining room was full of all our fellow passengers, and if I had to guess how many languages were being spoken, I would say a different language to each group of three, which made a hubbub of wonderful lilts, tilts and melodic sounds. After dinner, a long walk, and good nights all around, on went my swim suit to do a few laps to last me till I got back to my own section of Atlantic Ocean where the sun and the moon bid the shore good morn and good night.

The next morning, amazingly enough, the plane did take off from Dakar and landed in the capital city of Praia, Cape Verde. We were met by PC staff and while I was taken to the training center, Rebecca went back to her town on the out skirts of Praia. When we said goodbye to each other, we realized we were still comparing notes about this book, or about that film and that living check to jowl for three weeks had cemented our friendship. We promised to visit each other's towns in the year to come.

My living accommodations at the center were different from what I had left in Mindelo, now four of us crowded into one space. We were all PCVs, Jill and Roz would do the TEFL training, Suz was the health trainer, and I was to do cross culture training. Bunk beds were the order of the day and, since the four of us had trained together way back, we all had a good comfort level with each other. Because our living space was so limited, we figured out the night before we went to sleep, which two of us would take the first shift of rising and who would take the second.

The classes were in constant motion; the staff met regularly and repositioned themselves to meet the needs of the trainees. Cecilia, the Director of the training, did a fine job of holding a strong and opinionated staff together. The trainees came in all sizes, shapes, colors and ages. The youngest had just become 20 and the oldest was 75. We all worked hard preparing the lessons, counseling and listening. Then we had parts of the night free. I was walking down a steep hill one night lit by fierce moonlight, when I saw hibiscus plants and remembered the ditty, "hibiscus tight at night, open at first light." Dylan Thomas' verse came to me at the same time, "go not gentle into that long, good night, rage, rage against the dying of the light."

I thought of Vitorino and how we would laugh together in the moonlight when I read poetry to him in English and then translated it into Portuguese. We had not seen each other for two months and it would be another month before I would be folded into his comforting arms.

As the weeks of training rolled towards completion, Bernice invited me to her home in the town of Praia. The aroma of freshly baked peanut butter cookies greeted me at her door and we sat in comfy, stuffed chairs and compared notes from the last week's events. We discussed the upcoming Labor Day weekend and noted that it was no holiday here, just another work labor day. Bernice had a grand sense of zest. We had become fast friends and when I visited her, we went on long walks at the beach near her home, talked in the shade and giggled with tales of what we had done in the past years. But we both agreed to continue to live life to the fullest. Going back to the training site after the elegant visits with Bernice was always hard.

Training sessions wound down and the goodbyes began, and the PCT's began to leave by countries. The tiny island country of Sao Tome and Principe would receive three trainees to add to the eight already there,

Guinea Bissau received the highest number with 18 and Cape Verde received ten. As they left on the careening yellow buses going down the rugged mountain roads, I wondered if I would ever see any of them again. We had become so close in such a short time - but such is the way of the Peace Corps. We trainers could only hope we had done the job desired, prepare and train 44 people in three short months' time to handle anything that came their way. "Para bems and boa sorte" (good luck and congratulations) were said over and over till our throats ached. Then they were gone.

Flying back home to Mindelo the next day made me realize I had not been there for a very long three months. The lunar landscape came into view and then I knew I was home. Mario with his spiffy blue taxi picked me up and said I had been missed. The miniature American flag I had given him a year ago was still over his rear view window. Valentina gave me an enthusiastic hug and asked if I was now home for good or would I be going away again. Looking at her, I realized that when the time came to leave in one year, it would tear the heart out of me.

While unpacking and putting the gifts to one side, I heard a loud knock on my wooden door and there was Arlene. We hugged and laughed and then I heard the distinctive sound of Vitorino's car. I told Arlene to tell Vitorino I would be right down and to let him in. Running up the stairs I grabbed a small square pillow from my bed. I changed from my travel outfit to a loose fitting dress, and took the present I had bought him from Mopti, Mali and walked downstairs. He and Arlene were talking when I walked into the room and the expression on his face when he saw me was amazement, slight shock and numb - exactly the effect I wanted to create. I said in my best Portuguese "you said you would have liked to have had a child with me and I explained that I couldn't but, guess what - a miracle." I had put the pillow under the dress and looked about three months pregnant. His expression was so full of astonishment, I started to laugh and then the pillow fell out and he grabbed me and swung me around and put his head back and said, "A good, good joke, my Deana, but I am sad it is not true." Then we hugged and looked at each other with eyes that had not been dimmed of affection by time.

After Vitorino and I had reconnected, the light of dusk was beginning to sneak into my wooden shutters. I told him I had a present for him and he said he had one for me as well. We got our presents. I gave him the pipe I bought from a wood carver in Mali. He smiled. His gift was a small pipe, which fit snugly into my palm. We looked at each other and said "We gave each other the same gift." He got tobacco out of his pocket, taught me how to light my new pipe and smoke it properly. He told me that there would be many times he would not be able to be with me while I lived in Mindelo and he wanted me to have something of him near me. Then he said "When you leave, which you will do some day, you will have something to remind you of me." My tears would not hold back, they rolled down my cheeks silently and as he brushed them away with his lips, we stayed linked together by many links, the gifts of the pipes just one more link in our chain.

Diane with local fishermen

Old women who sat in front of church every morning

NAO FAZ MAL

"The Peace Corps makes its greatest contribution to foreign policy by not being part of it." Dean Rusk, 1961

Business is business, no matter where in the world you practice it. This is how I learned that fact. I had been taught in our three month training course that one must be culturally sensitive at all costs. We were taught the expression "nao faz mal" which means "No matter, no problem, that's okay." My boss, Senhor Evora, was a master at stone walling any project that he did not initiate. When I asked him for permission to do something, he would shrug and say "soon, nao faz mal." I wanted to get permission to get free cement for the old ladies in the tin shack town so they could have a house of their own. We had a policy in our project that stated people had to buy the cement, at a discount, to build their cement houses, but the old ladies did not have any money to buy the cement, even at the very good discount.

One night I went to sleep and tossed and turned - how would I solve this problem. I must have dozed off, for all of a sudden I awoke and said to myself, "By God, he is a shark and all this time I was treating him like a dolphin." My lessons from corporate America came streaming back into my head. I needed to have my clothes pressed, to make a good impression. So what do you when you want to iron your clothes and you have no iron, much less no electricity? You take the blouse and the skirt, fold them both where you want the crease pressed, put them under your mattress, and lie down on your mattress.

The next morning, with clothes pressed and looking sharp, I went to the boss's office. He gave the usual curt pleasantries and asked me to sit down. I said "No, not today, I have a need and want to discuss it with you." I had discovered the difference between the dorsal fin of a shark and the dorsal fin of a dolphin. Took me three days of haggling, cajoling, bullying, but I got the permission to get the cement for the old ladies and their home for the aged. Business was done, now on to the next challenge.

The next challenge was one that would stay with me for the entire two years I lived in Cape Verde. I remembered reading something JFK had said - "For we have not always recognized that the ideal contact is between peoples rather than governments. Governments come and go while lasting personal friendships and impressions remain." (March 21, 1961)

The challenge for me was to learn how to work with people who spoke another language, had customs that were different from mine and form lasting friendships. I thought this is why I went into the PC, to challenge myself, to work on a level I had never worked in before and be successful. PC does give you the challenges you need to have and then it is up to you to meet them and meet them well.

Correspondence still came flowing in from the States. My cousin, Father Michael Shugrue, sent me an invitation to attend his silver jubilee of ordination. My brother, Terry Shugrue, engineer for Turner Construction, sent me three very large posters that showed all the buildings that Turner constructed all around the world in 1990, 1991, 1992. They were most impressive. I gave them to my next door neighbor Pedro, Valentina's son, who was also an engineer. He hung one in their family home, one in his office in City Hall and then gave one to the Mayor of Mindelo. The Mayor hung in his office too! Turner certainly did get exposure in that country. Terry was proud of working for Turner (first and only job he has had) and I was very proud of my brother Terry. A friend's daughter, Aileen, sent me a most supportive letter and asked if I still had the teeny, tiny wooden Buddha she gave me. I glanced at my rickety wooden set of drawers and there was the Buddha sitting high on the top. Liz and Erv, whose college senior daughter Sarah died in the bombing of Pan Am 103 over Scotland a week before Christmas 1988, sent me a picture of a bench that Sarah's classmates had placed in their childhood playground in her memory. The memories pummeled me from all sides and every single time I receive mail, I became very quiet and melancholy. There was not one day that went by that I did not think about my four children and missed them greatly.

Then I would be pulled from my reverie by a surprise, something totally unexpected. I had never had a red dress, I was a redhead and my mother Leona said redheads never, ever wear red. I kept that piece of advice and never had a red dress. But that was to be changed in Africa. I told my American friend Suzette, a grand seamstress, that I wish I had a red dress. She persuaded me to buy some bright red material and made up a red dress for me. She brought it over to my apartment while I was in the midst of my thinking of Sarah's untimely death. Paula and Phil invited Paulino and me to attend the Mother's Day church service so I wore my new red dress. I said a secret prayer to my mother who I still missed and said to her, "Guess what, Mom, I am wearing a bright red dress, I have a brown baby in my arms and I am now living in West Africa." The mothers in the church were asked to stand. Each of us was given a glass dish in thanks for being Mothers. A children's chorus sang to us and even though I could not catch every word, I got the meaning and filled up with tears thinking of my children.

THE VISITS

There were five in all. Five people made the trek to a place you could not get to with ease. But made it they did and love them I shall for making the effort.

Maura, bubbly as the fizz in an American coke, pensive when necessary, was the first visitor one fine Saturday in November, 1991. I had written to my first born that I would see her that Saturday before the light changed. She wrote back "Why before the light changed?" I explained when she arrived.

The tiny, prop plane descended and her pretty fiery red suit proclaimed that she had arrived and her smile lit the air around her. We hugged, I held on a little longer than she did, to feel she was actually here. She looked around and said, "Now I know why you knew you would see me before dark, the airport has no electricity." She was learning about developing countries quickly. We could not find her bags; the attendant said he would bring them to my home later. As we were driven to my home, Maura commented, "You were right when you wrote it looks like a lunar landscape, it sure does"

After entering my home, "Your home is all stairs, your rooms tiny, but I love your big roof." We unpacked the one bag she was smart enough to carry on. I gave her some of my clothing and made her take a nap to rest up for the two weeks she would spend with me. Then the visitors arrived to meet her.

Bernice was in town, escorting two engineers from the States. Then Arlene, followed by Sandra, and on it went. I helped Maura with her Portuguese; she had standard Spanish in high school so could understand more than

144

she or I thought she would. I made a spaghetti dinner with fresh tuna that she said was the best she had ever had and I explained the tuna had been caught that morning and delivered to my home that afternoon. We went to the Piano Bar with Bernice. It was a cooking' night: my friend Cesaria Evora was singing and dedicated a song to the filha de Deana, the daughter of Diane. The music was good. We stayed past midnight. When Maura's eyes started to glaze over, it was time to tuck her in.

The first place to visit was our magnificent ocean. The next morning Maryann drove by saying "Pack up. I'll be back in ten minutes to take you to our house in San Pedro." We got our suits and were whisked away to the glorious surf. Maura watched in amazement as the Cape Verdean youngsters jumped in and out of the crashing waves. A delicious lunch of fresh fish and grilled chicken was served, guitars came out and Maura was serenaded. She absolutely glowed with all the attention and kept whispering, "They are so nice to me. Are they like this all the time?" "Yes, they make you feel like family." Maryann said it was time to take us home so Maura could rest as twilight was beginning to do its dance. Vitorino came by right after we arrived home to pay his respects, all spit polished and shined. Maura was reserved and polite.

Translating for each of them, I realized how difficult being a translator was, getting the emotions right for each of them. "Your daughter is very beautiful, she will turn a lot of heads in Mindelo, I will put the word out she is under my protection and she will be treated with respect." He said he would have his sons come by the next night and take her out dancing.

The next day was Saturday so I was off from work, and we were again invited to see the ocean. Vitorino picked up Arlene and took us to his home in Calhau, the outer edge of the island, next to the pounding surf where we spent the day. The rest of the day Maura and Arlene went to the ocean's edge swam and got to know each other. At the end of the day, Vitorino and I smoked our pipes by the ocean and were content to be quiet and watch the full moon rise and the emerging stars. The local fishermen came to shore and pushed their sailboats out into the darkness, ready to be guided by the stars. Vitorino told me when the moon was full, the catch was good. He drove back to his other home around midnight leaving us tucked in quiet. Swimming, eating and talking was the order of the next day. We went to a huge cliff, where the surf was pounding. I was afraid to go in when I spied three young men jumping off the side of the cliff. They invited us to come over, they really wanted the cute young things, but the cute young things did not want to risk the jump, so I went and we all held hands as we jumped into the air and then crashed into the water. We watched the fishermen clean the bright colored fish they caught the night before and each of us bought a fish for dinner. After a nap in the sun, Vitorino picked us up and back to town we went. I had my English class that night and invited Maura to join us. She answered questions about America, the students were very good with their English, and we all clapped with the success of the class. As we walked back to my home, Maura said it had snowed the night before she left Boston, and here she was, swimming two days later.

Her visit continued with visits to my office, meeting Paulino and greeting the women of the tin shack towns. Vitorino came by and said he would teach her how to dance Cape Verdean style. She said she knew how to dance and did not need him to show her. He got the message and schmoozed his way around her and in about 30 minutes, had her dancing Cape Verdean style. His sons picked her and Arlene up that night and they went out for a night on the town. Vitorino came by and said he went to the dance club and said she looked like she was having a grand time.

When I awoke the next morning, I saw Maura's dress (my dress, that is) still soaking wet from perspiration from night of dancing. "Mom, they really do take their dancing seriously, what a great time we had...when Vitorino's son drove me home, he shot by your door and I thought, uh-oh, where is he taking me. When I asked, he said he was going to make a u turn at the top of my road so he could let me out by the apartment door, not out in the middle of the road. What a nice, polite young man." A week had passed and now it was time to go and pick up my son Bill.

But first I had to be at the airport at dawn to meet an early flight from Praia. Patrick Ahearn was coming from the Inspector General's office of the PC from Washington and I was slotted to pick him up and act as his guide. I took him to Cafe Royal and discussed my job, frustrations, and joys, all wrapped in together. Then I took him to the two tin shack towns and introduced him all around, then dashed back to the airport to pick up Bill. He strolled off the plane like it was an everyday occurrence and his smile dazzled me. He only had two bags and he carried both with him. Maura's bags were still missing.

Maryann and Pedro invited us to their home; my tutor Yvonne and her fiancé David came to my home to welcome Bill, and he was put on the same schedule as Maura. Fresh fish dinner, a nap and then to the Piano Bar, this time taking Patrick with us. Cesaria Evora was in full swing again and, when she saw my son, motioned for him to come over to her. He did and then came back saying "She wants a whiskey. What do I do?" I gave him money and he bought the whiskey, she had him sit next to her and again, she dedicated a song to the filha (which means son in Portuguese) of Deana's. Both children were enthralled with her singing and again midnight came too quickly. Home to bed and they slept till noon while I had to go out to work.

We went out to do some shopping and they laughed at the method of buying eggs. You simply put the eggs in your pockets, no boxes or bags and had to be very careful if anyone hugged you - splat! Carmelita, one of the children I had met when I first came to Mindelo, came by and ended up playing and then beating Bill with a rousing game of jacks, much to his chagrin. Of course the American Ambassador and his wife happened to visit Mindelo that weekend, so we had them come by to visit while we were keeping an eye on Patrick, Bernice and the engineers. What a balancing act. I had told Bill not to let children in my home unless I was there - sticky fingers. Maura and I walked the Ambassador and his wife back to their hotel and then I realized I was giving an AIDS lecture at my home that night and had forgotten to tell Bill. We raced back and saw Bill standing outside of my home, trying to be polite while not letting anyone in. After all the students entered, I asked Maura and Bill to assist and almost instantly a bond was established between the students and my children. I took a back seat and watched the two of them give a terrific lecture on the danger of AIDS, in Spanish, in English and in body language. The class was a great success.

Vitorino formally came by and introduced himself and said he was glad to be in the home of Chefe Bill. I smiled ever so slightly and said "No, this is the house of chefe Deana," "no" said Vitorino, "When a man is present, he is the chefe." Vitorino winked at Bill and said "Ela e feminista, zangada com me" ("she is a feminist and now is mad at me.") They laughed, I did not. Vitorino knew how to get my goat. He invited Bill to go fishing with him the next day, Bill said fine. When Vitorino left, Bill said "Mom, I can't speak Portuguese, Vitorino can't speak English, and I can't fish." I told him not to worry. Vitorino came by to pick him up, very late that night they came back, smiling and chatting away. Bill said he had a great time, talked about the world, family and Cape Verde. When one makes an effort, the language barrier disappears. We all went to bed then as we would be getting up early to take a ferry from Sao Vicente where I lived to the island across from us -- Santao Antao.

Maura's alarm clock went off at 5am, Mario beeped his taxi horn and we three groggy Gallaghers stumbled into his taxi. The children's father had given each of them a sea sickness patch. I told them I ate a banana to avoid sea sickness. At the dock when we landed at Santao Antao, a Cape Verdean man, Bevindo, met us and we all had a cup of coffee. Bevindo asked them what the patches were for, they explained, and then he said he would like one, they each gave him theirs so Bevindo walked around with two sea sickness patches - and he never got on a boat.

When we got on the very, very narrow road to go to the north side of Santao Antao, Bill asked where the other road was coming back south. I explained that there was no other road, this was it. I told him that Cape Verde was in the Guinness Book of Records for having the most cobble stone roads in the world. When a van came towards us, we moved to the edge of the mountain, Maura and Bill blanched and I feel asleep as they white knuckled the rest of the ride.

When we arrived at the small town on the north side, we were told the Ambassador, his wife, and Patrick also were there too, so once again, we became a troop movement. We met Amy and Ross and had lunch at a tiny nook called RELAX. Amy was a TEFL teacher and asked Bill and Maura if they would come to her class. They agreed and the class asked them about some differences from the American way of life and the Cape Verdean way of life. Bill compared the dancing, Maura compared the food. We met a Brazilian cooperante who was very well funded by his country to work in a developing country. I had met him before in the capital city so knew him slightly. We all went to lunch and talked about his new computer - it did not have a user's manual. The next thing I knew, right after lunch, both of my children were invited to his office. They showed him how to work his new toy and he was very pleased (and relieved, might I add.) He invited Maura, Bill and me over to his very modern home for dinner where we had tasty food. After dinner, we all went to a dancing club. This island had only one club, Mindelo had five, but the action was the same. Maura taught Bill how to move, the girls lined up to dance with him, Maura had eager escorts, and I missed Vitorino. Midnight came and we three strolled back to our hotel; this town was quiet and more reserved than Mindelo.

Two days passed in business meetings for me, and touring for Maura and Bill. Then back to the ferry dock where we met Benvindo and he still had both of the round sea sickness patches behind his ear and said he was feeling fine because of the strong medicine from America. When we back home, even my children called it home now, we discovered Maura's bag had traveled to South Africa and was now back in Cape Verde in front of my apartment.

Too soon it was time to organize the despedia (farewell party) for my children. It had been great having them with me, working with me, meeting the people I loved; I could not believe their visit was about to end. The word went out, no invitations were sent and the night of the party came. The guests started to arrive. The first guests were the three young boys I jumped from the cliff with and now they were very happy because they got to visit Maura and Arlene again. Valentina bought over her fabulous chicken dish. The husband of my friend who worked at the bank took Bill into the corner and asked why the United States did not give his mother a car - he felt bad that I walked all over town. Bill explained that Peace Corps volunteers did not have a lot of money - they came to work, and not to make money. The banker did not say anything after that. The dancing continued and around dawn the last guest left. After sleeping three hours, we organized the luggage, got a ride and got to the airport. I told the children I was going to check on the bags, but I really went into the rest room, cried, wiped my eyes, and came back to the children. They never knew I cried. They walked on to the plane and both turned around at the same time to wave goodbye. God, that was hard to see. The props started and in the blink of an eye, their plane was just a little dot in the sky, I would not see them again for one more year and that was a very hard fact to keep in my heart. When I entered my apartment, it was so still, their vitality, energy and spirit were gone. I took a nap, did not wake until there was a knock on the door. It was twilight and Vitorino had come by to see if I was all right. We sat and talked about my children who I missed dreadfully, smoking our pipes and were quiet after the visits.

Ambassador Terry McNamara and his wife, Maura, Bill and Diane

Bill, Maura and Diane on ferry to Santao Antao

Bill and Maura at Relax bar

Maura and her mom

IN THE LINE OF FIRE

The concert was beginning late, but then no Cape Verdean concert ever started on time. That was just the way it was and after living in Africa you became used to it and accepted it or you would make yourself crazy. The band was full of young musicians; they melded as though they had played together for years. I do think African musicians have an ear that is tuned to new sounds and when they blend old and new together, it is oh, so smooth. As I sat on a piece of a wall that had been constructed for the audience, I mused about this concert and concerts in the U.S.

When my husband Bill and I lived in Annapolis, in the early 60's, we took our two youngest children to hear Dave Brubeck. He was young then too, the 4000 midshipmen roared and applauded after he played "Take Five". Years later I discovered that Paul Desmond wrote it, not Brubeck as I had thought. Many concerts came to mind: the New York city concert of Peggy Lee (who had perfect pitch,) the concert in Paris where Jesse Norman sang for the French anniversary of the storming of the Bastille, Ella Fitzgerald at the Boston Symphony Hall, Frank Sinatra, the concerts when our four children sang and made our hearts ache with pride. Much different settings than the one I was in now but the emotion was very similar. These concerts in Africa were social events as well, a chance to see your friends and neighbors. They also served as newspapers, television, radios and reports of who, why, what, when and where things were happening. I smiled at the differences and let the African music wash over me.

I had made a date with Arlene to meet her and her new beau and a friend of his after the concert. Not many Cape Verdeans had cars so cars weren't used to pick up your date: your feet got you there. PCVs don't have cars. I sauntered along the shore line, getting my feet wet in the surf and feeling mellow. As I rounded the corner where I would meet them, I saw the three waiting for me. They started to walk towards me when I heard a gunshot, like a huge bone breaking. I froze. I saw another flash to my left, close to where I was standing, a policeman shooting at a figure running across the Plaza. I saw the two young men had dropped to a sprinter's crouch and ran towards the fleeing man. Since I was the closest to the fleeing man, I thought, I'll give it a go, pulled my skirt up and ran after him. Arlene screamed, "Deana, stop, stop". She was right. I screeched to a stop and almost tripped myself. I saw the two men make a pinzer movement and close in on the runner, as they turned the corner and ran out of sight.

Arlene raced up to me and yelled, "You fool! You were running right into the line of fire." About two minutes later, the two men came around the corner with the runner. He was now walking on his tip toes as they had twisted his arms up high behind his back. The man who was to be my date took the runner to the police station and we three went to the dance club. When my date joined us later, he told us he and his friend were members of the elite Cape Verdean police who had been trained in Germany - no wonder they were so efficient. They congratulated me for my courage but chided me never to do that again. After a few hours of dancing, he walked me home past the spot where the shooting had occurred. It was all in a day's work for these two young men, but for me, it was an event I would not forget easily.

END OF 1991 AND BEGINNING OF 1992

The Thanksgiving of 1991 would be my last spent in West Africa, last year was my first. Being a Peace Corps Volunteer is a two and a half year commitment. Now I knew why they had us stay that long. You are just catching your breath, getting the lay of the land, and then it is almost over. The first Thanksgiving I spent on another island, this year I was invited to a lovely restaurant. My thoughts went back to that courageous mother I had met last Thanksgiving who I helped carve out a new home in a new cave as I enjoyed a sumptuous meal, surrounded by Cape Verdeans and PCVs. A roast pig was the main course and Pedro motioned for me to come to his side. He gave me a small plate with a piece of meat on it, "this is highly desirable and as it is your last Thanksgiving with us, you must have it." It was tasty, crisp and so tender. Maryann looked at me and smiled and said nothing. A few days later she told me what it was: the pig's ear.

Thanksgiving warned me that Christmas was soon to occur and I vowed that this Christmas would be different. I would not abandon my friends in Mindelo. Gathering all the little presents that Maura and Bill had brought me to give away, I began to wrap for the Natal exchange. Tarek played with the ribbon and I played Christmas music. I asked my English classes to sing Christmas songs in English, a large leap for them but they did well. Work at our Sewing Association started to slow down as the holidays approached. Our new chief, Senhor Neves, was a sensitive professional and a diplomat, and understood that the Sewing Association needed some down time. Senhor Neves was very different from Senhor Evora, who never thought about anyone except his own agenda. Received a thoughtful letter from my children's pediatrician, Dr. T. Berry Brazelton, with all of the answers to the questions Sandy from Mali had asked me about her son. I sent his letter on to Bernice so she could forward it to Sandy. Autumn leaves from colorful maples and oaks were sent by Cecilia, the training Director, and were immediately put in my small window. The sun made them dappled and I pretended it was a New England autumn.

The air was getting a tad cooler so I had to wear a light weight sweater when I went to the post office for the books that were coming in great numbers for the children's library. Boxes were stacked upon boxes in my little front hall. As I came out of the post office, election trucks were careening around the plaza, bellowing the name of different candidates, an independent candidate and the current party's choice. The pace was heating up. My political activist soul heated up but I knew we were not allowed to participate in any way which was very frustrating. The election was held and Onesimo Silveira was elected Mayor of our island on the independent ticket. He had received a PhD from Sweden, was Cape Verdean born and his wife and sons lived in New York City. Having met him in the past, I was very pleased he won; he was the type to move things along and did not have the mentality of "Wait till Lisbon tells us to move."

As the holidays came closer, Sandra invited Arlene and me out to her home in the interior for a holiday dinner. When we walked in, the first scent I smelled was roses. She worked for the agriculture minister and the gardens surrounding Sandra's home had roses next to her home; they were extraordinary. We exchanged gifts, sang Christmas songs and got very mellow. Five days before Christmas Arlene and Sandra went to Praia for the Ambassador's Christmas dinner. Valentina came over and asked me why I wasn't on the plane going to Praia (everyone knew what everyone else did.) I explained that I decided to stay at home; I saw a huge smile on her face. I handed out little gifts to the post office women who had been kind, the one legged shoe repair man, the waitress at Casa Benefica and the women in the tin shack town of Campinho that gave me a sense of the holidays. I received lovely gifts and cards came from friends in the States and I put my Nutcracker tape on full force. Maura sent Josa ping pong balls and he was thrilled with them. Bill sent a present to Carmalita, the young girl who had beaten him so soundly at jacks.

The Sunday before Christmas I was invited to go to a play and was thoroughly enchanted with it. Mary, Joseph and baby Jesus were all in place and the boys' choir was stupendous. Parents wiped their eyes, the actors and singers bowed to the applause and it was a very special night. I was beginning to be glad I had stayed home instead of flying away. Father Bernando told his driver to take me home and my feet got a rest from the cobblestones. Telephone calls to my office from Praia came fast and

155

furious: Bernice - "Do come, I'll make the peanut butter cookies you love," Arlene - "We'll have a party for you." I stayed on our island. Sandra's office had a children's party and I was invited and ended up dancing with 5 and 10 year old children.

Early on Christmas Eve, a concert was held in City Hall with guitars, fancy dresses and men in high spirits. I was folded into the group like an egg white into cake batter and felt like I was with family, which, I was indeed. Invitations came right and left to me for the next day; there were so many, I lost count. Maryann and Pedro, who were now like my sister and brother, invited me for Christmas Eve dinner, complete with cranberry sauce, mashed potatoes and American whiskey. I opted for the grog, cut with coconut milk and we sang carols with their Cape Verdean friends and families. Fire crackers exploded in the harbor and the Christmas pudding in my tummy gave me a feeling of being full: a new feeling for me.

Christmas day began with Canadian David driving up in his Russian car and saying, "Hop in;" you got so you never asked where you were going, you just went. We ended up in San Pedro in the home of the Swedish lady, Harriet, the head of the Swedish Clinic. Her huge home, on the shore next to the crashing waves, was all decorated for Christmas. We toured her new plants which were growing behind huge wind barriers, and we were given a gift of a fresh flower. Swedish food with a Cape Verdean flavor was served for breakfast and we toasted the holy day. Harriet drove me home and Mario, my faithful taxi driver, pulled up and took me to lunch at his home. His wife and sons had presents for me (thank God I had kept some extras available.) We talked about the Mayor and how he would change things more for the better. Lobster, chicken, and wine rounded out the holiday meal.

As I was coming home from Mario's, there was Dona Cuia waiting to walk me back to her home in Campinho. We met Antonia in the road, and danced to the music that was now coming out of all the tin shacks. I was taken to many of the tin shacks and it was always the same, "You stayed with us, you stayed with us, you did not go to the capital city, which makes us all very happy." Home for a quick nap and then David from the office came by and took me home where his lovely wife Norma cooked a delicious tuna dinner.

Of course, no type of holiday was complete unless you danced, so off to the dance club we went. A very, very tired Deana was driven home at 4 in the morning. Visions of children dancing, people saying Feliz Natal and great hugs from all of my friends made me sleep with a huge smile on my face. Christmas was over, but the spirit of Christmas lingered on.

The young women who always delivered yogurt to me did on the 26th, but, when I went to pay her, she said "no, this is my gift to you for the new year." With the traditional hug, I thanked her and gave her a gift. Vitorino came over and told me that on New Year's Eve, everyone got tossed into the ocean, so he advised me to wear every day clothes to whatever party I was to go to first, then after the traditional dunking, I could change into my fancy clothes to go dancing. Thoughtful my man Vitorino was.

In one day I was going to be 55. I decided not to look in the mirror for the next few days. I remembered reading about a French lady who, on becoming 75, put a very light piece of pale pink gauze over her mirror - how very French. Now, where could I find some pink gauze? Valentina must have sensed my melancholy as she brought over a chicken and rice plate with no explanation. Since I had about ten dictionaries in my apartment from the book collection that was growing by leaps and bounds, I looked up "melancholy" and discovered it was of Greek origin meaning depression of spirits, seriously thoughtful and pensive. Those three emotions would be with me throughout my entire PC experience. I found I walked on the beach alone with my thoughts when this mood hit me. When this happened, I would fling off my skirt and blouse, had a bathing suit under my clothes, took a dive into the waves and always felt refreshed. But the melancholy had to come first or the swim did not have the same healing effect. When I came home from my swim, I gathered up all of my Christmas trimmings and put them in a box for Sandra, so I could pass the baton on as the next Christmas I would be in the States.

Then my birthday came, December 31. I was 55 - the speed limit in the States, but there was no speed limit here, nowhere to speed to, really. The day started with sounds of children playing homemade instruments. I went to my small wooden door and listened to the little ones singing from door to door. I gave them all the small change I had in my pockets and their hugs and smiles stayed with me for the entire day. Arlene took me to a lovely luncheon at a new fancy restaurant named Jade: tiny with about six tables but real linen napkins and candle light made us feel quite special. Took a long nap in the afternoon (was getting very good at this exercise) with the shutters closed against the unrelenting sun. Maryann and Pedro invited me to Club Nautico for the New Year's festa. Decided not to take Vitorino's advice and wore some fancy duds my friend Fred has sent to me with Julie's shawl over my shoulders. Cape Verdeans clubs have chairs lining the walls, men go to the bar and the women get caught up on the gossip of the day. Maryann asked one of her husband's friends to dance with me; it was a much different crowd than the crowd at the dance clubs. These people were the top of their fields - professionals of the island, the movers and the shakers, the ones that did have some money and enjoyed their lives in Sao Vicente.

The first dance led to another and to another and then I never sat down again. Pink fireworks went up over the harbor and we all toasted the midnight hour and watched the young revelers swimming in the surf - a far cry from watching the ball descend over Times Square in my original home, New York City. The President, Antonio Mascarenhas Monteiro, and his gracious wife, Maria, came and we all talked about the future of our beloved country and what potential we had now that there was a freely elected President for the very first time. Mindelo lobster, wine from Portugal, Cape Verdean beer all combined to make it a grand festa. One of my younger dance partners walked me home at dawn and the pink and purple rays of dawn wrapped around us as we floated home. The year ended and I only had nine months to go. Wondering if I would get all that I wanted to get done finished, I fell asleep with the sounds of the surf lulling me to sleep.

THE LAST GASP YEAR

I celebrated the first day of the New Year by swimming in the ocean with my fellow worker Liz and her visiting daughter from Sweden. Seeing the two of them frolic together made me miss my four children, so I just threw myself into the swimming to a state of pleasant exhaustion. We decided to be adventurous and, since there was not one other soul on our magnificent beach, we took our tops off and I tanned some freckles on my bosoms - first time ever. Watching Liz and her daughter made me remember playing the same way with my children, who were now 30, 28, 27 and 25. Now I felt old indeed.

Back home in Brookline, I used to make New Year's resolutions at this time of the year but for some strange reason, I couldn't seem to do it now. Instead I went through all my clothes – not a long process – and gave the worn out ones to Donna Cuia for the women in the old age home; stains did not seem to bother them. That reminded me that one of the projects that I had to get going was the sewing association. Usually when one works in developing countries, the host country nationals who are most needy are chosen and assisted but I decided to do it differently for I had read about sustainable development and when I left, I wanted the projects to sustain themselves. I interviewed about 50 women from the two tin shack towns, and decided to work with the women from Campinho for they were more enthusiastic, needy and had a lighter spirit. They were also gutsier and stronger and did not put up with any nonsense from anyone. We would need that kind of resolve for the future. I narrowed the group down to twenty, using the rule that half would not continue and ten would be ideal.

At the first meeting the women, babies, bubbling teenagers and hanging on men who were curious were all there. The women were tired, after all it was 9 pm and they had all put in an arduous day with family. I spoke about the excitement of making money, of being able to move out of their tin shacks, of improving the quality of their lives and being able to afford the fees that were expected for schooling. That talk made them sit up and listen. They asked me to be the president, but I told them that the purpose of the association was for them to run it, to be responsible for its success or failure, and that I was only there to assist. After much bickering, the women chose Maria, mother of 7, thin and frail of body but not her spirit (after her seventh baby, she had her tubes tied, not a traditional decision.) I was thrilled with their choice because I knew she was hungry to learn and would be a good student. Rita was voted the treasurer, Leonora the secretary. As I tried to explain what each position meant and the responsibility it entailed, their blank looks told me I had my work cut out for me.

During the interviewing that took me about three months, I had asked each woman what skills they had and received the same answer, "I have no skills." After digging, questioning and watching, their natural sewing ability was evident. They could whip up a dress, a pair of slacks or a jacket in the blink of any eye. Sewing was a tradition that had been handed down from their mothers and their mother's mothers. Creating a sewing association was a natural.

We had to find machines, a place to meet and work. An old lady approached me on the street a few days after and whispered that she knew where there were sewing machines. Decades ago, the Portuguese had purchased them, given them to the women in the town, but then wanted them back when independence was being fought for in the early 70's. The clever women had hidden them in the interior – now all we had to do was find them. The word went out, via the grapevine which was most effective. A week later, the same old woman again whispered to me, "We have found them."

Knowing that we would have to have them checked out and oiled, I asked the general repair man of the town to come with me on an errand of mercy. We went bumping over the old sandy roads with the old woman sitting in the back, "Left here, no, right here, no back up, maybe here, no, maybe there." Not finding the place, confused and discouraged, we agreed to meet the next day to try again. The second day we hit pay dirt, we found a huge warehouse in the middle of nowhere that had been sheltering the sewing machines for many years. We got a few local boys to climb up, rig pulley system and get them down. The repairman looked thoughtful, clicked his tongue and said, "Yes, they are good, they will need work but it can be done." I hugged the old woman, picking her up in the air with a big hoot which left her slightly dazed but pleased. When I asked her if she would like to be part of the group she said quietly, "No, it is too late for me, let the young women have a chance, but I will watch." During the weeks of our organizing, I saw this woman in the background; our eyes would meet, a nod, and then she would be gone. It was almost as though she was the guardian angel of our sewing association.

Next we had to have a place for a real workshop. I began harassing City Hall, and Mayor Onesimo was most responsive, within a month, a room was found, windows were put into place and a real lock was put on. The sewing machine repairman was slow; he was so good that he had all the business in our little town. I would visit our machines, ooh and aahh over them and cluck about how long it was taking and finally, to get rid of me, he finished the repairs. Getting permission to use the project truck, getting a driver, (I was not allowed to drive) seemed to take forever but finally one bright day, they were delivered to the sewing room.

The word went out they were being delivered, everyone always knew what was happening and when, and 18 women, (we had already lost 2 that did not have patience) gathered around the five machines and touched them reverently. A quiet wrapped around us in that cement room that would become our workroom, our meeting room, a room of our own. There was no shouting, there was no noise, just 18 women and me looking and thinking about what might be. The grant for money to buy fabric materials had been written by me months before and one day a few weeks later, the Peace Corps Director called me at City Hall and told me a group in the States had obligated themselves to lend us the money. It was the "Boston Area Returned PC Volunteers Association." I got a young boy to run around the town and tell the women we would have a meeting that night. Seventeen women showed up, the numbers were dwindling, I feared that the ten I wanted might not go the distance, but I put that thought behind me when I announced we had been given the grant. Now there was shouting and yelling and smiles and it looked like we were going to be a sewing association after all.

About three nights later, the old woman who had found the machines came to my house and told me to be careful, there were people who did not want the association to succeed. She did not elaborate and when one of the members came the next morning in tears saying that the hinges of one of the windows had been jimmied and broken, I knew the old woman was right. Going back to the Mayor to hire a guard, I wondered who would want to torpedo our group - maybe the women who had not been selected

161

out of the 50, men who did not want it to succeed, or people who wanted to steal the machines and sell them. I thought of a quote from John Keats, "Oh, for a life of sensations rather than thought" so stopped thinking about who and got on with the sensations. The old lady arrived on my door step a few nights later and told me not to try to find out who broke the hinges, just to make sure the guard stayed at his post.

The next night I went for a long walk, to our work room. The guard was nowhere to be seen. I went to the local bar, not there, went to the group of men who always gathered on the corners to smoke and enjoy each other's company while their women worked in the shacks, not there. I sat on the stoop of our work room and waited. The night air was quiet and I fell asleep until the noise of someone walking in boots awakened me. The guard rounded the corner and was surprised to find me. I told him there were many men that were out of work and if he could not do his job, there were others that would and I promised to check on him from time to time. I suspected the old woman was also watching, but didn't see her.

While I was working on the establishing of the sewing association, the children's library had to be dealt with as well. PCV Brian lived on another island, one I had not visited as yet, and rumor had it that his island of Boa Vista had the best library in our little country. After I wrote and sent a proposal to John, he called and gave his okay and off I went to the island of Boa Vista three days later. I had learned in Cape Verde, always be prepared to move quickly because the chance might not come again. As our little prop plane was descended onto Boa Vista, I was struck by the island's beauty and realized why it was called Boa Vista, it meant "good view" in Portuguese. Looking at the shape of the island from the sky, I shuffled the deck of my memory and thought of the time I had awakened one night in my apartment when I first arrived in Cape Verde and puzzled about the shape of Africa. I had run down stairs, lit a candle and looked at the map of Africa on my wall. There it was, Africa was the shape of a heart.

Boa Vista had long, white beaches stretched out, surrounding the island, so different from our island. High winds buffeted our plane and we hit the ground with a big bump. A little yellow cab came up to the plane and the driver said he was asked by Senhor Brian to come and fetch me. When I arrived at a cement apartment, much like mine, it so was quiet I took a nap. Brian arrived hours later. We went for a swim; he explained that he had no water so a swimming bath was the order of the day. We compared stories of how long we had gone without bathing in pure water - we tied. The beaches were magnificent and deserted. We rolled down the huge dunes and laughed when we hit the shore of the ocean and just continued to roll until the water sucked us in. Dinner was in a lovely restaurant where everyone knew Brian and everyone traded stories of the day. Later I went to bed with plans of how I would run a library.

The next morning as Brian fixed me fabulous blueberry pancakes, I saw a conch shell on his shelf that he had sawed in half. I asked him how he did it, being the engineer that he was, he instructed me. I went to the beach and dove and dove until I found a perfect shell, gave to Brian to cut it in half and tucked the two halves into my back pack for the trip back to Mindelo. He then took me to the library, a fairly new wooden building in the middle of a square. Brian had made an appointment for me to meet the man in charge, but he was not there. Brian had to go to work so I wandered around the square, saw a chapel and went in and prayed that some of my projects would be successful. A young girl came in and yelled to me. She was talking in Crioulo, but as each island had its own variation of Crioulo, I did not understand a word, but understood the meaning - something was happening outside of the church.

Outside the dark and cool church, the sun hit me and then I saw what she wanted me to see - the opening of the library. We both ran across the plaza. I thanked her. I still don't know how she knew I wanted to see the librarian. Brian's island must have been the same as mine; everyone knew what everyone was doing. The librarian showed me around, explained the process, and how it was run. I flew home the next day with my shell present and a head full of ideas for the children's library in Campinho.

When Vitorino came to visit that night, I told him I had a present for him and he scolded me for spending money on him. Laughingly I told him it cost only one or two dives and gave him one half of the shell and showed him the other half. He chose the one that was slightly bigger, telling me that of course he was the "chefe" and should have the bigger side and as long as we each kept our half of the shell, we would always be in each other's memory. He said he would put his half in the ocean house in Calhau and would always think of me when he looked at it. I put my half on my windowsill and the light of the moon and the light of the sun gave it different colors constantly. I had just read a book of poems by Yeats and remembered, "silver apples of the moon, golden apples of the sun."

WHEN YOU LEARN ANOTHER LANGUAGE, YOU GAIN ANOTHER SOUL

One evening at Cafe Royal, an administrator from Shell Oil asked me if I could teach English as a second language. Frances and I decided it sounded like a good project. We would teach adults who worked during the day in evening classes. We worked out a curriculum and rules of the classroom. Six women and four men showed up the first evening and were most motivated to learn. When I asked the students why they were there, one woman said she worked for Shell and would automatically receive a higher salary if she spoke English. One man said he did not have a job but if he had English, he would have a very distinct advantage in the job market. A young woman whose mother worked at Shell said she wanted to go to college but could not speak English; if she could, she could pass the entrance examination. I brought my trusty New York Times Sunday paper with me and gave the first assignment: read one sentence and then tell me what it means.

One afternoon, I took Paulino to Frances' apartment for his usual visit with her. She had a great ability to make him laugh. She looked very sad this particular visit and I asked her why. She said that Kristin, the PC nurse, had asked her to come to Praia and to settle her accounts in Mindelo. I knew she had been having trouble with some of her projects; some did not get off the ground. Arlene heard about the request from PC so came in and we helped Frances pack. To lighten the mood, we reminisced about the fly in the beer story during our crazy training days in Guinea Bissau. This is the story: first month, a PCV finds a fly in her beer, throws the beer away. The second month, the PCV takes the fly out and drinks the beer. Third month, PCV gets a fly in her glass of beer, drinks the beer and the fly and says "needed the protein." Arlene and I took her out to dinner that night and we three were a sad trio. The next morning, Mario drove the three of us to the airport. We hugged and said we would see her when she came back, but Frances never came back to Mindelo.

THE HIKE FROM HELL

Diane hiking in brown hills

With the coming of the New Year a new form of government began. For fifteen years, since Cape Verde's independence from Portugal, only one party had been in control: PAICV. The citizens of Cape Verde had experienced their first multi-party election. Antonio Mascarenhas Monteiro won as President and Onesimo Silveira won as Mayor. The Mayor held his first meeting with all of us who worked in City Hall, complete with jacket and tie, and the meeting started, believe it or not, on time. He introduced all of his cabinet and outlined each of their responsibilities. This was not the fly by night disorganization that governed before: this was professional. The next day the Mayor asked me to come to his office with a list of projects I was working on with time frames for completion. I ran to my home and worked into the night writing about all that I wanted to accomplish in my remaining nine months.

To get away from the stress of the job, Sandra invited Arlene, Liz and me to go on a hike in the interior. Shorts, T shirts, good walking shoes, hats for the intense sun that never let up, my always present water bottle and my trusty sun screen were the order of the day. Sandra said it would take an "hour or so", I should have listened to those last two words "or so." The more we walked, the more it felt like the mountain seemed to have moved further away. We left in the early morning to avoid the hot midday sun, but got caught right in the middle of the scorching heat. At noon time we were still far away from our destination. We noticed that each of our steps got slower; our conversation, bubbly at first, was reduced to short queries: "Can we stop for just a little rest?" Over the ridge, under mountain arches, the scenery was still monochromic, brown, tan, ivory and beige, not a hint of green anywhere.

Finally, after four hours, we heard the ocean's roar and all scampered over the final ledge to see the magnificent blue Atlantic Ocean with huge rollers pounding a deserted beach. We four raced to the beach, flung off our sweat drenched shirts and shorts and tumbled into the cooling water. As I limped out of the ocean, I spied a hammock and silently thanked the clever person who had found a place to put it. I was asleep in the hammock in a second, the others played in the surf, picked up sea shells and relaxed, stress left all of us.

As the afternoon wore one, we decided to stay and see the sunset. Not one person had we seen, not one other sound had we heard of another human being, just we four in the middle of west nowhere. We sat silently watching the rollers increase and decrease, we watched the clouds gain dark hues and begin to do their falling act. We did not speak, just watched, smiled and felt good. The sense of urgency that we all had at the beginning had completely gone. Walking back in the early evening was easy and the twinkling stars that came out to find us were dimmed by the emerging moon that followed us back to our town. All in all, a very mellow day, and I was secretly proud that I had kept up with the youngsters.

CARNAVAL

The tension was rising, the air was vibrating and the word Carnaval was all that was heard on the streets. Since this was my second Carnaval, I thought I knew what was coming, but I was wrong. This year, perhaps because of the new government, or because there was a spirit of newness in the country, there seemed to be more money flowing for the parade and for the parties that were about to begin. I noticed a lull at the office, people strolled in when they felt like it, and no one put in a full day of work. One colleague said "Deana, don't fuss, it is 'interval para Carnaval.' "

I decided to have a party at my home and many PCVs from all of the other islands arrived to stay in my home. The spaghetti, warm CV beer and laughter began. A huge jug of wine was donated by the attending Ambassador and his wife and many friends from other islands dropped by: Brazilians, Italians, Portuguese, a wonderful mix. I noticed Vitorino deep in conversation with the Ambassador and when I asked later if he knew who he had been speaking with, he answered "all men are the same, he loves Cape Verde and that is our commonality."

On the night before the parade, the children were wildly excited; the oldsters were elegant and controlled. All people from the stores, the tin shacks, and the streets were mingling together in a joyful celebration. That night was the grand costume ball and in response to Vitorino's question of what I was wearing, I showed him a rather boring outfit. "No, no," he fumed and proceeded to tear through my clothes, picking out wild combinations, restyled my hair and selected my makeup. Slipping his hand into mine, he said "I want to be proud of you, even though I am not with you in person tonight, I am with you - never forget that."

Arriving at the ball, I found the mood was high and the dancing just beginning. Hours and hours of whirling, laughing, pausing only until the next partner came along was the practice of the night. We quieted down when Cesaria Evora sang her mournful songs but got up again and danced to Manecas Matos's band and his fast beat until it was time to go home.

The next day, with the official parade and its floats and dancing, I knew, as the Cape Verdean I had become, not to go to work as I had the year before. At the face-painting table I became a yellow bird - bright blue dots over my brown freckles and big wild eyebrows. At the dance club that night the bouncer routinely said "mundo pagamento" (the world pays to enter) but recognizing me said as the one who helped his aunt with moving her to a cement house in the tin shack town, added "except Deana."

MOTHER AND DAUGHTER

I must have a welcome sign, so I made one, put it up on my front door and hitched a ride to the airport. The wind and the clear, bright sun were all in place. My dear friend Cynthia and her daughter Heather were coming to visit me - Cambridge, MA to Cape Verde. The Cape Verde month of March would be very different from New England's month of March.

The plane was a just a speck, then it became real with its props fighting cross winds caused by trade winds bouncing off the surrounding mountains of brown sand. When they descended the short and rickety steps from the plane, tears came - just as I had when my daughter Maura and son Bill came to visit five months before. I thought - God, they made this trip just to see me —I was *so* honored as Cynthia and I hugged and spun each other around, looking to see how we had changed; daughter Heather stood quietly waiting for her turn to be hugged and welcomed. Once home and fed, they gamely agreed to go to a concert. Two hours later I pried them from their make shift beds I invented with old cement bags tied together on my second floor area, and whoosh they were right in the middle of our best club listening to a Cape Verdean group from France. Then we noticed film cameras all around the club and the next thing Heather knew, the cameras were beaming in on her. We were told that the film would be shown in France in a few months and they thanked us for letting them film us. Then I noticed Cynthia was fading so went to find a taxi - none found. Just as we had begun the five mile walk back to my house, a man stopped his car, asked where we were going, and gallantly took us aboard in his stalling, bumpy truck. Cynthia looked at me and said "Diane, do you know him?" "No, but it is okay." We were two New York City born women, one questioning, one not.

Jet lag made them groggy the next day, so I let them sleep and went to work. That evening Arlene and Maryann joined us for dinner where Cynthia

170

regaled us with her fluent Portuguese. I had forgotten that she told me she had studied Portuguese and she was thrilled I was living in a country with a language that she knew. They unpacked presents and told stories from the States and five women smiled with each other's company in the candlelight in my little apartment.

Because nothing is a secret on our island, Vitorino came by the next evening to welcome my two Boston friends and invited them to his house on the ocean. The full moon was out and when I told Cynthia and Heather that here the moon was feminine and the sun was masculine, they thought about it and we all agreed we liked it that way.

The next day Maryann took them out and showed them our island as I bounced off to work. The sewing machine shuffle had not finished getting the machines from the repair shop to the tin shack town. Mother and daughter gamely piled into the truck and helped with the transfer. Cynthia took pictures of the women reacting to the delivery and I told her if she told them she was going to send the women prints, she must do that. So many people took their pictures, promising to send and never did. I knew that Cynthia would send them and in a few weeks, her pictures arrived. All the women were thrilled.

One island visit would not do, so the next day we took the ferry over to Santao Antao. We visited a grog factory on the island where bulls pulled a stone around and the stone mashed the leaves and parts of the tree to make the grog. Of course we all had to sample it and went back to the ferry and Mindelo with a slight buzz.

The next lesson of their visit was discovering how to ration water when there is none. I noticed before we had left that the water faucet was down to a trickle but did not focus on it. When we came back, Heather wanted to wash her hair and said there was no water coming from the faucet. We three climbed up to the roof. I had Cynthia climb on my sturdy stool. Looking into my small reservoir where my water was stored she exclaimed "Wow, it is dark in here". I handed her my flashlight and we realized why it was dark - not a drop of water was there. I went to plan B. My neighbor, Valentina, who had many more people living with her in her home than I had, never ran out of water and told us to bring our jugs over. We got the jugs all families have and she graciously filled them up. I noticed Heather used a very small amount of water - she was learning.

No visit to Mindelo would be complete without a visit to the Piano Bar to hear Cesaria Evora. Cynthia had heard of her in the States and was thrilled to meet her. As we walked home, Cynthia asked me how big the island was - she said the island where she and I were born was about 22 square miles. I said that was about the size of Sao Vicente and we realized both the island of Manhattan, where we were born, and the island of Mindelo, were the same size.

Then their visit of two weeks was over, it went so fast. There I was at the airport again, saying goodbye, and it still hurt to say goodbye.

Cynthia , Josa and Diane – Pacim Truck – picking up sewing machine for sewing association

Bathing beauties

Cynthia and Diane in front Diane's home

SPRING

Back in the States, it was spring time which always reminded me of lines from John Steinbeck's Travels with Charlie: "How can you ever appreciate a magnificent New England spring unless you have been through a less than magnificent winter?" The seasons in Cape Verde were summer, early summer, midsummer and end of summer.

This April the wind started to pick up quite a bit and I asked Pedro why. I didn't remember last year's spring being this windy. "All hurricanes are born just north of Santo Antao, the island across from our island, and we get the tail end of the fierce wind." The wind was so strong, it would sneak through the cracks in my wooden shutters and rattle my ivy vines which were now healthy and strung all around the front walls of my apartment. All the vines had grown from the one vine the old woman with wrinkles gave to me when I first came to live in Mindelo. I went to see her one day a few months back, but her cement apartment had another person in it and I learned that the old woman had died. I felt so sad when I walked home, over the same route she had used. I used to go and visit her from time to time but we never exchanged names. Now she was gone but her gift lived on.

With the coming of April I realized I had to decide whether or not to go to Ireland for the Irish Shugrue family reunion in June. I counted all my money in hand - made out a budget and figured that if I sold some of my tee shirts that my friends in the states continually sent to me, stuck to rice and bananas and purchased NOTHING, I could maybe save up enough money for the flight. This would not be easy but would be worth the effort. As I began my frugal campaign, I concentrated on what I had in my storage bin. Maryann had given me a red onion - a real treat so I promised myself that I would use it sparingly in my one egg omelet that I made every Saturday morning. That onion lasted for two months and every morsel was

174

appreciated. Instead of my routine of using a tea bag twice, I would use three times - not too bad - just a little weak. Decided even my kitty would have less to eat as well - fish was very expensive so would buy the heads and tails instead of the whole body. Maryann continued her generous habit of inviting me for dinner and lunch from time to time and I would wolf down all of the food served. She was a polite lady, and never said a word about my new behavior. I was too embarrassed to tell her why I was so hungry all the time. One night at dinner Pedro said to me, "You will never be the same person when you return to the U.S., Africa has taught you many things and one is how to be patient."

But I had more important things to think about than missing Cape Verdean dancing. The sewing association was about to begin purchasing supplies. When the money came to me from the Boston Returned Peace Corps Volunteer Association, I went flying to the tin shack town of Campinho. When I told the association women, they were very quiet until I finished my tortured explanation in Portuguese. Then shouts went out and we all hugged each other and made plans to do the necessary shopping the next day. I would go along to advise if necessary. We went to the material store but the clerks were not polite to my friends. I decided to step forth and smile and say good morning - the tone changed and the clerk became very pleasant. The funeral store lady did not give my friends a hard time; she was used to having women in from the tin shack towns with old, worn out dresses and no shoes. With each purchase, I showed Rita, the association's treasurer, how to enter the amount in a rough ledger she and I had made the week before. The women were clever. We would go into one store and get a price, which they would discuss outside, go over to the next store and get another price, discuss and run to the third store. When they figured out which was the best deal, they would smile and saunter into the store that had the best deal. Their confidence was growing by leaps and bounds and I hung back, watching with pride.

Then another miracle happened. My dear friend Yvonne sent me samples of lovely material from her interior design business that she had on Cape Cod, Massachusetts. The women made patchwork skirts from the samples and never had been told how to create this type of pattern - they just did it.

PACIM was going to be relocated and job descriptions were changed due to the recent election of another political party. Everything was frantic with the move and the new office was very loud, located in the middle of town. When Sandra offered me her home in the quiet interior, I jumped at the

175

chance to be in a quiet space. We agreed to exchange homes, she to stay in my apartment in town where there was a lot of action; me to the peace and quiet of the interior.

With my backpack on my shoulder (I had learned how to pack with a minimal amount of "stuff"), I got a ride on the road to the interior and was deposited into a blackness that swallowed me whole. Sandra had told me to walk along the road until it took a turn and then to head off the road on an eastern line. I did and was amazed when, after about 45 minutes, I saw the outline of her building and the agricultural station that was next to her house. The key was right where she said it was. The scent of fresh roses filled the air. I lit a candle, silence greeted my every action and I sat on her small bed. The next thing I knew the sun was knocking on my eye lids and I realized I had slept in my clothes and had not moved an inch since sitting on her bed.

The day passed quietly and dusk came before I knew it so I decided I would walk to the restaurant Ranchero Carmel. I looked at the stars and figured where the house was, where the restaurant was and beamed myself onto a route that would get me there. I dragged some large boulder like rocks and put them in a row that I hoped would guide me to and fro. Finally found myself on the road with the lights from the restaurant blinking far away. As I walked on the road, a car stopped and the driver asked if I was okay and then said when he recognized me "oh, Deana, would you like a bolea (a ride)" and I said "no thank you". It was fun to see the cars come with the white lights - diamonds my mother, Leona, used to call them and then became rubies when all that could be seen was the back lights.

When I went in, the owner Manuel said, "I didn't hear a car when you drove in". I explained that I had walked and was staying at Sandra's home. A half hour later a delicious smelling chicken was wrapped 'to go' and a glass of grog was given to fortify me for the walk back to Sandra's home. When I got off the road, I had a slight panic attack, wondering if I could find the small boulders I had placed so carefully. The moon was only a quarter shape so did not supply a lot of light but somehow the boulders did appear and the stars and moon combined to light a safe trip home. Three candles lit my dinner and I put on a Mozart tape and all was right with the world. I guess I must have dozed off again, my new habit, and a car horn awakened me. It was Vitorino with his son Hercules. They heard I was staying in the interior, had just come back from night fishing and showed me their results - eels, groupers and fish of many colors. They shared a small cake with me that they had taken to their fishing expedition and I shared my grog. We listened to my Mozart and I listened to their tall fish tales and then they left. I walked a little way to watch their car headlights fade into the distance, counted my stars and fell into bed. The stars and the silver moon stood guard.

The next morning I hitched a ride to Club Nautico where the artist Baptista's show was to be hung. All the paintings the committee had gathered were stacked and my days of being an art gallery owner came back urging me to assist. Remembering my dear partners put yet another lump in my throat, but I realized one was coming to visit, one had sent the quilt samples and all the others had been most supportive with letters and care packages. The diversity of Baptista's work was evident, from a magnificent oil of the Pope, to a little child asleep, to a naked, sensuous woman lying down, all showed what promise the man had who was cut down too early in his life.

Two days later we had the art opening. Pedro had hung an illustrated poem Baptista wrote for me and placed it in a small alcove by itself. Reading it made me cry while remembering the day it had been given to me. Mayor Onesimo Silveira opened the exhibition with a dynamic speech about the artists and poets of Cape Verde and how we must support them. Pedro thanked all who had lent the committee their pieces and thanked me for having the soul of a Cape Verdean. The hall quickly filled up and the citizens of Sao Vicente were able to savor the work of one of their own. It was a muted gathering of respect and homage. I took one long look at this exhibition that spoke volumes about the life of Cape Verde, the Catholicism, the children and most, of all, the pride Cape Verdeans have in their heritage.

CLOSE OF SERVICE
LIFE IS AN INCOMPLETE SENTENCE

Information had been sent to all twelve volunteers in Cape Verde about the upcoming "Close of Service" seminar given three to five months before the volunteers would leave. The teachers in our group were scheduled to leave late June/July so once again the "saying goodbye dance" would begin. I would be going to another island for two weeks and thought this would be the time to say goodbye to my dear kitty Tarek. Acting on Vitorino's suggestion that I should put Tarek out near his work place so he could keep an eye on him, the three of us got into his car one evening at dusk. His first time in a car made Tarek become very quiet. We pulled into the area where he was going to live, I opened the door, and when I put him on the car hood, he looked at me, looked around and sat down. Vitorino laughed but just then, out of nowhere, another cat approached. Without a look back, Tarek was off the hood, onto the road and out of sight. Yup, it was a female. I slipped back into the car as Vitorino drove me home. I burst into tears. He consoled me until I fell asleep dreaming of the tiny kitty that was given to me as a gift so long ago and now was back on his own in his own territory.

The close of service workshop was going to be held on the island of Fogo, (volcano in Portuguese), but first we went to Praia, the capital, to join the others. The next morning all twelve volunteers and four staff members climbed onto a rickety prop plane - discovered only 12 seats for the 16 of us so we drew straws and four stayed to catch the plane the next day. By now, we were all used to inefficiency and took it in our stride. At a small shop at the airport I saw 2 samples of handmade pipes. I asked the woman owner if she could have two made that I could pick up when we returned after our conference. Yes, a perfect gift for Vitorino and me. The ride to our hotel took us past the volcano, huge piece of earth jutting right out of the earth and touching the sky. Arlene and I were put in the same room, with a view of a swimming pool. I was so glad I had my bathing suit - it was always in the bottom of my backpack. After a tasty dinner, we went to our rooms to get some rest before the bittersweet sessions that were about to begin. Arlene fell asleep first and then I hit the pillow but was awakened by someone talking in a low voice in Portuguese. I opened my eyes slowly so the person speaking would not know I was awake, and looked around. No one was there. Then I realized that Arlene was talking in her sleep in Portuguese since that was her first language.

In between the close of service sessions given by an excellent African American trainer named Arnold, we were treated to excursions. We saw the famous volcano and I asked our guide how often it erupted. He said every 40 years or so, the last time it went off was in 1951. He smiled and said it was a bit late but maybe we would be lucky and have it go off while we were there. We were treated to the local wine whose grapes were grown in the ash. It was red and very strong. I bought a small bottle and watered it down every time I had a drink. The children in the villages around the volcano were light skinned with blue eyes and blond hair. I asked the guide why they were so different. He said they were descendants of the French royalists and were called "children of the priests".

Back to the sessions and a theme I would hear more and more - re-entry will be difficult. When Arnold asked each of us what scared us most about coming to Africa, I said not getting the language and not being able to translate my sense of humor. He asked what scared us most about going home and I said not having my family and friends understand my African experience. Arnold told us life is an incomplete sentence - so just go with the flow. At breaks, I would go to our room, put on the suit and relax in the pool. The sessions ran from high humor, to quiet lectures, frayed nerves and frustration. Resumes were discussed and interview skills, and we all began to realize that indeed we were about to "go home." Then it was over, the last time all twelve would be together as a group. We took the usual pictures, only this time the subjects did not have the gleeful smiles and wide eyes that we had in our picture in Atlanta two plus years before. We had changed, Pedro of Mindelo was correct: we would never be the same again.

The session closed, address list was passed around and we boarded the truck back to the airport quietly. I went to the small shop; of course the pipes were not ready. We bid farewell to the island that had been our home for our last week together. The volcano erupted in 1994 - no deaths were reported but houses were destroyed and there was great damage - a little late in erupting.

Now only eight flew out while four waited to go the next day. It was now 1 a.m. so Bernice, her friend Manuel and I went back to Bernice's home for a quiet night cap, or we thought. About 2am, there was a knock on the door. Bernice went to the door and I heard two men's voices, then the pitch to their voices got higher. Manuel went to the door. A heated discussion began, I walked to the kitchen and went to the knife holder and chose the biggest handle in her holder. I walked to the door, whispered to Bernice that I had the biggest knife in the house and was prepared to use it. She was still talking, Manuel was arguing and I decided to step forward to address the disturbing situation and pulled the huge handled knife from behind my back and held it in the air. Bernice and Manuel looked at it and began to laugh. I thought that rude since I was willing to risk life and limb to protect us and then I looked up and saw that what I was holding was indeed the biggest handle in the collection, only it was the knife sharpener rod, not the huge, sharp knife I had envisioned. I broke up, the potential troublemakers broke up and the situation changed when we all broke up laughing. The men left and Manuel left, shaking his head and Bernice and I giggled as we went to bed.

The trip back to Mindelo was uneventful until I turned the key in my door. My next door neighbor Valentina came huffing and puffing over and said she was mad at me for leaving and not telling her where I was going. She thought I had left for good. I felt bad and told her I would be in Mindelo until October.

My projects now only had five months to be completed. The human resource rule of not learning a new job until eighteen months on the job was right, I was just getting the hang of it all, and now would have to leave. The sewing association women were making clothing at a fast clip. When Winnie came to visit, I took her to the tin shack town and she bought a skirt, liked it so much, she bought another one for her daughter. The women were so pleased; the bread bags were selling well, they were making maternity clothes and they were saving up their money to buy cement to make a house for themselves.

Every time a plane landed in Mindelo, more and more cartons of books for the children's library arrived. I was running out of space to store them in my small front hall. I received good news about the children's library.

Soule, the Administrator from Shell Oil, told me my proposal had been accepted and they would supply me with the money to buy the wood for the book cases. I went to the music store to find the carpenter who worked there part time, but he was gone. The owner said he had a present for me. He gave me two tapes he had made from originals saying he knew I could not afford them. What a sweet and caring gesture. I thanked him quietly. Bana was a very famous singer. Went home and played them and thought about when I would be listening to these in another country. I became very sad until I remembered a story that Pedro told me about Bana. Bana is about 6' 6", and he sent his son to the store to buy milk. When the boy returned, Bana asked his son where the change was. Son said, "Man said no change due." Bana took off his large shoe and said to his son, "Take this back to the clerk and say, this is my father's shoe." He did and came back with the change. I met Bana months later and asked him if that story was true, "What do you think, Deana?" "Yes, I think it is true." He smiled and nodded yes.

Things were revving up and more visitors were coming as well. Jean wrote that she would be arriving on June 20th, to depart July 4th, so I made my plane reservations for Ireland and the Shugrue family reunion with all the money I had managed to scrape together so we could depart the same time. How organized! But now I had to organize my AIDS lectures and train someone to give them after I left.

There was a Cape Verdean born man, John, who lived in the States and had a home in Mindelo as well, and he heard about my giving AIDS lectures. He asked if I would give one at the high school. I had been trying to get into that place for 1 ½ years. He invited the island's only ob/gyn, Dr. Rosario, and the school principal, a few teachers and other dignitaries. The hall was surprisingly full for a Saturday morning, introductions were given and I was off and running. I described the overall picture of the devastation AIDS caused; Dr. Rosario gave the ways it could be transferred. When a question was asked that seemed a little sensitive, we would look at John and he would nod to the appropriate person on the platform to answer. The lecture went smoothly and two hours were over before we knew it. I ended my section by saying "if you contract AIDS, you have a one way ticket to the cemetery with no return trip". After the lecture, one woman told me she was glad she came with her high school daughter. She thought there was medicine for AIDS and the U.S. would send it to the poor countries soon.

I decided to go back to the office to file all of my lecture material. The phone was ringing. Gabriel Evora was on the line and said he had seen me go to the office and wanted to speak to me about something very important. He said that the government was going to cut the number of employees and he wanted me to protect his buddies. It took me a few minutes to realize that this man, my former boss, was speaking in perfect English - something I had never heard him do. I assured him that the proper people would be cut. Then said I was quite surprised to hear his English - he had never used it before when I was struggling to speak Portuguese and begged him to speak English to help me understand. He never did, until he wanted something and now he did and I was not about to assist. There were all kinds of Cape Verdeans: the bad and the good. Evora was the former, Paulino, Amelia, Pedro, Maryann and Vitorino were the latter.

JUNE

The June reunion of the clan Shugrue was fast approaching. I had purchased my airline ticket, now I had to get money. I looked around my apartment and gathered tee shirts, baseball hats, ballpoint pens and compact discs and put signs on the walls of the deserted houses on our road - yard sale – only I had to say "inside house sale".

The first buyer was Elisio, Arlene's friend, and he scooped up many of my CDs. Some of my women friends from Campinho bought hair combs I had brought with me as well as office supplies, scissors, thread, beauty supplies. The sale went on all day and of course the women used it for social purposes. Rita, the treasurer of the sewing association, came by on the way to visit her father who was gravely ill in the hospital. Maria Louisa, the president of the sewing association, bought hair ribbons for her four daughters.

The day wore on, I wore out and finally it was all done. I heard the sound of slow and mournful music and recognized the funeral dirge. I peeked out of my wooden shutters and saw Rita, our association's treasurer, holding her mother's arm - her father had died. I quickly switched into my funeral garb, black blouse and black skirt, and joined the procession going to the church. After the long service, the trail of mourners walked ever so slowly to the cemetery. The dead had to be buried the day they died. We all went to the home of Rita's father. Suddenly I realized that half of the town would be in her family's home and with a panicked feeling, I rushed around to find Rita. We had just collected money from the sale of clothing and Rita, as treasurer, was holding it all. When I finally found her, I quietly asked where the money was. She smiled, patted her bra and skirt and indicated that the money was on her body and no one would lift it from where she had put it.

VISIT OF MY BEST FRIEND - BOSTON VARIETY

All of the Boston pictures were in place on the walls of the room where she would sleep for two weeks, her bed was neatly made with my prettiest flowered sheets, the floor had been scrubbed, and the Sahel sand was out the door. One of my very dearest friends was coming. I rode to the airport with a light heart. Jean came into view, smiling, her head held high but the usual quick step was a bit tentative. I ran over to her and hugged her. She kept saying," I'm here, I really am here." We laughed and drew back to compare the actual with the memories - two old friends sharing again.

My faithful Mario the taxi driver came over and asked where her bags were, she told me one bag was lost. As Mario's cab took us to my apartment, I explained that this very morning our sewing association was having their first sale and it just happened to be in my front hall. When the sewing women saw her, they did the welcome hug and proudly showed her their pieces hanging amidst my hanging "all over the place" ivy. Women were coming in and out of my apartment buying. The association women clucked with joy over each sale. The women collected the money, distributed it amongst themselves and then said it was time for a celebratory drink. With my precious grog, we initiated Jean into the Mindelo life. Each of the ten women grabbed one of my hats (Jean commented "some things never change - you had a hat rack at home in Boston, now you have many hats here in Africa"). She gave me letters from my four children, friends and the New York Times - what joy she brought. As the light faded, so did Jean and to bed she went.

The next two weeks spun around Jean, meeting Maryann, the woman who had become like my sister, who took us to her home by the ocean where we swam like kids. Arlene came and bonded with yet another mother figure. Vitorino came to pay his respects and as he left, after a short visit,

184

whispered into my ear "I think she is nervous about me so I will visit slowly." With a kiss on my ear and a squeeze of my hand, he left quietly. Maryann treated us to fresh tuna for lunch during the week with her delicious gin and tonics.

Jean said she wanted to paint in the morning so when I came home from work, I was surprised to see her not on the roof drawing and painting but sitting in my cool front room. "The light is just too brilliant, I must have more subtleties and shadows - your African light is outrageous." She began to draw inside during the blistering hot mornings and paint in the cooler and less bright afternoons. She loved the shapes of the roof tops and told me she was so happy to be getting such a new perspective in her art. The restaurants, the few stores and my office were all visited. Then I introduced Jean to Paulino. He was very shy with Jean but, being a grandmother, she won him over quickly.

Before we went to bed each night, we would talk about the day's events and discuss Cape Verdean culture. Each morning, I would visit the airline office, was told that Jean's luggage would "come the next day," the African "wait dance." I had told my evening English class that I would bring them another visitor - my children, Cynthia & Heather had all done their share of telling about America so now it was Jean's turn. She took the posters of her oils and prints and showed them in the class, explaining how an artist creates. She spoke in English, I translated into Portuguese, but soon I noticed that the class was listening and understanding her so I became silent and she gave the entire lesson.

On the weekend we were invited to Calhau to spend the night in Vitorino's ocean home. He picked us up early so we could spend the entire day playing in the ocean, walking the beach, snoozing in the shade and talking about how different it all was here. We watched the fishermen go out late at night in their small boats with the huge sails and heard them slip back into shore the following morning. The fish were all colors, brown sharks, green moray eels, orange groupers and others brightly colored as well. Jean took out her sketch pad and did drawings of everything that surrounded us.

Jean got to see how some Cape Verdeans work - when it suited them. Arthur was the carpenter I had hired to make bookcases for the children's library. The books from the States were coming in fast and furious and I needed to get them out of my tiny front room. There was always one delay after another. Finally the day came and Jean and I went to see them. The bookcases were perfect. Arthur said he did his best job because he wanted some of the young students to become interested in carpentry. We begged and borrowed trucks - mostly with our smiles and a shrug and "if you don't help me, I don't know who will." to get the books to the school house that had been built only months before. To the students' oohs and aahs, the four individual pieces were put into place and we told the children the books would be coming shortly.

It took a month to catalog, place and establish the children's library of Campinho. We had a big reception, the head of the Education board came, all the teachers and children were in place and Jean got to see how an idea given by the old women of the tin shack town produced what they needed: books to educate their children. The grand number was 1,812 books, all donated by my friends and friends of friends from the States. Seeing the children's faces light up when they saw the books for THEIR library made all the work and sweat worthwhile. We brought all of the postcards that my friend Jay had sent and they became the library cards for each child. One project down, twenty-something to go.

The English class I had been teaching twice a week was to shut down for the three weeks I would be in Ireland on vacation. Jean suggested a scavenger hunt in English. She and I stayed up for hours thinking of articles to hide around the school that would be difficult to locate by name. When we explained the procedure at the beginning of the last class, frowns and confused looks greeted us. So Jean hid something they could see, I was blindfolded and then I ran around the classroom trying to locate the object. Finally they got the object of the game and a mad dash began through the two floors of the school. Nothing was safe, window sills, drawers, chairs, tables, under, on top of and inside. The scurrying lasted about one hour. Then Jean blew the whistle. We counted all of the objects found and Dilma was announced as the winner, which was nice because her father had died two weeks before and she had been very sad in class. Dilma's mood brightened when she heard she had won. I dismissed the class and we said our goodbyes and Jean and I giggled on our long walk home about all of the funny mistakes of the hunt and admitted we were too tired to pack for our upcoming trip. Jean was leaving after two weeks and planned to visit Portugal, so I decided to go with her and then when she went to the States, I would go to attend my family Shugrue clan meeting in Ireland.

We went to say good bye to Paulino and his mother Amelia and realized this was the day they were being moved from their tiny tin shack to a real room with cement floors, a flush toilet and a sink. Amelia was so frail we did the packing and I held Paulino as a small cart took their meager belongings to their new home. Amelia received a key and we all walked into a brand new, freshly painted room. Since the census I took a year before had indicated Amelia had no living relative in Cape Verde, she was entitled to live in this room and would not have to pay rent - it was called the place for people who have no help. We left them smiling and touching and examining all the parts of their new home. I told them I would be back in a few weeks, but when I left, I noticed Paulino looked sad and came to take my hand. I explained again and he left my side and stood with his mother, they had security with each other. It was just Paulino and Amelia in the one room apartment. My heart shuddered when I left, they were so alone and weak and I prayed to God to help them survive.

Jean Cain visit 1992

Vitorino came to say goodbye, Jean discreetly went upstairs to bed and he and I sat still for a long time on the makeshift sofa he had made for me and did not talk. Finally he stood, told me to be careful and said "Tenho sonhos cordo rosa," I wish you pink dreams. As I went upstairs to my sleeping room, I realized this was the beginning of our goodbyes. It was too sad to think of so I lit my candle, finished my packing and then watched the moon do her dance of the skies as I fell asleep. The morning of our departure Yvonne came and gave Jean a can of tuna made on our island and hand lotion for my trip. All the neighbors waved goodbye and faithful Mario took us to the airport, I noticed Vitorino's car parked off the side of the airport road and blew him silent kiss with dry eyes. The tears would come later.

My last visitor and I left the island looking at the lunar landscape of Sao Vicente in a mood of quietness that surprised us both.

BACK HOME TO MINDELO

After returning from vacation in Portugal and Ireland, my life in Mindelo began once again with Valentina, saying many people were asking for me. As I was writing notes for the library that night, I heard the distinctive roar of Vitorino's car. We picked up right where we left off, in each other's arms. I gave him the pipe I bought for him in England. He said it was too expensive. I asked him how he knew; he said the fancy box told him so. A renewal of our passion filled the night and I got lost in his arms. When I got quiet, he seemed to know what I was thinking. He said, "Even though we will be parted by thousands of miles, our hearts would never be." Falling asleep in his arms, I realized I would leave part of my heart with this man who had become so very important in my life.

The local Peace Corps Director, John, said he wanted to meet with the sewing association women. They were nervous but handled him well. Their books were in order: president, treasurer, secretary beamed at the end of the meeting.

Mayor Onesimo heard about the success of the sewing association and asked me to extend my Peace Corps service for just one more year. John asked the same, Vitorino as well. I felt torn, pulled and sad. I explained to the President that I missed my four children too much. He said he had twin sons who lived in New York City with his wife and understood my feelings. Even my musician friends got into the act to try to get me to stay. I took a torn traveling bag to my one legged shoe repair man to stitch and he asked me how much longer I would stay. I explained, he got up, stood on his one leg, came over to me and gave me a hug.

Then there was Arlene, who had become like another daughter, and was about to leave. I took her to a new restaurant with table cloths and we had chilled white wine, a rare treat indeed. We toasted each other, our friendship and the Peace Corps. We reveled in the new restaurant and hoped this would be a harbinger of things to come. It was so hot my Tic Tacs melted in their plastic case and I dug them out with my nail file.

Some plusses, some minuses of living in Cape Verde, the plusses out weighted the minuses hands down. Example - party giving. Now was the time to produce Arlene's despedia- a traditional going away party always given by the departing person. All of the professors Arlene taught with at the high school came and bought bowls and plates of food. The young men she had met and stolen their hearts came with beer. Vitorino came with grog for her to take back home, gift after gift was tucked aside to be packed. I watched and silently practiced saying good bye. Then we all went out to the clubs and danced till madrugda. Saw a shooting star on my walk home and went for a swim alone, watching the sky hoping to see another.

Two days later Arlene left. During the airport drive we both got quiet and did not talk. When the plane arrived, we hugged. She said she had left a few things in her apartment for me to have. I walked back to her silent apartment and took a wooden string lamp shade and a piece of metal with figures cut out in a village scene. They became part of my life, as she had.

The goodbye wrenching continued. Bernice wrote me asking when I was coming to Praia; she was leaving the Embassy the next week, peanut butter cookies at the ready. Winnie, wife of the USAID Director Tom, sent a note saying she and Tom were going to their next post, Ougandougou, Burkina Fasso. An invitation was extended. When I was going for my PC interview, my daughter Claire gave me good advice. "Impress them, Mom, capital cities always keep the same name like Ougandougou is the same, the country used to be called Upper Volta." During my interview, I just let Claire's tid bit drop, ever so subtly, - thank you, Claire. I started giving away my Newsweek magazines, in which I read a line, "keep learning, marveling and laughing", Marta Munzer MIT graduate, electrochemical engineer on her 93rd birthday, my kind of woman.

The events I had attended in the past with a casual air, I now went to with the desire to imprint them in my mind. Bia Dos Gatos was the August musical festival at Cat Fish Bay. I told Vitorino that I was amazed that there was always a full moon at the beginning of the festival, he laughed. "We plan the festival around the moon, my love." We took Paulino to the festival and, when Vitorino threw him up in the air, he would laugh like a merry three year old. Paulino never had a dad to play with.

When I came home from the music festival, there was a note from the Mayor under my door: USAID people are coming tomorrow morning for reports, you go on at 8 am. Instead of relaxing with Vitorino, I burned the midnight oil and wrote reports on the sewing association, Project PACIM, the school library, my AIDS lectures. The next morning I gave the presentation and asked the examiners if they wanted to see the areas I worked in. "Not necessary" was the response. I forced them to go and see the devastation of the tin shack towns, the poverty of the homeless, the prostitutes and dirty children running in the dirt out of control. After that tour, it was easier to get money from USAID.

Paulino – I still had one more project to accomplish with him, get him in to school. I pulled all sorts of strings, chits outstanding were called in and he got into a school for free. When I ran to tell Amelia, she just looked at me, and her eyes of poverty did not understand my message. I walked the 45 minute walk to his tin shack every morning, raced back to my home, bathed him, and walked him to the new school. Then I hired a neighbor of his to walk him, but after a week, I realized Amelia could not get him ready and I had to be at my office every morning at 8:30. It was a great effort, but it did not work. What would become of Paulino? Every time I complained to Vitorino he consoled me, grog mellowed me out and a midnight swim cooled me down. Paulino was a problem I could not fix.

As I mulled over my departure, I got a note telling me to come to Praia for one last training session for the new volunteers. How typical of Peace Corps. I had so little time on my own island to wrap everything up and they took me away. I told Vitorino and he said "This will be good practice for when we have to say good bye soon." He was so centered, damn him.

END OF TRAINING IN SAO JORGE

The training was winding down and I was winding up so I could be ready to return to my work in Mindelo. The trainees were getting itchy too, three months was just about the right amount of time to train. I passed out my reprints, my favorite one being about the bumble bee. "According to aeronautical tests, the Bumble Bee cannot fly because of the shape and weight of its body in relation to its total wing area. The bumble bee doesn't know this; so he goes ahead and flies anyway." This is the Peace Corps philosophy, exactly. Then the famous and well known Ghanaian quote: "If you educate a man you simply educate an individual, but if you educate a woman, you educate a family." - J.E. Kwewgyir Aggrey, Ghanaian educator (1875 -1927). And finally the famous Mark Twain quote "Travel is fatal to bigotry, prejudice, and narrow-mindedness."

Another sign of my impending departure: the post office lady asked me when she should start holding my mail and what address she could send it to. I sent letters to my friends saying "Do not send mail; I shall be home soon" but I had no clue when I would be home. Sandra came over and gave me a stunning ebony wooden sculpture of a Masai woman standing, holding a kalabash, her present to me from her trip to Kenya. In turn, I gave her posters, tee shirts and lectures in Portuguese and Crioulo on AIDS. She promised to keep that part of my project going in her neighborhood. A trip to the travel agent and I was booked to go to Praia for my report giving and farewell. Tried to catch up in my daily log, some days I would have a scrawl so squiggly I could not read. Would I ever write a book about my almost three years? Well, if I did, I better have the notes. Older volunteers did the logs, the younger ones did not.

The sewing association was selling their clothing like mad; they were beginning to get the concept of paying back the loan they had received from the PC group in Boston. The books had been carefully ensconced into the book cases in Campinho and the teachers were allowing the students to take books home. Engineer Pedro from my office came to my house to get the green marble plaque that the Arlington, Massachusetts Sweet Adelines had sent with the books they had purchased in memory of their director's mother who was from Cape Verde. I had had been storing it in my bedroom for safekeeping.

As Pedro and I walked up my long cement staircase, I suddenly remembered that I had put signs all around my bedroom in English about loving, sharing and Vitorino had added the Portuguese words. Anatomy lessons were everywhere so I raced in front of Pedro, saying my bed room was a mess and grabbed all the papers off the walls, blushing. Pedro shook his head, got the plaque and went down stairs as I clutched the papers and laughed to myself. The large American eagle was most impressive and the children silently looked at the words in English knowing that maybe, one day, they would be able to read English from the books this group had sent. I would see a student walking with an English book carefully tucked under their arm, holding the precious library card that had been made from Jay's Mexican post cards. They would smile and I would return the smile; if only I could show my friends who had so kindly sent books their smiles.

What should I take home and what should I leave? The one animal skin that were gifts to me from my three month training in Guinea Bissau definitely went into the duffle. Posters sent to me went to the members of the sewing association and clothing went to my friends in the tin shack town of Campinho. My two wooden stools that were the sum total of my furniture I wished I could fold and take but knew it would not work so planned to give them to the sewing association. I did take the small and very light stool that I bought in Mali, made from the baobob tree. The ivy that was now entwined totally around my front hall I would leave for the next tenant and I remembered the kindness of the old woman who had given me the cuttings when I first arrived.

One last part remained of the sewing association puzzle: open up a bank account. We had a meeting; I explained the process and told them to get dressed up. The next morning we five walked into the bank. It was the first time in a bank for most of the women. We were given a hard time and I could not figure out why. Then I was told that the women must have shoes on to do business in the bank. I told them to go back to the tin shack town, borrow shoes and bring them to my apartment. When they arrived (the devil made me do it...) I had them take a shoe from each pair and switch - so no one had on matching shoes. We walked into the bank to raised eyebrows but we were treated like real customers - which we indeed were.

We explained what we wanted to do; eyebrows raised told me that the bank officials were surprised to see the money we wanted to deposit. But first, we had to have birth certificates, proper stamps to open an account, then a document saying where they lived. Each time we brought back the necessary document, they gave us a new hurdle to jump. But we hung in there, gathered for a meeting outside the bank to see who could go and get what while the rest of us would wait. Finally the deed was done, the account was opened and the women glowed with pride when they went back to their neighbors with the news, they had money in the bank! I told them they did it all themselves and they had. What a sweet moment it was to watch their new found walk full of confidence and pride. I thought of a quote I used to have on my fridge at home. "Whatever women do they must do twice as well as men to be thought half as good - luckily, this is not difficult"- Charlotte Whitton, Mayor of Ottawa.

When I went back to my apartment to continue the packing, I found a tube of toothpaste and smiled with glee. I had been skimping like a dying miser for the past few weeks. But I must not blow it - must remember I was going on West Africa so back to the skimpy miser behavior. A letter was delivered to me - unusual - I usually picked up my mail. But this looked important so the postmistress had it delivered. Was it another death or an accident? Would I have to go home early? No, this was glad news from my son Bill, "Dear Mom, Great news, I'm engaged to Mary Blumenthal with a possible date of June 13, 1993, all are very happy." I smiled, and thought of what it would be like to have a daughter-in-law.

Events continued to happen around us that made us realize how frail we all were. PCV Nat Creamer who lived on the island of Mao had been evacuated for personal reasons. He would be missed; he was a prince of a guy. I wrote a letter to his parents telling them they should be very proud of what he had accomplished and that he would be remembered by all.

There were loops to be closed before I left and one of them was the AIDS condom lectures. I continued to give them and was always on the search for a bright person to train to take my place as a lecturer. Finally found two young people who had the energy and commitment to continue the lectures. I asked if they would continue - heard "Yes," so our lectures became three way lectures. I led, they followed, and as the weeks went by, I put myself into the background and they led. That made me feel my work would continue for, after all, the Peace Corps mission is to teach and leave and have the nationals take over. Talk about sustainable development, the eight sewing association members were tearing up the town, making clothing for dozens of people and putting the money in the bank. Sometimes we nine would have heated discussions about the direction of the association. They were not easy women to deal with but I remembered I had decided to choose strong women so they would succeed and be strong models and not wimps.

Now the calendar was telling me to get organized about what to bring home, what to give away. I had Vitorino take down the wood and string lamp the old man had made for Arlene. I had to search for days for a box but found one and packed it to go on the boat "The Jenny" that sailed to the States monthly. I also packed the huge Senegalese leather and straw hat and the iron cut out sculpture with bizarre shapes and sizes.

One morning I awoke with a wild red rash, on my chest, on my back, all over. It was Saturday and the clinic was closed so I went to see Maryann and Pedro. "Allergic reaction" said Pedro, who wrote down what to buy, and Maryann put the salve all over me and the relief came quickly. I opened a box of Wet Ones that my son had sent and they were all dried out because of the intense heat. When Vitorino visited that night, he got furious with me. "You're doing too much, you are running yourself down, and God is telling you to take it easy". He washed me with soap that had lye in it that he kept in his car and the redness quieted down and so did we, in each other's arms as we fell into a deep sleep.

I decided I would give myself a despedia. I started to make a guest list and a list of food and liquor to buy so that I could acknowledge all my friends and thank them for their friendship.

GETTING READY TO CUT THE BONDS

The United States was starting to creep into more and more of my life in Cape Verde. A letter from Jean saying my art gallery partners were planning a Christmas party and hoped I would be home by then. Les, who worked in Praia, visited our town and we went to dinner at the Senegalese restaurant. The owners visited our table with admonitions to make sure I visited their French restaurant in Dakar, Senegal. I asked how they knew I was leaving and going to the West Africa and they replied "We all know you are leaving." Les chatted with them about his visits to their country and I got quiet – it was not going to be easy to break the bonds. Les invited me to his new home when I came to sign the final papers for PC. I filed the invitation as I had learned to do while living in Africa.

Sandra and I decided to have a farewell visit to the island across from ours, Santao Antao. Mario, my faithful taxi driver, beeped his horn right at 6:30 am. He said he would give me a free ride to the airport when I left. I murmured thanks quietly and he said not to be sad, he knew I would come back to visit. He pointed to the American flag I had given him, which was still proudly waving from his dash board and smiled, "You might leave here, Deana, but you will never leave our memory." Sandra met me at the boat and off we went for the usual wild ride, Cape Verdeans vomiting left and right. I grabbed the banana I bought the day before and munched it down and fell asleep which was my answer to sea sickness. As I left the boat, the old Captain who had become my friend said, "When you return, join me in the cabin so you will remember the sunset over our islands." The van took us to the north side of the island, the ride was bumpy and long, and I told myself how smart I was to wear my bra - a habit I had long lost. We got another ride to the small village of Pauol and the small pensaio (hotel) was perfect. We both flopped on the small beds and slept with the sound of the surf lulling us.

After our nap, we walked around the small village, not a long walk, not a big town. We saw a huge German Shepard dog barking and scaring two little girls. Sandra immediately went to the master and told him to stop his dog, but he paid her no mind. I went over to him and told him the same thing and he bowed and did - wrinkles won out. We had a small dinner in the hotel and fell back to our room. Spiders were doing their jump rope acrobatics on our walls with the fresh breeze off the ocean that made our gauze curtains dance. We talked about Charlotte's Web and sleep wrapped up our night.

We had been told of rock paintings that were mysterious, the Rocks of Janela, so headed off in that direction. A half hour later, we saw huge boulders jutting up from a sea of tall grass and there, in white, bold strokes were strange markings. A cross tilting towards the far away ocean, a figure running, unusual markings all around a type of writing but nothing made sense. We sat near the base of the biggest boulder and made up stories about how they got there, how they were painted and why.

As the sunset was beginning to paint its lovely colors, we walked back to town. Sandra went ahead. I took out my pipe that Vitorino had made for me and began to smoke. When I got to a fork in the road, I sat down on a huge boulder. Some children saw me, pointed and yelled, "Bruxa, bruxa". I had left my dictionary in our room so continued to smoke when an old woman came up next to me, cackled, pointed to me and said "Bruxa." I smiled, nodded yes, figuring she was friendly and if she agreed with the children that I was a bruxa, it must be all right. She took out her pipe, sat down next to me, motioned that she wanted some of my tobacco and we smoked in silence until the light was gone. People passed by, smiled. When I got back to our hotel, I asked Sandra what bruxa meant. She said witch and only witches smoked pipes in Cape Verde. Sandra said that this island was the only place where bruxas lived. I fit right in.

After dinner, dancing and back to our hotel, Sandra fell asleep and I got out my pipe, went to our small balcony, and watched the ocean play out over my pipe smoke. Maybe I was a witch after all. Swimming, visiting friends of Maryann & Pedro's filled our next few days, but always at sunset, I went to the fork in the small road and sat and waited for my bruxa friend. Never heard a sound, she just arrived, smiled, took my tobacco and we sat in silence, watching the gray moon start its rise. The stars pulled out of the light and into the darkness which illuminated their sparkles. This indeed was the definition of mellow.

Knowing this would be my last night on the island, I motioned to my new found friend that I was leaving the following morning and would always remember. When our smoke was finished, she stood, bowed and smiled, her tobacco stained teeth shining, I bowed and my newly stained teeth grinned back at her. She disappeared down the dark road, the only light being the one from her pipe. She didn't know I had put most of my tobacco into her cloth bag when she was not looking. I turned and sat back down in "our spot" wondering what her life story was and felt I had made a friend.

The next morning, our host gave me a leaf wrapped around a small object. I asked him who had given it to him, "you will know when you open it up". The leaf held a very small pipe, made of a tough wood I had not seen before in CV It had a small etching on it, scratched by a sharp object. I could not see it clearly in the hotel's dim light so went out to the brilliant sun. It had two stick figures on the side, woman's figures. I looked at the spot where we had sat, no one was there, but a memory had formed there.

Our mellow weekend came to a close and we fell asleep on the ferry back to our island. In the next few months, whenever I smoked my new pipe, I thought of my friend the bruxa and how she accepted me as a fellow bruxa at least enough to share some of my tobacco and make me a pipe for me to use and remember.

Now the leave taking was getting very real. I wrote my invitation and Pedro put sail boats and balloons all around the border for my despedia. I started giving them out to my neighbors on our road. I went to the tin shack town and gave invitations to my favorites, they got sad and quiet. Vitorino came to visit, he laughed about the bruxa story and told me to remember him every time I used the pipe he made for me and the pipe the woman made for me. In the last few weeks we were beginning to just sit in each other's arms on my roof, not moving much, just watching the moon and stars. I knew he was thinking of my leaving when he started a sentence and then stopped and just hugged me. Our times together got quieter and quieter. When he would leave after we shared our bodies, I could not go to the shutters and wave good bye - it hurt too much to see him drive away.

Diane with pipe Vitorino made for her

Bruxa (witch in Portuguese)

Bruxa – gave me this pipe as a fellow Bruxa

199

The other man in my life was beginning to look skinnier and more malnourished. I had asked Kristin, our PC, nurse if she could give me some vitamins for Paulino. He had his head shaved again for the lice he had, scabies were making red welts on his arms and legs. The women of the tin shack town kept saying "take him to America, Amelia cannot take care of him." Amelia would look at me and nod yes, but I turned and walked away saying I could not take him back with me. I reread the letter Lisa, my predecessor, wrote about the adoption process. It was complicated, costly and time consuming. I knew I could barely get myself home, much less bring a four year old with me.

Friends began having farewell parties for me. Harriet, the Swedish clinic director, had Maryann, Sandra and me out for a delicious dinner in her magnificent home by the ocean. She toasted and thanked me for having the soul of a Cape Verdean. We drank to Cape Verde and all her wonderful, generous and unique citizens.

With two weeks to go – I divided up my possessions, what I would sell, what to give away and what to send home on the Jenny boat. Most of my stuff I gave to the women in the two tin shack towns, Vitorino got special things like sharp knives, tool kits and anything he could use for the desalinization plant. I took our project truck to the harbor and loaded one metal barrel and 14 boxes for their trip to America. The sales began: everything into my tiny front hall, kind of a yard sale without the yard. The men bought the cassettes, the women sheets & pillows and clothes. As I watched my clothing walk out the door, I wondered how my clothes would look on others. An apron a friend had sent from the Boston Long Island Homeless Shelter was my cash box, change went in and out. It had been decided that another volunteer, Ray, would take over my apartment when I left. He asked if I would please let the ivy stay that had grown all over my walls, I cut a piece and put it in water to see if I could root it and take it home. It died - was not meant to leave.

The children from the tin shack town of Campinho came and sat silently in the road outside of my door saying nothing. A teacher from Campinho came to bring one of her children home and mentioned that the doors to the library cases were broken. They had fallen off their hinges as the children used them so much. I laughed thinking it was so great that they

broke with use, then realized the books could be stolen so ran into town and tried to find Arthur, master builder. Finally I tracked him down and laid him out for the hinges that did not last a mere month. I had not paid the full amount due, so had him by the short hairs. "When the hinges are replaced by strong ones, your money will be paid." He growled but a child told me the next day, hinges were fixed, books were secure. Only then was he paid the remaining money due.

Each night Vitorino came by, sometimes full of grog, which made him loud, sometimes startling sober and quiet. We spun from babbling about unimportant things to looking at each other and growing quiet with our own thoughts. One night he looked down and said, "I really did not think you would go, PC wants you to stay, the President of the Island wants you to stay, and so do I." Tried to explain how it was time to go home, I missed my children desperately, my job was over. The sewing association was up and running and profitable, the children's library was functioning, the AIDS lectures were being taught by Cape Verdeans and my job at the project in the tin shack towns was over. The President told me he used my memos to him as examples of how people act in business when they want to change the situation.

The invitations to my despedia had all been delivered. Amelia, Paulino's mom, said she did not have any clothing to wear. I went out and bought each of them something to wear. Presents started to arrive at my home. The restaurant man, to whom I taught the concept of "take home." dropped off white doilies with a hand drawn picture of a red headed witch on them. He smiled and I smiled and wondered if he had heard the story of Deana, the bruxa. My one legged shoe repair man, Antonio, gave me a heart shaped box made of sea shells. Bella, the artist gave me a batik she had done of a man and woman dancing very close with wind floating all around them. Serafim, maker of boats, gave me a bottle of grog.

Friday was our traditional night when Vitorino and I went out to his house on the ocean in Calhau. When we arrived, I walked right into the ocean, with skirt and blouse on and laughed when I realized I forgot to take them off. Flung them to Vitorino who was lighting his pipe on the shore, my bathing suit bothered me so I tossed it to him too. Swimming naked and alone in the dark, feeling small fish pass me by, using the stars to guide me, the moon to light him, I drank the sights and sounds in and promised I would never forget.

Finally Vitorino roared for me to come in, he did not like it when I swam out too far. I felt like swimming to the continent so I would not have to return to the shore and have our goodbye hugs. He had bought my favorite kind of grog, made with coconut milk, and I drank a little too much, he drank a little too much and we both fell asleep. The dawn light played with our eyes until we opened them and realized how late - or early it was. We raced back to the town, he promised to come to my despedia that night, and we parted.

I slept for two hours and then hit the deck running to get the party organized. Found the musicians and reminded them to come at 8, checked with the food lady and she said her chicken would be the best it ever had been in honor of Deana .Borrowed tables from here, chairs from there, got lots of candles from hardware store. All of a sudden, there was Cheryl, PCV from Guinea Bissau, on my door stop. She needed a place to stay, but I was not my usual hospitable self and said straight out she had to find another place to stay.

The light over the ocean was beginning to change, telling me sunset was near and I still had a million loose ends. Whose car did I hear but Vitorino's. He walked in very tall and straight and not at all like his usual fun loving self. He sat on one of my stools and told me to guess which hand had a surprise in it. I had taught him this American game two years before. He had made another pipe for me; this one had a metal edge to it as I had cracked the bowl slightly on the one he had made the year before. He took me up to my roof, played a CV tape, we danced, and he sang very quietly in my ear. The light faded, the sun disappeared and we still danced slowly.

We were jolted out of our quietness by Hamilton's voice yelling on the first floor, "Everyone is at your party" Vitorino left, I dressed and went to the big room I had rented in the town hall. When I walked in, the music was blaring in perfect Cape Verdean rhythm, the smell of cooking chicken filled the air and the bar was crowded with all of my friends. Yvonne and David gave me a shark made out of bone, my two women friends from the post office gave me a Bella batik, Project PACIM made a presentation of a black and white tapestry they had all contributed to, Ricardo Neves gave me a Cesaria CD. My friends from the bank laughed with me at the stories of my early days of depositing my checks and not knowing the Portuguese numbers past twenty... not that my checks were much higher.

Antonio, the one legged man, asked me to dance with him. I froze, said I had to check the chicken and would be right back. Went into the kitchen, talked to the wall, muttering, how the hell am I going to dance with a one legged man, I don't want to embarrass him, what to do? Finally came out of the kitchen and saw Antonio dancing with the sexiest young girl with complete ease, using his crutch as a leg. When he finished, I told him I was now ready to dance, the chicken was fine and he laughed and said, "You were afraid, but now you see I can do it." God, he was fine on the dance floor. I said as we finished our fifteen minute set, "how I wished I had danced with you in the past. He laughed and said I was not ready until this night. How wise he was.

Every once in a while I would look around for Vitorino. Paulino and his mother never showed. One of my best young dance partners Mick and I danced and he whispered, "Don't be sad, you will always have us in your heart." The music continued, the chicken was enjoyed and then around 3:30 people started to go home. Hugs, kisses, and long looks at each other finished the party. Joaquin from the Peace Corps office drove me home and I sat on my bed, staring out at the ocean and moon and did not sleep.

Faithful Hamilton knocked at my door about an hour later and said to get ready, Maryann would soon be here. I raced around, threw stuff willy nilly into the small bags, and there stood Maryann, not a tear on her cheek, but a sad look in her eyes. Her car slowly crept to the airport, not like it usually did when we were off to a swim. The airport shuffle and then the toy plane came in over the ocean and turned to make its descent. Maryann and I hugged, not a word was said. I climbed aboard, the door shut.

Through a tiny window in the plane, I saw a red car next to the huge sand dunes near the runway, and a tall man was standing by it. He lit a pipe and motioned in the direction of the plane. It was Vitorino, doing what he said he would do, wishing me well in his own way. I touched the pipe in my pocket, as tears came streaming down my cheeks, closed my fingers around it and nodded back to him. He never saw the gesture, but he knew I had done it. The little plane took off and then turned to go back over the end of our island. As we were still low, I saw our tin shack town Campinho and a group of my women friends, standing alone in a clearing, waving white scarves over their heads towards the plane. Suddenly, my tears stopped, I smiled and felt happy, comforted by all the goodbyes, all given in their own ways.

Diane dancing with Valentina

Antonio, one legged man who repaired shoes for all who had two legs

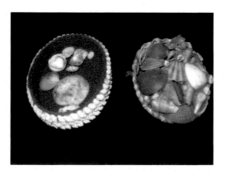

Shell Case made by Antonio for Diane

THE LEAVING OF CAPE VERDE

Never realized how different each island was in Cape Verde until I looked at the island of Santiago where I was about to land. It had green all scattered about, tall buildings and fancy paved roads. The faces that greeted us upon landing were neither friendly nor familiar. I realized I had become an elitist about "our" island being the best with the best people, the best heart, and the best soul.

After the airport luggage dance, I found my friend Shelia, Cape Verdean staff member from the Embassy, and she took me to her Victorian home. After looking at me and realizing what kind of shape I was in, she gave me a glass of wine, a tuna sandwich and put me in her bed where I promptly fell asleep, awaking four hours later. Then she drove me to the home of Les & Katy. As she left, she invited me to go out dancing that night, I said I could not "play," I was "played out." Katy was a perfect host: dinner and to bed.

The next day filled up with Peace Corps paper work and severing the ties officially. Kristin, our PC nurse, went over me with a fine tooth comb and declared me fit as a fiddle – then when she looked at me again, she amended her findings with "very sad eyes." Maryann called me at the PC office and told me the famous musician Louis Lobo made a tape for me as a farewell gift and she would send to the States. When she said goodbye, there was a slight catch in her voice which I immediately heard. We hung up quickly so we would not break up on the phone. PCV Rebecca with whom I had traveled to Senegal and Mali also called to say goodbye.

A visit to the airline told me the departure time was dawn, as usual. Then I would be off to visit my friends Winnie & Tom who had just been transferred to Ougandougou, Burkina Fasso. I called Vitorino at his office. He was surprised but asked if I had seen his car next to the airport when I left. I murmured "yes" and he told me not to be sad.

Antonia from the embassy came over with the black bead with white spots that I had ordered, called the "eye of God." She put it on a small chain and hung it round my neck. "Now, God will protect you when you leave 'your' country. Never forget us, Deana."

A sleepless night passed, then onto the plane, and hello Senegal, once again. I was surprised by the number of beggars and crippled children begging at the airport. A cab took me to the PC office across from the Grand Mosque. There I met Maura Sene, PC staff, a charming woman with an Irish lilt to her voice, about my age and who had married a Senegalese while visiting Paris as a young woman. I went to the PC guest house for the night and listened to the chants and prayers coming from the mosque. Volunteers came in and invited me to go to the American Cultural Club to hear the election results. Red, white and blue streamers lined the ceilings, the walls and most of the Senegalese who were busy having a good time. The other two volunteers and I were the only Americans. Midnight, then came 1am, then 2 am. At 4:50, William Jefferson Clinton who I had voted for by absentee ballot was declared the winner and we all limped home.

The next morning, I went back to the PC office, an oasis in the midst of a most confusing city, and asked for directions to the French Embassy so I could pick up my visa. Once there, the French woman gave me a hard time; the day wore on and then lunch time was announced - 2 hours of course, so everyone left. I stayed because I did not want to lose my now valuable spot in line, fell asleep and was awakened by people coming back. The line crawled on and I became totally frustrated. I spied a most distinguished man who was strolling through the hall approached him and asked if he could assist. "Not a problem, give me your passport" – and it was returned with the visa ten minutes later. He bowed, I bowed and I thanked the French for their manners - at least of this gentleman.

I returned to the PC office and had dinner with my new friend Maura. She took me on a tour of the city, and I understood why she loved it. It was a combination of Europe, Africa and yet unique. We went to dinner in a hotel where the restaurant on the dock jutted out over the ocean. The surf pounded under our feet, white wine relaxed us and we became old friends. Talked about the joys and sorrows of raising children and where our journeys had taken us. We promised to stay in touch.

The airport shuffle began again and we had an uneventful flight to Ougandougou, Burkina Fasso, where Tom Luche met me. Lightning and thunder and torrential rain began - wind shield wipers and puddles, it was so weird for me to see and feel after living in Cape Verde.

Winifred Luche, security guard and Diane, Waga

Tom Luche and Diane and security guard, Waga

*Diane's final trip in Africa November, 1992 arriving at home of Winifred
and Tom Luche – Burkina Fasso – 5 bags and skinny Diane*

"Love Letters" with Tom Luche

Diane walked on the back of this crocodile – Waga

We arrived at their magnificent home, complete with security guards, a pool in the front yard and manicured green grass. I took my shoes off and walked in the rain and grass. Winnie came to their veranda and told me to come in from the rain and we hugged and laughed. She was not feeling well so Tom & I went out to dinner at L'Eau Vive which was a restaurant run by Catholic nuns. Smiles, service, and a sumptuous feast made me realize I was in Francophone Africa. At the end of the dinner, the nuns handed out cards and we sang Ave Maria (in French) but I sang it in Latin (my high school nuns would have been proud.) We returned to their house and, with the sound of rain, I went quickly to sleep.

No one was home when I dragged my sorry ass out of bed the next morning. Winnie had put up a picture of Tom and me when we did "Love Letters" together in Cape Verde. How thoughtful. I made a cup of tea and enjoyed it with some French bread and hit the pool and laughed with the pleasure of it all. Then I thought of Cape Verde and all my friends and cried in the pool. I noticed small birds diving into the pool and asked Winnie what they were..."bats, my dear, but not to worry, they never hit you - they have sonar." We went to the American Club and watched tennis.

Winnie and I had a lovely quiet dinner after Tom had left for Ivory Coast. Winnie got me up to speed about the doings in the States; she told me Millicent Fenwick, 82, U.S. Congresswoman from New Jersey, had died. I had interviewed her in the States and remembered her smoking a pipe, showed Winnie my pipe that Vitorino made and we got quiet about our mutual memories of living in Cape Verde. I told her that I always thought of Cape Verde as the lost continent of Atlantis.

It seemed my thoughts were still with Cape Verde but there were things to see in Waga, nickname for the capital. The former President Sankara had gathered artists to do sculptures on existing boulders in the interior. At the entrance to a national park, there was a huge stone banana which everyone was allowed to sit on. The works were wonderful: funny, engaging, sad, angry and gentle.

As we drove home, rather, were driven home, Winnie told me we were invited to a ball the next evening as it was Nov. 10th. I told her my brother had taught me the importance of the date of the Marine Corps birthday! Winnie lent me an elegant, long dress, black pumps and beautiful jewelry. The Marine Corps band was in full swing when we arrived and the two of us were swept away to the dance floor. I had forgotten how to dance American. The Marines were good dancers but did not move the way the Cape Verdeans did and I had a hard time teaching myself to move the way I used to move.

In the morning, the next place to visit was the African market, with Winnie's friend as my guide. I bought bright material for my three daughters, and my future daughter in law and small gifts for friends. Then Winnie and I tucked in and recovered from the Marine Ball, watched movies and ate French goodies. Saw a framed quote Winnie had hung "Laissez Chaque Homme Exercer L'Art Ou'il Connait" - Winnie translated - Let every man practice the art that he knows. Winnie took me to the home of her friend, Zarah. I was impressed with her paintings copied from a John Singer Sargent book of Berbers: on horseback, shooting, at the market. Zarah and her husband had adopted a Berber child and then had one of their own. She told me her stories of Morocco. Berber pictures were on all the walls and when I began to think maybe I should go there, Zarah gave me names of friends in Morocco. I had no particular time to get back to Boston and felt liberated from schedules now that my PC job was finished. Had a unusual green patterned dress made for me with gold weavings on the front, was a perfect fit - no tape measure needed. It constantly amazed me how African women knew how to sew, tailor, and design clothing so it was just right and perfect. A pattern was never used. It was a gift they never even knew they had.

Off to the market for fresh veggies, fruits and even batiks put on cards, purchased a dozen and the artist gave me one free to keep for myself. Went to a rug making school and watched the artists make magnificent weavings. Went horseback riding with Zarah and met the riding instructor, Mr. Morrow. He had trained in England, was a member of the Ghana Calvary and put us through our paces. I had learned English style as a little girl, then Western after college in Colorado, but I learned more about the horse and having a good seat from this man than I had ever learned from any of my former teachers. He had us walk under the horse, a first, take the saddle off and put it back on, lie on the back on the horse, over the head, jump off and then JUMP on, walk, trot and canter in the ring before he allowed us to go out on the trail. I was aching even before I got off the horse, but uttered not a word of complaint. The trail was a wonder. Up and over huge hills, we rode down at a canter, and we madly jumped over puddles. I thanked him and he said he hoped I would return.

The next day was Sunday, so Zarah took me to the very large Cathedral in the middle of the city. There was lots of singing, and kneeling and praying out loud. I felt like I was back at my high school, Our Lady of Mercy Academy on Long Island. Some memories just never leave one.

After church we walked on the streets of Waga which were full of red dust and gray dirt on the sides with bicycles and mobilettes racing in helter skelter fashion. We went out every other night for dinner, one night to an excellent Vietnamese restaurant, the next Hamburger House. I went back to my riding class and every single part of my body was in revolt. We rode into the country side, Mr. Morrow's crisp British voice always keeping us crisp. Villages, women walking with perfectly balanced jugs of water on their heads, children everywhere were enjoyed by all the riders. Three days of this and my body was almost getting back into shape but then the French desserts would take over and next stop: Fat city. A round of tennis with Winnie, horseback riding, laps in the pool, were all in a day's work.

ADVENTURE # 713 - BURKINA FASSO AND THE CROC

Winnie said everyone did it. She said she would be right next to me when I did it and told me not to be afraid, so, of course, I went right to it.

After a long drive into the interior; over dirt roads, through villages surrounding us, past strolling donkeys carrying heavy loads, Winnie and I arrived at our destination. Because Burkina Fasso (the former Upper Volta) is a land locked country, the colonial French had created bouragaes, bodies of water in the interior to be used as needed. This bouragae looked benign enough, kind of muddy water, no waves, no tides pulling, no signs of life moving in the water until I looked closely and there, two strange little some things emerging over the surface of the water ... and another pair, and another pair. Soon there were about five pairs of some things moving in our direction.

A tall, elegant Burkian man came up to me and said," Would you like to see what is in our water?" I looked back at the water and there was a small crocodile surfacing, walking towards us. The man said "Do not move quickly, do not be afraid, go the cages over there and bring back a live chicken." Did as told, the chicken had a string around his neck, the crock spied it and began an advance. The man said "Stand there, when I tell you to get on the back of the crocodile, do so quickly." By now I was rigid with fear. The crocodile turned, the man held my hand, "Please step on his back now, hold the chicken over his head and do not shake." As I walked on the back of the crocodile from his tail to his head, dangling the chicken on the string, the croc lifted his head and took a swipe at the chicken. The string was pulled out of my hand, chicken was grabbed, I jumped off, and the crocodile took chicken to water, happy croc, not so happy chicken. Terrified Diane stood still. Winnie came towards me, "Diane dear, well done - a cool drink is waiting for you." I gulped the cool drink, still looking at the water that no longer had pairs of eyes on the surface.

I have the picture to prove that I really did it.

"A MAN NEEDS A LITTLE MADNESS OR ELSE HE NEVER DARES CUT THE ROPE AND BE FREE"

Zorba, the Greek, Michael Cacoyannis

That quote from Zorba should be the icon, mantra, of the Peace Corps. If you don't take the risk, you might as well be dead. Having just walked on the back of a croc, I thought, why not go to the Ivory Coast and then hit Morocco? I told Winnie of my decision and she was pleased and helped me do the usual African dance of transportation. This time I would take a train to Ivory Coast. I still had to go through the agony of making reservations. We went to the train station and the gates to the station were locked. Thank God I had Winnie to expedite as her flawless French got us the information that the tickets were sold only on the day of the trip. Had to get a visa for a trip to the Ivory Coast so - off to the French Embassy, but this time I had Winnie and it went very smoothly.

After those two tough trips, nothing else to do but hit the tennis courts, where I was told that when the bats hung in the trees they sounded like metal swings rocking on a southern porch. At tennis I met Jeri, who gave me her card and invited me to her home in the Ivory Coast. I said I might just take her up on that.

It was now November 19th so took Meflaquline for malaria because I was on the continent and had the wild dreams that came with the territory. I never had to take them in Cape Verde, there was no malaria there. The train station was crowded, but Winnie's driver got me through the process and there I was in a cabin for a 28 hour ride. We left on the dot of 8:30 am, the scenery spun by me: green trees, tall grass, donkeys pulling cart loads of wood, white egrets soaring up beyond. About six hours into the trip, it was time to go to the bathroom. It was terrible, so back to my cabin, hoisted up my skirts and made a neat shot into the empty soda can. Now it was a can of something else. I made friends with the porter who was in

213

charge of our cabins, smiled and chatted, not sure of his language or mine, but we understood each other. About bed time, the porter put fresh sheets on my second tier berth, and turned down the lightweight blanket, having earned a decent tip.

At sunset the huge red orb began its descent. Dark, inky blues, Kelly greens, yellows and burnt sienna took over the sky and I watched the panorama play itself out. Distant slash and burn fires showed with teeny, bright pin point lights. Baobob trees showed their predictable arrogance and then the stars started their light show. Twinkling, stationary, they all seemed to revolve. I opened the train window and smelled the night fires in villages, animal scents, and flowers making an African potpourri.

A knock on the door announced two huge men, armed with rifles, scowling and using tough James Cagney voices, asking for my papers. My porter came, spoke to them in a language that I did not have a prayer of understanding. They bowed, I bowed and off they went. The porter had earned another tip, a tad smaller than the last, but nonetheless a tip. Mosquitoes began to circle so on went the Skin So soft. They did not like it and left for to juicier quarters. My small paper fan accompanied me to my upper berth. So did a nip of Dewar's that Nedda had sent to me months before and with some stale dead cheese and crackers made my dinner high on my perch. I leaned out my window and saw the train head light pierce the ink surrounding us, a single beacon of strong, intruding light. I had begun to fall asleep when I heard guards coming down our corridor and my cabin man saying that I was a Peace Corps person. Footsteps got fainter and I was rocked and rolled to sleep.

When the first light began to show Kamate, my cabin man, knocked quietly and told me that breakfast was ready. Struggled up, dressed and limped with stiff bones to the cabin where coffee and tea and breads were being served. Realized I had not talked to anyone in the past 12 hours, but upon reflection, thinking that had been just fine. I took my plethora of pills with tea that was dark and wonderful. Thought about the names "the dark continent" and "the third world" and wondered why those who coined the terms did not call it "the first world". After all, Africa was where man was born. I had been told it was "about" ... one always had to be wary when one heard the word "about" ... a 22 to 28 hour train trip. The train ride was beginning to wear thin. It had been 20 hours and I could not get a straight answer from Kamata, even with another tad of a tip.

A live chicken was taken onto the train at the next stop, one, quick flick of an expert wrist and he was history. The people in the cabin next to mine had a small Bunsen burner and I smelled the chicken being cooked. The older woman leaned out and put her head into my cabin and asked if I would like a piece, I smiled and went immediately to her cabin, surrounded by children, elders and visiting relatives all asking questions, clucking over me and making me feel like one of the family. We laughed, smiled and enjoyed each other and then - miracle of miracles - were told the station was near. We rushed to get organized, their family, my family of one and the next thing I knew I was standing on a wooden station in Abidjan, Ivory Coast, a country I had only seen on a map and never dreamed I would someday visit.

The platform was a mass of people, rushing here and there. I asked if anyone knew where the PC office was. A man responded "Are you a Catholic?" and I replied "yes." He smiled, told me he was a priest and would take me to his mission office and get the PC address. At his office near a church, he put me in a cab and gave the driver money. I thanked him for his generosity and landed at the PC office. There I met a charming young PCV, Cedric, who explained that the current director did not allow PCVs from other countries to stay in the guest house. I smiled weakly as I did not have a lot of money to spend on hotels. He saw my worried look and offered me a cup of tea. We discussed my predicament, he called hotels and either they were full or too expensive. I was starting to get discouraged, but then remembered Jeri's calling card In my back pack, hauled it out and called her up. She was most gracious and said of course I should come right over and stay with her and her husband.

Cedric and I arrived at Jeri's home where an American military meeting was in progress in the living room, so we were invited to the patio where we enjoyed a cool drink and each other's company. Cedric took his leave, telling me to keep in touch with him. A maid showed me to the guest room where there were lots of fluffy pillows, a huge double bed, an air conditioner and ceiling fan. Just Jeri and I sat down to dinner, as her husband Randall had to go to the office and do a report. I slept in the luxurious bed which finished my trip of the day.

Singing birds, heavy rain and my ceiling fan were wake up calls. Their house staff person, Jerome, made a luscious breakfast for Jeri and me and off we went to the commissary. After stocking up with more food than I had seen in a year in my Mindelo home, Jeri took me on a scenic ride through the capital city of Abidjan. A huge Catholic church dominated a large section of the city. Jeri told me about that the largest Catholic Church in the world in the interior of the Ivory Coast, in the town of the President's mother. The French influence was visible in the architecture of official buildings and it seemed to me that there had been positive effects of their colonial presence.

We visited the Marine House, where a poster blaring "ONCE A MARINE, ALWAYS A MARINE" greeted us at the front door. It reminded me of a time I used information my Marine brother Richard had given me. Richard told me that if I ever got into trouble in a country to find the American Embassy and ask the Marine guarding it if I could enter. "November 10" was the pass word to be used. Well, I somehow managed to get into an argument in a West African country during my PC stint, in a bar of all places, and the people I was arguing with were getting quite agitated and I became fearful. I said I had to go to the bathroom, and would be right back. There I found a loose board in the back of the bathroom, pulled it out and ran like a woman possessed. I kept looking up at the sky to find the American flag flying, found it, beamed in and the Marine guarding the Embassy shouted "Halt, identify yourself'. I said "November 10th", he said "Proceed" and I slipped into the Embassy. Perhaps the P C button I had on my blouse, or the frightened face of an old white woman out of breath also helped. My angry companions coming to a halt in front of the Marine asked if he had seen a white woman running. The Marine responded, "Continue on your way," then he turned to me and said, "What the hell is this all about." He told me to go to the cafeteria, have some tea and rest until the Ambassador came the following morning. I met the Ambassador the next morning, told him my story, he told me to be more careful in choosing companions and to learn to "button my mouth" in foreign countries. I assured him I would take his advice.

The next day was Sunday so off to the Cathedral, which was complete with a stained glass white God who rode on a white horse, white soldiers on a ship, and a black choir that did not quit. The three dozen singers' handkerchiefs fluttered from their hands, they closed their eyes, raised their heads and moved in time with the music. The congregation whole heartedly participated. After Mass, Jeri took me to the church tower by the elevator and we saw the amazing view of the city. Ten to fifteen sky scrapers, modern office buildings all clustered around a huge lagoon surrounding the city. Trees were abundant and I drank them in gratefully after the drought ridden Cape Verdean landscape. Back at the house, we walked in the garden where she showed me aero phages plants that affix themselves to the trees, long vine like attachments that used no water, no food, just hung on the bark of the tree.

When I talked with Jeri about going home from Ivory Coast or trying to see one more country, she encouraged me to go to Morocco. Randall found out I could get a PCV discount but only catch was that I had to go to Belgium to get to Morocco. I thought that I had not been to Belgium as yet, so said yes to Randall's proposal.

After all that heavy thinking about my next trip, Jeri suggested getting a haircut, taking a swim, and get some Christmas shopping done, all of which I completed. Jeri was used to giving parties for the American and foreign community. I marveled at how all the details were taken care of, all the guests were happy. Jeri told me no tour would be complete without a trip to the Grand Bassaam, an area outside of the city on the coast. When I saw the lovely old French buildings, pounding surf and fine restaurants they all told me of the French influence. Men were making brass carvings over an open flame, so of course I purchased gifts, as well as some of Ivory Coast's famous batik table cloths and straw dolls. I saw a small mask in one of the vendors stalls, was told it was an antique. My shopping sense said it was not, but it looked so lovely I bought it anyway. I asked the guard at the Embassy a few days later if could possibly be authentic. "Nope, not on your life, but is a nice piece of sculpture".

Next on the schedule was cooking food for Thanksgiving. I wondered where my four chicks would be and felt a huge twinge of guilt for not being there with them for the third Thanksgiving in a row but reasoned that I would be able to spend the rest of my life with them on turkey day and might never again have the opportunity to visit new cultures, new countries and meet new friends. Stuffing, veggies, even cranberry sauce started filling up the kitchen. Jeri let me help with the cooking and organizing, which I thoroughly enjoyed. Now I knew why Jeri purchased so much at the commissary. We had been invited to the Ambassador's home for the Thanksgiving celebration, so Jeri had offered to bring some food for the dinner. A picture of Nancy Reagan in red ruffled dress made me realize in whose company I was. A young American boy, complete with Boy Scout uniform, presented a speech about what Thanksgiving meant for him. Then the Ambassador took the floor, welcomed all of us to his home and asked us to have a moment of silence to remember all who were not with us this day.

I had called my son Bill a few days earlier with travel questions and at exactly midnight, he called as arranged with the answers. He "suggested" that I go to Lisbon, might be safer than Morocco and told me I had five strikes against me, first, I was white, 2nd, I was a woman, 3rd, I was old, 4th, I was poor and 5th, I was traveling alone so come home "RIGHT NOW, MOM!!" I told him I appreciated all of his advice. He gave me the information I had requested and then said a quiet "goodbye, Mom, please take care of yourself," and I knew I had to get off the phone quickly or else my voice would break and I would cry too.

I packed my one bag for my next trip and was lulled to sleep by rain. After I said a fond goodbye to Jeri, Randall's driver took me to the airport, most efficiently got me exactly where I should have been, but when I offered him a tip, he said "No, it is my job to make it easy for you." Thank you for offering." And away I went to another undiscovered country - Belgium.

BRUSSELS TO MOROCCO ON THE WAY TO BOSTON

The pilot advised us we were about to land in Brussels. It was rainy, chilly and 5:30 in the morning. Went to a Statler Hotel across the street from the airport – I booked myself for just the time until my next plane departed for Morocco that night. I asked them to ring me in four hours so I could see the city. When their call came, I dragged my sorry ass out of bed, had a hot shower, (such a divine new experience) and turned on the radio. Suddenly there was Elvis singing his blue suede shoes off and I was abruptly shocked into another world.

I took an express train into the city, fast and efficient. I watched huge tower clocks whiz by, bronze statues surrounding the towers. I took to the pavement, enjoyed wonderful coffee and pastry and saw an art gallery with a sign in their window, "Grand Opening tonight - 6:30 pm." As it was 6pm and people were scurrying around, on top of ladders, I ambled in, asking if they needed some help while explaining I had an art gallery in America and next thing I knew, I had overalls on, was on top of a ladder and hanging art, just like my old Bare Cove Gallery days. I secured eye hooks, put wire on the back of frames and set the crooked ones straight. Then off came the overalls, someone gave me a long dressy scarf and I mingled with the crowd that came pouring in. About an hour later, I took the train back to the Statler, grabbed my one bag, and took off, happy about the 10% discount just because I was a PCV. I was on my way to Casablanca. Another adventure was about to begin.

Casablanca came into sight: home of Rick's Cafe, Ingrid looking soulful, Sidney the sinister, Bogey - "of all the joints ..." what a city! I had checked my money in Brussels and realized I was getting poor once again. I figured I would do cheap in Casablanca, explained what I needed to the taxi driver and he brought me to the front of the Hotel Excelsior. There were

Moroccan men in the lobby, Moroccan men walking in the street, Moroccan men everywhere; not one woman in sight. The room was pleasant, with high ceilings and the ubiquitous ceiling fan. The bed was narrow and there were only a few token roaches along with the running water. I took a bath and hit the streets for dinner.

When I asked the desk clerk to recommend a restaurant, he said that women did not go out by themselves in the evening. I thanked him politely for his advice and said I would be very careful. I had put on my long, baggy skirt, long cotton jacket and plain scruffy bag which I thought would help me fade into the background. I was wrong.

I began my saunter, saw the famous Casbah, steered clear of it, looked in shop windows and then felt a presence behind me. Saw his reflection in a store window; tall, white, wearing jeans and an expensive shirt. When I stopped, he would stop. When I crossed the street, he crossed the street. There were still enough Moroccan men on the streets to make me feel secure, but I knew I was in trouble. Casually looking around, I saw a Holiday Inn. I beat a path to the door, told the desk clerk that I was a visitor, PCV and nervous about the tall man behind me. I asked if he would pretend I was a guest, give me a key and say "Good night, Mrs. Brown" in a loud voice. Clerk nodded, "Good night now, Mrs. Brown. We will see you in the early morning." A wink from him, I got on the elevator, got off at the 11th floor, took the stairs to the 15th floor, read a book (always have a book when traveling) and waited an hour. Back in the lobby, I saw that the stalker was gone. I gave the clerk the key and walked quickly to my hotel. Sometimes it pays to have a New York City street attitude but important to remember to heed the local cautions as well.

The next morning, car horns, motor bikes and pigeons awakened me. I was in a major city and these were sounds I had forgotten. I went to "Rick's Café", had a delicious breakfast and then went to a taxi stand where I watched the various drivers. Finally I picked a man who was middle aged and had an honest face. His name was Tahar and he gave me a tour of his city. Corniche Boulevard, a wide two lane paved highway, was where the very wealthy lived in stark white houses with manicured lawns and tall gates. One beach was named "Miami Plage" and another "Tahiti" and of all dreadful things, there was a brand new McDonalds. Tahar was very proud of it, I tried to explain what junk food was, but could not get the message across.

Since it was a Sunday, people were strolling on the beach like an Atlantic City scene. Then we went by a part of town I knew existed but had not yet seen: the other part of town where the very poor lived. Tin shacks, dirt roads and people who had the look of poverty. Thought of our tin shack towns in Mindelo: the poor are the poor no matter what country they live in. We stopped for lunch, my cabbie treated, and he noticed my back pack was ripped. Tahar took me to one of his many cousins' home and said he could fix it. I looked them all in the eye, kept saying Peace Corps, and left my bag there - hoping I would get it back. Tahar took me back to the hotel where I took a very long nap, and went down at 4 as arranged. There was Tahar, bag repaired, candy in a cloth for my next trip. I gave him small presents for his children and he took me to a place where I got a ride to Marrakech. Tahar did the negotiating, said he bought two spaces for me so the other passengers would not crowd me.

Off went our long car to Marakesh. Tahar must have told the driver to take good care of me. I was always politely addressed. The driver bought me tea when we stopped for gas. One of the young men shared some of his cookies with me and, all in all, it was a most pleasant experience. I decided to do the cheap hotel here, too, so chose the Hotel Ambassador, same class as Hotel Excelsior but this room had a huge double bed and no roaches. After reveling in a huge tub with hot water, I took the stairs down, hoping to keep moving and avoid getting stiff. Breakfast in the lobby was tasty: hot milk, apricot jelly and French rolls. Ate some, put others in my newly repaired bag and hit the streets to soak up a new city that I had only dreamed about.

As it was the last day of November, I wondered where in the world I would be on the last day in December, my 56th birthday. I bought quite pretty postcards and was surprised by the price, thinking it was high when I did my calculations. When I asked the clerk if the price was correct, he assured me that it was. When I stopped for lunch, and heard some Moroccan men speaking English, I asked them for their help and explained the high price of the post cards, adding I was a Peace Corps Volunteer. They got angry at the price, took me over to the Tourist Bureau and told the man in charge in Arabic that I had been gypped. The Tourist Bureau man took my arm, apologized and we walked to the postcard seller's stand. As soon as the owner saw me with the Tourist Bureau man, he started to talk quickly in Arabic and looked flustered. The Bureau man said to me, ever so quietly, that the man had made a mistake and the postcards were now free for me.

I said that was not necessary, that I would pay, but the Bureau man said he did not want a bad story about Morocco going back to America.

The Tourist Bureau man got a tour taxi for me. The driver took me to the Palace of one of the former kings, Yacoubel Mansour, who had four wives, and 12 concubines. All the wives were treated equally it was said, but my driver said that Bida was his favorite. The Palace was made of cedar with floral decorations on all the walls. The French found and used a very old cemetery behind the Palace, thus saving it and the Palace from destruction. I saw a few women who were veiled. The taxi driver explained that the veil was not a religious rule, but the husband's rule. My driver told me that women leave the house just two times, one to marry and one when they die.

When I visited a rug factory and saw a small, pale peach, pale blue Berber rug, I put it on my credit card that had not been used for almost three years and had it shipped to my home in Brookline. The rug would remind me of my wonderful trip to Morocco.

At the souk, the huge outdoor market, there were performing monkeys, jugglers, dancers, exquisite fabrics by the bolt. I took pictures: water sellers in colorful costumes with ornate silver hats and beautiful, heavy silver cups, and everywhere were children playing games, and elegant, mysterious looking veiled women. Bought a black/green large shawl, tied it around my waist and, voila, my drab, beige outfit looked quite nice, back to the hotel for a quick nap and then to the famous casino.

Since I had not had a good dinner for a few days, I treated myself to a tasty dinner and a floor show. First came the belly dancers, their grace was amazing, then came the acrobats with wild contortions and then, the last performer, and the most dramatic, the snake charmer. Since my table was so close to the stage and now close to the cobras, I ordered another white wine. The charmer began his seductive playing and out of the basket came not one but two hooded cobras. The white wine went down quickly and was refilled quickly. The audience got quiet, I got slightly buzzed and then it happened. One of the cobras began to get nearer and nearer to the edge of the stage, the charmer played louder and then the cobra disappeared. The charmer played the first cobra back into the basket, the patrons were yelling and running out of the restaurant and I sat with my freshly filled white wine, very still. The waiters had left and the audience had left; there was one cobra, one charmer and me. Maybe I was too tired, too mellowed, maybe the flute playing got to me but when the charmer found the cobra, he yelled in a triumphant way and brought the cobra over for me to see. I smiled weakly. Back into the basket went the cobra. My waiter thanked me for staying so calm and said the charmer would like to buy me a glass of wine. I slept well that night despite the cobras in my dreams.

My friendly driver Ambari took me to Volubis, an ancient Roman city with a magnificent arch still intact with the name Guea II carved over the top that the King had made for his mother. All around it were covered onion fields and I was told that the covering would stunt their growth so they could sell in the winter for more money. Thorn bushes protected the crops and proved very effective. Next were the royal stables: King Moulay Ishamel had built them to stable 10,000 horses. As a horse woman, I noted the stalls were well constructed and reflected his love and caring for the horses. I remembered my friend Mohammed el Baz, born in Morocco and now living in the States, told me that when he came to America he was surprised that dogs were considered man's best friend. He had always been taught that the horse was man's best friend.

I had been told that no one has ever seen the two queens, one Berber and one an Arab, but my guide paused and said everyone had seen them as they travel the city frequently. The King is an Arab and we saw his huge farm in Yacob with gates all covered with sculpted roses. When we drove by a beautiful pine forest, the scent reminded me of the Maine woods. Coke signs were everywhere and horses were always part of the scene. Each town has one market day to sell and Ambari stopped so I could get a feel of each of the different towns. We went to one of the King's palaces. He has one in each major city and each one is always at the ready for a visit. This one was built in 1967 had seven doors, one door for each day of the week. The shinning brass all around the gates was polished with lemons, and I was told only Moroccan lemons would do. At a brass store I watched an old man teach a young man how to etch with a heavy nail and hammer into a piece of brass. I bought a small brass piece for each of my children and one for my home. The salesman was most gracious. It was not a very expensive purchase. He bowed to me and then gave me a piece of old silver as a cadeau, a gift, so I would remember Marrakech. I went back to the hotel, packed for an early morning departure and told myself one day I must come back to this enchanting city.

The only way to travel that I had not tried in Morocco was by train. Ambari, the nice taxi driver, took me to the station, talked to the porter and my two small bags were put in a state room. The other occupant introduced himself as Mohammed, he was old, older than I, so we had an immediate commonality. As I was getting settled in my seat, the taxi driver knocked on my window, I rolled it down and he handed me a pale pink rose, said something in Arabic and bowed. Putting the rose to my lips, I blew the traditional goodbye kiss but this was something special and he was so kind to me. When Mohammed saw this gesture, he smiled and bowed to my taxi driver and we three smiled with an old, new bond. The train took off, the wheels clicked and off to sleep I went. When I awoke, it was late afternoon and the sky was beginning to change color. Two dry "Wet Ones" were used and put away for another day. I pulled down the writing desk top and wrote on the first expensive, then free, post card from Marrakech. Snow topped mountains loomed in the far distance, then came heavy fields of tall yellow grass and short green grass and horses, always horses, grazing.

When we pulled into the Fez station, I looked at my map and discovered the Hotel Palais Jamai was on the other side of the town. A huge castle wall surrounded the area the hotel was in. The desk clerk and I haggled, 900 dirhams for a room with view of the Medina, 600 for a view of the city - frugality ruled and I went to a room looking over the city, watched the sun set, heard the call to prayer, sat on the magnificent Moroccan rug and prayed along silently in thanksgiving for my safe trip. There were some worn leather chairs, brass rubbings on the walls and I felt a sense of comfort in my new room. The half moon hung over my balcony, clouds trickled about and the city came alive. Dinner in my room consisted of cheese from Burkina Fasso, Belgian chocolates, French rolls from Marrakech, stale crackers from Casablanca, salami from Ivory Coast, lots of fresh water and I was full. I ventured out to take a walk around the bazaar, being wary of tall, white European men. The hour and my feet told me it was time to head back to my room.

The next morning I hit the deck running and told the desk clerk I needed a plumber for the non-functioning toilet and someone to fix the non-working radio. I borrowed a typewriter from the front desk and wrote and sent an article about the train ride from Waga to the Ivory Coast as requested by the public relations man at the American Embassy in Waga. I had read in a recent newspaper from the states that Father Robert Drinan had just celebrated being a lawyer and a priest for 50 years, so, since I had the typewriter at hand, a letter went off to him with my sincere congratulations. Breakfast consisted of one roll I had saved from the night before. I took a walk around the beautiful gardens, talked to the gardeners and compared flowers in America with flowers in Morocco. When I returned to my room, I found a welcome bunch of fresh flowers on my night table so I decided to munch my salami with fresh crackers for an in room lunch, took a nap and then found a new guide. There were a group of guides outside of the hotel and I went into my close look at one and all and chose one I thought I could trust. His name was El Sid and he took me on a walking tour, including a rug factory where I watched very young girls weaving beautiful patterns in and out in and out with very fast movements. Visitors received tea served in the traditional manner, poured from a great height to create a foamy brew.

Since my last two meals had been frugal, I got all dressed up for a hotel dinner. After all, the Palais Jamai was one of the most famous hotels in the world, enough of stale salami from weeks ago. I was the only white woman in the dining room, the only woman for that matter. Prompt and courteous service brought me Moroccan lamb on a skewer with a plate of couscous on the side. While I savored my white wine, I watched the other diners enjoy themselves.

The next morning El Sid took me out of the city to show me the country side. Morocco has no scarcity of water, wells are five meters deep and the result is public fountains all around the city of Fez. How different from dry Cape Verde! Sheep in pastures, horses in fields and always, snow covered mountains forming a magnificent and almost incongruous backdrop. Fences made of huge aloe cactus and telephone poles dotted the landscape with tall towers interspersed. I saw pictures of the current King Hassan II with his two sons; his three daughters were never in any pictures. Herdsmen on magnificent Arabian horses roamed the plains, keeping sheep and horses in line. When we got out of the car and stretched, a rider came up to say hello to us. El Sid and the horseman talked and smiled, and the rider spun his horse around, looked at me and said to me "We will see you again, In Shallah Boukra - (if God wills)." I said back quietly, "se deus quizer" Portuguese for "if God wills". El Sid took me back to my hotel after a full day of touring and I went out onto the back patio to watch the setting sun over the old city.

When I entered my room that night, a scent filled the air; it was the peach rose the Marrakech taxi driver had given me, still sharing its beauty on the table next to the door. I decided to stay one more day; one can do that when one does not have a schedule. I had the desk clerk call El Sid the next morning and he took me to the healing waters of Moulay's very hot springs. The facility was very modern and stark, my bathing suit, which was always with me, was not to be used. Birthday suits were the order of the day. I was led down steep stairs into the women's baths, a clean, large room with individual tubs all around in a circle. Submerged in a huge, deep tub with lulling music in the background; my body was grateful. When a crisp woman's voice came into my quiet space, "do you wish to repose?" a nod was all I could muster. After I got out of the tub, I was wrapped into a large, terry cloth bathrobe and led to a chaise. One hour later, I was escorted to a new room, robe off, assisted onto a cool wooden table and the old body was massaged with reverence and delicate strength. Every single part that had been abused during my three month trek was brought back to a calm life, muscles were massaged, tendons were stretched and my body was totally rejuvenated.

The drive back to the city took us through olive groves and deposited me at the Palais Jamai, weary and content. El Sid told me not to go out that night, but to rest for the next journey. I heeded his advice and tucked in early with the scent of the single rose by the front door and the huge bunch of flowers in my bedroom. During the night, I got restless and went down the hotel corridor until I found a balcony. Watched the old city still alive and yet, parts still sleeping. The moon hung over the ancient city with a protective aura.

El Sid had arranged for me to go to Tangier with a driver friend of his in a Mercedes Benz station wagon. Two other passengers came and we were off to a new city. The driver took us past a huge cemetery, and told us that separated burying had occurred in the past, Europeans, Jews and Moslems all totally apart. Harraick, my new driver, said that does not happen now. We passed a marriage cart with a white clad, shy bride and beaming groom accompanied by the smiles and laughter of family and friends. Fields of cotton, groves full of oranges and lemons, and eucalyptus trees all filled the landscape and five hours flew by. We made a stop for tea and cookies and again, the driver treated me. I was learning hospitality is another name for Morocco.

Since this was most likely to be my last city to visit, I decided to go to the most elegant hotel, the El Minzah, right smack dab in the heart of the city. In the lobby was a huge picture of the unsmiling King flanked by two handsomely carved royal chairs. My room over looked the garden, where I spied a pool. I ran down to get the dust of the journey off, dove in and almost froze. I did not linger in that pool. I got dressed and walked to the American School and to get the telephone number of Noel, a British teacher whose name have been given to me in Burkino Fasso as a must see when I hit Tangier. There was a sense of New York City and Paris in this new city: new to me but an ancient city in this country. I had dressed down and no one paid any attention to me, and that was just the way I wanted it. When I left the hotel, no taxi drivers tried to grab me to be their customer. They waited for the rich tourists to sweep in. That was fine with me. Shank's mare was to be my mode of transportation.

I had been told not to miss the Forbes Museum, some distance from the Hotel El Minzah. I decided to walk to it anyway, as cabs would be too expensive. I passed by elegant, private homes with tall and imposing gates guarding them from the street. The Forbes Museum is situated on top of a hill and is quite large. Inside are huge displays of military units serving in many, many wars, all in miniature. What was most fascinating was the integrity of each battle, the absolute dedication to detail, all done on perfect scale. Then I noticed every battle had a prominent battalion or squadron or grouping of black soldiers. They were all in full regalia, each unit documented with accuracy and all of these groups were in the foreground. Read that Malcolm Forbes was born in Scotland but had lived in Tangier for the past twenty years until his death. There was a large oil painting of him sitting on a wild motorcycle, smiling at all of us.

As I rounded a corner, fascinated by the fine detail of all of the dioramas, a garden came into view. I gingerly stepped outside and took a deep breath. I had not seen so many flowers, so many plants and so much loveliness in one spot for the past three years. There were statues interspersed in the garden and the total effect was calm compared to the battle scenes I had just seen. As I began to walk quietly into the garden, I heard a step on the gravel path to my right. Thinking it was another visitor, I continued my walk until a man's voice said "Please, do not walk in the garden." Turning slowly, I saw a short, elegantly dressed man approaching me and he said, "This garden is not for the public to visit, it is private." For one of the few times in my life, I did not argue. He asked "Are you new to Tangier?" I explained that this was my last city to visit before I returned home after living in West Africa for three years. He paused, "Come back here at 5:30." I walked back to my hotel, showered, fluffed up the hair as best I could, took a taxi and was back at exactly 5:30.

227

The gentleman was waiting for me outside the museum. He extended his arm and escorted me in to the garden. He indicated that I sit in a large, hand carved wooden chair with huge arm rests and a fan like back facing out over the ocean. A servant appeared from nowhere and poured us a lovely tea. Not a word had been spoken. The gentleman pointed to the sky that was by now filling up with amazing Technicolor hues, all shades of the rainbow. We sat in silence and watched the sun go down and disappear behind the Rock of Gibraltar in what was one of the most peaceful sunsets I had ever experienced. "You are sitting in a chair where only beautiful women have sat." I asked who had sat there last and he smiled and said "Elizabeth." An hour passed, the servant came and took away the tray of tea and delicate cookies, the gentleman thanked me for coming and said his man would drive me back to my hotel. I stood; he took my arm again and escorted me to the car. I thanked him quietly.

The next morning I called Noel and he sent his driver to pick me up at my hotel and I was driven to yet another hill. Noel had two houses, one to work in and one to sleep and live in. Fireplaces were going in both houses, bookshelves lined all the walls in both houses, and a manual typewriter sat in the center of his working home. His driver said Noel was not feeling well so the visit would be limited to one half hour. Noel's grey hair, his 65 years and his British accent all told me I had met a fine, bright gentleman. He had just completed a book on the history of South Africa where he was born. I gave him a copy of my old Newsweek and he was so pleased there was an article about the DeBeers diamond cartel in S.A. We talked about being driven to write and how it was his passion. I told him I had been keeping logs of every day I spent living in Africa and he encouraged me to write a book when I returned to the U.S. "You have a story from another perspective. Share it; do not hold it to yourself." His servant Mustafa served tea and we discussed Americans and Brits and how they love to explore new countries. He planned to sell some of his property in Morocco so he could buy a flat in London. He told me about being a journalist for the Montreal Star and covering Broadway 1952 - 1957, exactly the time I was beginning to study acting in NYC. We figured we lived in the same city at the same time and saw many of the same new plays and laughed at the thought of it all. He pointed to another hill outside of his window and said the large building there was another of the King's residences the King had not visited for 30 years but it was always at the ready. He told wild stories of when he had been a jet setter and I told my simple stories. The half hour visit was now into its fourth hour. When he began to pause more frequently, I asked to take my leave, but he protested. Thirty minutes later we shook hands and I left a dedicated writer nodding off in his wing back chair with the light from the fireplace playing on his well earned wrinkles.

A quiet tea and roll in a cafe was my dinner and nine hours of sleep took over. I had not, as yet, ridden a camel so began the hunt the next day. At a seaside town I found the camel, the owner and the sea. I told my city driver to come back at sunset and had not one but two camel rides. I took the first one with the owner holding the lead rope, then two tourist couples came and were timid about riding the camels. The owner said, "This American lady did it, you can too, she will hold your ropes and it will be very safe." I became the leader of five camels and loved every bumpy, jolting, jarring movement. When the ride was over, the owner said as a thank you for taking the tourists, I could ride to the sea wall, a good distance away. I smiled, he hit the rump of the camel and the two of us were off at a lopsided, weird angled lope skimming the soft waves of the ocean, running across the sand pell mell. As soon as we reached the wall, the owner lot out a piercing whistle, camel turned and made a mad dash back to his owner with one worn out and marvelously happy rider. I took off my shoes, walked the long stretch of beach and sat down when the need for a nap over took me immediately. I wound the strap of my bag around my arms and neck so if anyone was going to rob me, they would have to strangle me first. My hat from the Banana Republic store in Boston covered my face and the waves lulled me to sleep.

Morocco

When I awoke, the sun had shifted to the west, telling me it was time to move and eat. At an outdoor cafe, I had lamb on a skewer, cold beer and look at the town of Ajilah. My driver appeared on the dot of 5, and took me back to the hotel where I put feet up to read a book and relax. After doing the counting the money exercise again, I decided to have a light dinner. Down a side street I melded, melded into the crowd, found an outdoor cafe, had tea and toast and a sweet. I noticed a woman wearing a lovely robe with hand sewn embroidery. When I asked her where she purchased it, she wrote down directions to a woman's cooperative where I purchased five, one for each daughter, one for me and one extra - a special gift for whom I did not know yet.

It was now December 7th, Pearl Harbor Day in the States, I was sure I was the only one in Tangier who would remember that infamous day. It began to rain heavily so put on my wind breaker jacket and was snug and dry. Felt it was time to think about returning home to Boston so I entered the telephone building. What a nightmare, hundreds of wall phones, people yelling into the receivers, some crying, some laughing, all talking a mile a minute. The lines were long, the building had no ventilation; it was grim. Finally my turn came. I got daughter Maura by some miracle and she was astonished by my voice. I told her I would be home in a few weeks or so. When I hung up, I had a funny feeling, perhaps my newly found freedom was about to come to an end.

Back at the hotel, I called Barbara to come and join me for tea, she was the American lady who had married a Berber whose name had been given to me by Jeri from the Ivory Coast. She was a bright and interesting woman and we talked children (she had three), schooling, countries and the world. After about two hours, she left saying said she would pick me up for dinner at her home the next evening. I protested saying I had to pack, and rest before the next big trip, but she answered "fine, I'll pick you up at 5". I lost that argument.

The next day I scrambled around the city doing last minute errands, bought my airline ticket, checked the leather stores for treasures, took one more walk through the bazaar, drank one more tea at the Cafe De Paris on the corner across from the French Embassy. Barbara arrived on the dot of 5 and away we went to yet another hilltop. The car climbed up and up and up, and the city lights disappeared behind us, the trees took over and we ended in a grove of eucalyptus trees, their scent playing on the gentle wind surrounding a huge home. Three large dogs were at my side the minute I opened the car door. Barbara said not to worry; they were just checking me out. Her husband, Farid, opened the house door and gave me a warm welcome. A roaring fire was going and Farid asked what I would like to drink and as I was about to ask for the traditional tea, he added, Scotch, rye or bourbon. Scotch got the nod.

We three hunkered around the fire, laughing, sharing and feeling like we had known each other for much longer than a few hours. A servant called us to dinner. The dining room faced the entire city; a panoramic view filled the entire, huge picture window, it was almost like a movie set it was so perfect. A piping hot chicken lemon soup began our dinner, the servers coming and going in a most quiet and gentle way. The dinner was eaten at a lovely pace, the conversation flowed on and we stayed at the table for about three hours. Barbara gave me her mail to be posted in the States, Farid called the El Minzah and said I should be given the customary 20% discount and the evening came to a lovely and gracious end with two new friends. When Kenza came to say goodbye, I told her to call me when she came to Wellesley College in Massachusetts the next year and she would be folded into my family. Alia, their middle daughter, and the youngest Rita came to say good bye as well. The scent of the eucalyptus trees stayed with me for the entire ride back to the hotel.

As I slowly did last minute packing, I was alarmed to realize that part of me didn't want to leave and part of me did want to go back home to the States. I decided to take one last swim in Morocco, so did some laps in a frigid pool and watched the stars cover an inky black Moroccan sky. After a warm bath and thoughts about the magnificent country of Morocco with all of its various pulses, I let the evening chanting lull me to sleep.

The jarring telephone awakened me and I was off in a petite taxi to the airport. I looked down at the city from the plane that was disappearing underneath our wings and promised myself I would return to this fascinating country one fine day. Many hours later, the steward tapped me gently on the shoulder and said we would be arriving in New York soon. What a strange sensation it was to hear "New York". I had lived there half of my life and now it sounded so foreign.

We landed at the JFK International airport on a bitter cold December day. The Moroccan air that I had just left was warm and soothing, this New York air cut right through my light cotton skirt and blouse, even my jacket provided little protection. After going through customs, I walked out to a place that said "Official Greeting Area" and there, on a huge wall, wonder of wonders, were those cherished words:

"Give me your tired, your poor, your huddled masses, yearning to breathe free. Send these, the wretched refuse of your teeming shore. Send these, the homeless, tempest tossed to me: I lift my lamp beside the golden door." - Emma Lazarus 1849 - 1887.

This is the inscription for the Statue of Liberty in New York Harbor. I smiled, remembering, as a little girl the first time I had seen those words with my father, mother and younger brother Richard long ago. How safe I was then. Now I felt like one of those tempest tossed persons.

Spotting a Red Cap, I asked him to take a picture of me in front of this inscription. He took my camera and started to back away, I asked him why and he answered politely that he wanted to get a long distance shot because I looked like 50 miles of bad road close up. I thanked him for taking the picture, not the remark, and then sat down on a bench and cried silently. I had thought coming back home would be a lot easier than when I went to Africa to live, but I was wrong.

I finally realized this culture shock response to coming home was not going to get me to Boston, so I stood, shook myself, took a deep breath and walked to a public telephone. I dialed Maura's number, she answered and I said, "This is Mom, I am coming home by plane to Logan airport tonight." She got quiet, I got quiet and she said "I will meet you."

In Boston, I was met by Maura, and Bill and his fiancée Mary. I looked at them and realized I had been out of their lives for a long time, got choked up as they gathered round me. They asked me where I wanted to go for dinner and what I wanted to eat. I said quietly, "Maura's apartment, hot Campbell's tomato soup, grilled cheese sandwich, a dill pickle and a Sam Adams cold beer". All were served up quietly and chocolate chip cookies rounded out my perfect first meal back in America. The three of them looked at me and realized I was a very different person than the one who had left almost three years prior. That night I slept in Maura's bed waiting for the Sahel sand to cover me, the moon to nod at me and the stars to light my bedroom. None of this happened.

December 1992 JFK airport, New York at the end of my journey

The next day, Bill drove me to my dear friend Win's extra apartment outside of the city where I would stay by myself for one week, getting my bearings. Win gave me a hug, the keys to his apartment, said to sleep well and call him when I was ready to go out for dinner. I went to see my faithful dentist, Dr. Di Maggio, who looked at my teeth and said there was lots of work to be done. A week passed, I went on long walks in the country, checked the stars and the moon every night and then was ready to go back to the city. I thanked Win who drove me to Boston where Dodie and Bill had a Christmas party and had invited me. I kept looking at my dear friends with new eyes.

That night it was arranged that I would go back to my own apartment. Andrew, Dodie's son, drove me to my Brookline home. I asked him to walk in with me as I was a bit timid. He did, gave me a hug and left. I sat down on my sofa, put an Afghan throw my children had put out for me and fell asleep there; the bedroom was just too scary to be in. My dear friend Annie saw my kitchen light on the next morning and brought over her welcoming hugs and an African violet. My two San Francisco daughters, Katherine and Claire, came home for the holidays. My two Boston children told their siblings to watch me, that I was different. I walked down my hall to the bathroom to take a shower, fumbled in my pockets for a match, and then realized I had electricity. Oh yes, I remember now.

Christmas week came and there was no food in the fridge. I gave the children money as I did not have the courage to go to the huge super market after shopping in my small outdoor door market in Africa. Then we ran out of beer and wine; I gave them a $10 bill, they looked at me, smiled and kicked in the rest. My friend Nola took me out to dinner, dressed up with my pearl necklace just like we had in the days when we were both professionals in Boston. She picked me up in her car and said we would be late and should call the restaurant. I said I would make a call if she would stop by a public phone booth, she smiled, got out her cell phone and I said, oh yes, I remember now. I found myself saying this over and over again. Win took me out to dinner at a great steak house. When I finished eating my first baked potato in three years, he asked if I was through with it, I said yes and he said he would love the potato skin. Oh yes, I remember now.

One night I was taken to the theatre and an African memory came back. My elegant, black velvet theatre purse did not have its zipper completely closed, so when my date, Richard, handed me my evening bag, my Swiss Army knife that had been my companion for the past three years, hit the floor with a clang. It was cold as ice now, but I remembered when it was very hot the night I had used it in West Africa. This is what happened.

On a warm autumn night in October of 1990, I had been chasing sleep for hours. I was so tired. My bed had a back board of rough wood, a thin mattress that I suspected had been used during WWII with empty cement bags piled on top and a sheet that was much too heavy. Sleep would not come. Finally, the eyes closed and I dozed off. All of a sudden, a bright light shone on my face. Nothing stirred: no noise, no rustle, just a steady light right in my face. The sweat began to form on my fore head, trickling into my eyes and making them sting with its salt. I slipped my left hand under the sheet and was careful not to make a movement or sound that would indicate I was awake. My hand touched the Swiss Army knife that was on a cardboard box next to my bed. If I was going to be killed or hurt, so was the intruder. My fingers grasped the handle. The blade was sharp. I opened my eyes, threw off the sheet, jumped up and screamed, "What do you want, what do you want?" and swung my knife through the hot, dry quiet night air. The answer was silence. I looked around and then saw my intruder. Tears came to my eyes and I collapsed with relief for I had knifed the moon. The African moon was shining through my open window. It had turned its usual corner and spilled its light right into my small, cement sleeping room; no wonder there was not a sound. I started to sob with relief and then laughed for this moon would become my protector, my companion, my constant during the next three years on this little island in the middle of the ocean. I put my elbows on the wooden window sill and looked at my new friend. Clouds lazily stroked it, its beams muffled by the clouds at times, bright when the clouds finished their fondling. After a while, I crawled back into my narrow bed, pulled up the sheet and let my moon take care of me for the rest of the night.

As I sat in the Colonial Theatre that winter night in Boston, feeling the Swiss Army knife in my hand, I smiled at my recollections but could not, of course, explain them to my questioning date. I had returned to my home, had worn the pearls as in the past, but there was a different heart under those pearls now. I had resumed using my evening purse, but there was something different in it that had never been there before.

THE CHAPTER BEFORE THE LAST CHAPTER

During the entire two and a half years that Paulino and I became attached, his mother Amelia used to beg me to take him to the U. S. with me. To people who have lived in any developing country, this is not unusual. We understood that because the mothers knew they could not take care of all the children they had, if one went to a country where they would be taken care of, that child would be fortunate. I asked the women of the tin shack towns why they had so many children "Because if one of our children goes to live in another country, they will send money back to us."

I explained to Amelia that I was much too old to raise her son. She told me she knew she would die soon and wanted to make sure he had a good life. Amelia had two older daughters who she had given away to other families who could feed and shelter them, but no one wanted a boy. Birth control was not allowed in the strict Catholic country of Cape Verde. When Amelia died, it was a certain fact that Paulino would hit the streets and would most likely die.

The women of Ilha d' Madeira teased me when I carried him the long distance to the clinic. "Deana, Paulino is like your son, his hair is red like yours." They were right about the color; when a child is malnourished, the hair becomes a strange hue of red. He also started developing sores in the corners of his mouth. There were times he was just too weak to walk, so I would put him in the hospital and they would give him IV's, and then send him back to the tin shack town. Maura sent me baby vitamins and baby aspirin, but they disappeared when I gave them to Amelia. Even our PC nurse, Kristin, gave him vitamins which disappeared. I finally kept the vitamins at my home and gave them to him when he stayed with me.

When I came back to the States, I kept thinking about Paulino and what would happen to him when Amelia died. I was leery, knowing it would be a volatile issue and might be viewed as white woman saves black baby. I developed pictures of him and took them to the Cape Verdean communities: Fall River, Brockton, Providence, Scituate. I went to Dorchester to Catholic churches and told them about Paulino, all in Portuguese (not easy.) No one was interested in adopting a little boy from Cape Verde. I went to adoption agencies and asked for their help, was told no one wanted a boy soon to be 5. I went on radio stations, television talk shows, wrote newspaper articles and sent mailings to my friends who had Cape Verdean contacts. I tracked down every possible lead and always got the same response, thank you very much but no thank you.

There were many risks if I brought him from Cape Verde to the United States. There was no risk if he stayed in Cape Verde, he would, simply die.

So, after one year of thinking of Paulino, I took the gamble and went back to Cape Verde in May of 1994 to see if it was possible to bring him back to the U.S., that is, if he was still alive.

THE LAST CHAPTER
"YOU MUST DO THE THING YOU THINK YOU CANNOT DO"

Eleanor Roosevelt

"What do you mean I need a visa - it will take six to nine months for the process - I have to have the birth certificate of the mother first? What do you mean, it can't be done?"

This was what I heard in English, in Portuguese, and in Crioulo. This was not going to be an easy walk on the beach, but I had no idea how tough a walk it would be. All I wanted to do was bring a little boy out of an African country and take him to the States for another family to adopt. The people who lived in the tin shack town of Mindelo, on the island of Sao Vicente, The Republic of Cape Verde, West Africa, were squatters. This was their last stop, their last place before they rested forever. No electricity, no sanitation facilities, no running water, no nutritious food, no schools.

Paulino, the son of a squatter, nevertheless deserved to have a life with nutritious food, sound health and an education. He would not receive it living where he lived. Paulino Gomes Silva was a survivor. But he did not have a prayer of a chance living in Cape Verde. He would grow up never seeing the inside of a school, would never get off his island of birth. He would never taste a nutritious meal, be able to write his name or read a book or play without hunger pains in his belly.

Amelia, his mother, was a domestic, a term people used when they had no known occupation and no ability to make money and support a family. Amelia had given birth to four children, two older half-sisters of Paulino, and a still born baby.

When Paulino was tiny, Amelia tied him to her back with a piece of cloth. When I carried him, I also tied him to my back - much easier. I remembered seeing a woman carrying a baby on her back and I noticed she had a natural rest for the child - her ass. It was like a ledge. So when Paulino rode on my back, I would thrust my ass out and walk like an African mother. This walk reminded me of my dance teacher, Martha Graham. "Stand on that line, there is a thread that comes from the middle of your instep. It goes through the absolute middle of your body and comes out on the top of your head." Miss Graham had to teach us to walk the way African women did naturally.

Paulino went through the next two and a half years living in his mother's home but visiting and often staying overnight with me. I took him swimming when friends came for the weekend. He had never seen a beach before; his mother had been too frail to walk him the long distance. He took to water with no fear, he splashed and ran and laughed. He spoke in Crioulo, his island language, a mixture of Portuguese and local slang. I understood the basic words: I want to eat, I want to drink, and I want to pee.

There was the lesson of peeing in the bed. We slept like spoons; I would hold him all night. The first night I awoke with a warm feeling and then my nose told me, pee in the bed. Off went the thin sheet, out went the boy, whisk went the sheets and he was on the floor. He looked at me as if to say, there must be a lesson here. He never wet his bed again. I'm not sure If Dr. T. Berry Brazelton, or Dr. Leroy Eldridge, my pediatricians, would have approved, but then, where were they when I needed them?

When I came back to the U.S. the end of December, 1992, culture shock, re-entry - the full catastrophe, as Zorba the Greek would say, pummeled me. I would sometimes get sad in the midst of a swirling party and not know why. For one year and three months, I divided every pay check I received in half and put one half into a special account. I never told myself why I was doing this, I just did it. Later I realized I was saving up for air fare to Cape Verde to get Paulino out.

In the spring of 1994, I met a student at Simmons College where I was recruiting for Peace Corps. She had been one of the seniors I had tutored at Madison Park/Humphrey Center in Roxbury. Since she had been to my farewell party in the States when I left in 1990, she asked how my experience had been in Cape Verde. I told her how I had been touched and that I was saving money to go back. She told me of her Cape Verdean cousin's travel agency that had a special discount rate for Cape Verde. I called, he said yes, it was true and quoted me a fare that was exactly half of what another agency had told me.

One of my bridesmaids, Mona, lived on Long Island near JFK airport where I was to depart for Cape Verde. We had not seen each other for thirty years. I called her sister-in-law Betty, got Mona's number, told her I was going to Africa by way of JFK; she said "stay with me." We had a reunion with all of her family, all of whom I had grown up with on Long Island.

The next morning Mona's husband Tom took me to JFK. It was pouring rain. What would it be like going back? Was Thomas Wolfe correct, you can't go home again? Would people I loved have died? Would they have forgotten me? What, what, what? These questions haunted me. Tom asked me if I had my ticket. "Yes," I replied. "Have your passport?" "Yes, Tom, I have traveled all over the world, don't you think by now I would have it down pat." Why did I snap at Tom, I must have been very nervous.

The check-in clerk looked my ticket and passport, and then asked, "Where is your visa?" With a turn in my stomach, I said, "What visa?" "Cape Verde visa, you must have a visa." "What do you mean? I have to have a visa?" Gulp, sputter, I then stammered. "Well, you see, when I was in the Peace Corps, just one year ago..." Tom asked if he could speak to the manager, then the manager came to the desk, and that is when Tom and I did the pincer movement. He did the New York Irish charm; I did the Peace Corps story. He was our age; he listened and told us to stay where we were. Tom told his young son to take me to the bar, get me a double Scotch. Tom and the manager took my passport, driver's license and my Peace Corps staff card. Tom found us thirty minutes later and said "You're cleared. You will have a big problem getting into the country, so be prepared." Tom walked me back to the counter, the check-in clerk smiled, and I left thanking Tom - he was a much better traveler than I.

I had my carry-on bag. One always brings a fully packed bag with enough clothing and necessities to get you through the first few days, just in case, God forbid, your bags are lost. Mona had said to me when I told her I needed to go to the drug store to buy a few last minute things, "If you don't have it, you can buy it there." Right? Wrong! She didn't know Africa. I was shown to my seat, it was in business class. The check in clerk had upgraded me - wide seats - good wine – delicious food. My seat companion was George, cameraman from CBS, going to South Africa to cover the first multiparty election in history. We talked about freedom, opportunities, commitment. He wished me luck in getting Paulino out; I said I was going to try my damnedest.

I looked at the monitor that showed where we were in flight: North America, then nothing. Cape Verde finally came on the screen. "Look George, that is where I am going. That was my home." The Cape Verdean stars welcomed me; I had forgotten how clear the sky can be with no street lamps, no city lights, and no pollution. Tears came to my eyes, but they didn't roll down; my man Vitorino had taught me how to swallow my tears. I had forgotten how the stars gave off such light and how the moon came through with dependable brightness. A small group of us disembarked at the airport of Sal, a small airport in Cape Verde and the turn in my stomach came back. No visa, I told myself, you must be careful.

Hustle, bustle, the luggage carousel went round and round and then, no sound. No more bags. My three huge bags, stuffed to the gills with presents for everyone, were not there. Now, I not only had no visa, I had no luggage. The customs man said, "I do not find a visa in your passport." "Well", I said "umm, you are correct, you see" the Peace Corps dialogue spilled out. His eyes glazed over. What did he care? "The manager will be here in six hours, you may not enter until he talks to you." I had a seven hour layover before I took the puddle jumper plane to the island of Sao Vicente so I walked around with my one small bag and slept on hard benches, watching the sky go from total darkness to a magnificent sunrise. Purples, oranges, violets and mauves all welcomed the new day.

The head of the Customs Police came towards me. This is not going to be easy, he is not smiling. I bowed, smiled and went into my patter. He listened."Did you work in Ilha d' Madeira in Mindelo?" "Yes, I did." This was all in Portuguese so I kept checking my vocabulary in the index of my mind. Finally the headman said "200 escudos." Then he leaned over and said "Thank you for what you did there." He had remembered me; what a gift he gave me! I had kept some Cape Verdean money when I left a year and a half before. I gave it to him. He returned, visa in place. I bowed, he bowed, and my perspiration stopped. How many more hurdles would I have during this trip?

I fell asleep again on the chairs - no money for the expensive hotels nearby. A gentle hand awakened me. "Miss, may I ask you a favor? My grandson

241

needs to get to Mindelo, could you take him with you? He has a ticket." A small nine month old fat baby was put into my arms. I smiled, the baby smiled, and the grandfather said thank you. He said if I ever needed anything, to just call him. I asked what he did and he told me he worked for South Africa Air. File that name; you might need him for Paulino. "May I have your number, Senhor?" With his name and number in my hand and his grandson in my arms, we got on the plane. Both the baby and I nodded off before departure.

The next thing I felt was a gentle hand telling me we had arrived. I looked out and there it was: the same building, the same lunar landscape, and the same black taxis. I spied faithful Maryann, who with her husband Pedro, had invited me to stay in their home. When she saw the baby in my arms she laughed and asked why I did not tell her of my miracle. A grandmother came up and took the baby. Maryann asked where my bags were. We laughed at my story, jumped into her truck and off we went to their home in the town.

Maryann allowed me to take a little nap but awakened me an hour later to tell me "many people want to see you." We loaded the truck with all the food she had been preparing for the party and we went to their new house high on a hill overlooking the ocean at Lazarette. With the ocean once again pounding in my ears, and with the clear blue of the sky as a backdrop, the party began. I reveled in the friendships I renewed.

Then I wondered if I would see my man today, or tomorrow, or perhaps, not at all. The sunset started doing its magic dance, and we packed the dishes and I walked around a corner of the porch. A strong hand shot out and grabbed my forearm. It was Vitorino. My breath came in spurts, my face flushed and I felt lightheaded. I looked up and there he was, smiling, the face I had dreamed of for the past 1 ½ years. I started to give my body to him for an embrace, but he backed away and said, "Welcome, Deana." We shook hands but the grasp was intimate, as intimate as two dancers on a moonlit dance floor. We made small talk: "Did you have a nice flight, how is your family, are you well?" Our hostess told me to help pack the dishes and then said softly, "Bring them to the city house and then you are free." Vitorino and I got into his car. We did not speak. His hand covered mine and we both smiled as we looked out at the sunset and drove towards the harbor town. He jumped out at my hostess' home and gave her the bowls. Maryann walked around to my window and gave me a set of keys. "Come home when you wish." We drove away to his home near the sea, to renew,

242

to touch and to be one again.

The next morning I awakened to the sound of the sea wafting through my bedroom in the home of Maryann and Pedro. I told Maryann and Pedro about my plans for Paulino. They said it would not be easy, it would take some time, but they would support and help me all they could. During the next two weeks, Maryann woke me every day by saying, "You're late. You have a lot to do." My first visit was to the small Catholic Church in the middle of town. As I turned the corner, I saw the same four women who had always been sitting on the bench. They looked at me and smiled and gathered the strength in their old bones to stand and hug and cry with me. Their eyes followed me as I went into the dark church to kneel on the hard boards where I thanked God for allowing me to come home.

I felt complete when I emerged. I was greeted at once by the lady who baked the tasty Portuguese bread and she called to me to come to her bakery and have a roll with her. The lady at the photo store called a greeting and some of the children from the tin shack town of Campinho gathered round me. The mayor, Onesimo Silveira, came out of his City Hall office and we discussed how "our" island was doing. He had planted flowers and bushes and trees in the plaza in front of City Hall. I remembered four years earlier when I walked into that same hall with a fear that had made me sweat. I made my visits in town and retreated to the cool oasis of Maryann and Pedro's home for a wonderful lunch. We all took the traditional rest after lunch and then I hit the road again. I started giving out the presents I was smart enough to put in my carry on. Smiles, hugs, and I heard many "we have missed you."

My friend Cuia filled up with tears when I entered her cement house. She was wearing the Ship & Shore blouse I had given her a year and a half before. Her neighbor, Antonia, laughed and swung me around, showed me the Elvis poster that I sent to her. Joanna, who lived in the old age home, showed me a picture on her bedside table of herself and my daughter Maura in November 1991. Then she got very quiet and told me her remaining leg would be coming off soon. I told her I would pray for her. Maria, the woman in the next room, came in dancing on the stump of her leg. The "other Maria," who is blind and almost totally deaf, was led into the shack. No one said a word. She felt my eyes, my mouth, my ears, and then my hair. When she touched my hair she said, "Ah, Donna Deana." We all clapped - sounds she would never hear but she knew we were happy for her and felt our mouths for the smiles that were there. Then all the women

243

told me I was "gordo," which is fat in Portuguese and they thought I looked much better now than I did when I lived in their town. I had lost thirty-eight pounds when I lived in West Africa; I had put every single pound back on since arriving back in the States. I smiled remembering that Vitorino had said the same thing the first night I had arrived as his hands felt all the familiar places he knew so well.

I left and my feet instinctively took me to my old narrow pathway. I stood in front of the apartment where I lived, loved, cried and learned more than I ever thought possible. The wooden shutters were closed and dirty the front walk not swept. My next door neighbor Valentina came out and smiled, we embraced. I left with a promise to come back for a lunch.

I walked to the airline office and asked if my bags had returned from their trip to South Africa. I told the inefficient man in charge that I must have my bags. He gave me a shrug and I firmly told him I would return the next day. From the airline office I strolled to the post office and knocked at the door in the back where my packages used to be. Although there was no one in sight, I knocked and said with a put-on angry voice that I wanted my packages and I wanted them now. I heard voices, and the door opened slowly. When they saw it was me, the clerks squealed, "Donna Deana is back" and the dance of the returned was played again.

The next morning, Maryann told me my three bags had arrived at the airport and she would pick them up. Thank God. After hearing that good news, I walked to the other tin-shack town, Ilha d' Madeira, the one where Paulino lived with his mother. Will they still be there? Will they be alive? Will his mother allow him to go back with me? The cry went out, "Donna Deana is back" and then Paulino ran to me. I felt my eyes fill up with tears, I couldn't seem to move quickly, but he did. He leapt into my arms and I lifted him up with a hug and buried my face into his shoulders. A shudder passed between us. Funny, it was a shudder I could not control. In that moment, I told myself he deserved to have a better life.

His mother quietly came up to me and we hugged. She was frailer than she was when I first knew her. The three of us walked into her small cement apartment. I noticed Paulino was full of scabs and was scratching. I wondered if she knew that I was going to ask her permission to take her son to the States, took a deep breath, and asked and she said yes. I told her I would come back the next day and we would start gathering the necessary documents. I tried to keep my joy under wraps and walked slowly out of the area. Then, when I was far away, I kicked my heels up, yelled to the sky and said Gracias, Deus, thank you, God.

When I arrived at Amelia's apartment the next day, she told me she wanted her aunt to go along with us. That was the first time I have ever heard of any aunt. We went to her home where she was gracious but reserved. I explained what I wanted to do and she said she would go along with us and help. We went to the clinic where Paulino had a blood test for AIDS. "We will let you know in a week." Whoops, here we go, African time against U.S. time. I told her we needed the information as soon as possible as there were many documents I must get and the blood test would tell me if it was all possible. A smile, she said "Yes, Donna Deana, since you helped my mother many years ago, I shall help you today." They don't forget.

I meet my friend Ana Filo Da Cruz on the street, we laughed and hugged and talked about her new son. Then she spied Paulino's scabs and said he had scabies and I must get rid of them at once. She was a pharmacist and gave me the correct medicine. She said his mother must be treated too, but we both knew that Amelia was not capable of treating herself. We discussed the problem and then I asked the aunt if Paulino could stay with her until his scabies were cured, yes. The severing process had begun for Paulino and his mother. Ana gave me the medicine and cautioned me against getting scabies myself. Scabies are wildly contagious.

Being an optimist, I took Paulino to have his passport picture taken. He was in borrowed clothing, and would not smile. The picture came out gray and black, just like his expression. Paulino, his mother and aunt walked back home, I walked back to Maryann's. I did not sleep. Now I was worried about all the steps that had to be taken.

We went to the registry where I requested a birth certificate for Paulino. We were asked for Amelia's birth certificate. Amelia gave me a blank look, never had one. Thank God her aunt was along. She explained the situation. The clerk told me to go and buy five selos. My Portuguese being a bit rusty I thought that meant candles. I raced to the hardware store, without a second thought, returned with five candles. Now the Portuguese word for candle is velas, not selos, so the clerk asked why I had candles, I replied "You said selos, aren't they candles?" When we realized the mix up, we all burst into laughter. She had wanted me to buy stamps, which is "selos," for the document. We finally got a certificate for Amelia and then I asked for Paulino's. "No, no, we only do one family birth certificate a day." In a New

York second I was explaining why I needed them. Paulino got cranky, Amelia felt faint and the aunt told me she had to go. I told them in no uncertain terms that no one would go anywhere until I got the birth certificate for Paulino. They realized I was serious and in a moment it was produced. I bought the four of us a cup of coffee and we were all silent. Would all the paperwork get done in time to get the visa by May 3rd, my departure date? The thought nagged me constantly.

We were a very funny quartet. Paulino, bopping along without a concern in his young life, Amelia brooding and thinking about what she was participating in, the aunt, Nano, using this as a social occasion to tell all how lucky her grand-nephew was going to be when he got to the United States. The four of us developed a pattern. Since we always seemed to arrive about one hour before closing time, I worked out a routine. I told Paulino to pretend to be tired and lie down. I then placed him in front of the door. I told Amelia she should look frail and sick and ask for a chair, Nano should find the relative/friend she knew behind the counter and engage them in a lively conversation. It worked; when things looked grim and we were about to get kicked out, Paulino would go to the door and lie down and be asleep, a chair would be given to frail Amelia and Nano would have a chat with whomever she spied. What a trio!

Next we had to get the permission paper. A heavy lady, not in body but in spirit, said, "You must have three witnesses for the mark of Amelia" (thumb print, Amelia did not know how to write.) "Nano can be one, I can be another and you, Senhora can be the third." Not so fast. "You can't because you are a stranger, Nano can't because she is a relative and I can't because I work here." OK, plan B: hit the floor Paulino, faint Amelia, visit with friends here Nano. I ran down the three flights of stairs (not one of these document places were on the first floor.) At 12:30 most of the people were at home, but I spied a 'slide and glide' dude coming down the street. I called to him and explained our situation. He looked at me and said, "Don't you remember me, Deana?" Who the hell was he? I took a guess and said, "Oh, yes, aren't you that good dancer I met some time ago"? He smiled, nodded, (lucky guess on my part,) and up he bounded the three flights of stairs and signed his name.

Now we needed two more, I spied another young man, the only one on the deserted street. Same plea, he shook his head no. My dancer friend yelled from the 3rd floor window, "Do it, Fernando, Deana is my friend." Up he bounded. Now I had two people to sign the papers, one to go. Ah ha, an old curmudgeon ambled by. I explained, he looked at the stairs and said, no way. My face fell - he got the picture and went to the first door he saw, pounded on it with his cane. He asked for the father and the father came to the door. The old man explained to him and he looked at me. Now because an old man and old woman had asked, he had to respect us. Up he went, witnesses all, the heavy woman gave each one a glare, but the deed was done and another hurdle taken. I was told the passport would take a week, so I explained that we did not have a week, we had today and then we had to fly to the United States Embassy on another island. Come back tomorrow I was told.

We did, got the passport, then hit the airline office to book our flight. "All filled up Deana," I was told. An old lady who was standing nearby told me to get to the airport early with a standby ticket and smile a lot with boy in hand. I did and we flew that day. We arrived at the capital city where Arlene, the PCV who served on the same island as a teacher as I did, took us to the Embassy. She had talked to the consul on our behalf before we arrived. We met the consul and he proceeded to grill me like I have never been grilled before. Later I was told about the live organ black market. Poor families sell their children for great amounts of money, the children are taken out of the country, killed, and their organs are sold on the black market. The Counsel knew of no Cape Verdean who ever dealt with this black market. The story filled me with disgust and every time I looked at Paulino, I thought "how could any human being ever kill a child for his organs?" My nightmares, which were already terrifying, got a new wrinkle. I would wake in the night, no matter where Paulino and I were, in a cold sweat, thinking I had lost him, that he would be stolen and sold and killed. The visa was given to us the next day.

Finally we returned to Arlene's home, where she asked her maid to watch Paulino while we went out for dinner to the home of our friends Les & Katy. Both worked for bettering the life of Cape Verdeans through different organizations, so they listened to our story about Paulino with great understanding.

We flew back to our island and I called the South Africa Air grandfather whose grandson I had taken to Mindelo. He said he would do what he could about a ticket for Paulino. Four hours later, the deed was done.

Throughout all the days of the visits to the official places, I saw Vitorino in the evenings. He encouraged me and gave me the strength to continue. We were as comfortable with each other after 1 ½ years apart as we had been before. He fixed the pipe he made for me in August of 1990 and scolded me for not keeping it cleaner. I laughed and went for a swim in the ocean while he worked on it. When I came in from my starlit swim in the warm, clear Atlantic water, my grog was ready, and, as Cape Verdean music filled his house, we danced, laughed and shared.

During the two weeks I was there, friends came to take me out for lunch and dinner. Yvonne was as gentle as she had always been, David was his usual cheery self, and Maryann and Pedro were always there to give me a lift, a hint, and a hug. I had told Vitorino that my feet were feeling abused so he went and got argila, the radioactive sand from the mountains of our island to soothe and comfort. He also gave me a bottle of grog with coconut milk to take home. I sampled it and the taste brought back the memories of the nights near the ocean with him a year and a half before.

It soon was time to leave. I went to the home of Nano where Paulino had been staying. He was not ready. We had to find his clothes, wash him in a tiny plastic tub and then walk to the home of his mother. The look on her face that morning will haunt me for the rest of my life. The look said I so love you that I shall give you up. It is what every mother has said to her child when parting. She gave him a little bag of hard cookies and whispered something into his ear. He looked at her, paused, then took her hand and brought her over to me. I did not move. He took my hand and this 4 ½ year old boy took control and led us to the door. He took one look back, did not smile, and walked out, with his mom on one hand and me on the other. His great-aunt Nano walked behind and not a word was said during the forty-minute walk to Maryann and Pedro's home.

Maryann met us at her stairs. Her face had a look of understanding. The silence was complete as she took Paulino's hand from mine and told his mother to say goodbye. Amelia kneeled and held him. His Great Aunt Nano gave him a package and told him something quietly, then with his mother moved toward the door. Maryann moved toward the stairs - Paulino and I stood still. He reached for my hand, his skin was healed and his touch was soft. I remembered that little hand and the first time I felt it four years earlier. His touch, the touch of the old woman who lost her second leg, the touch of the blind woman feeling my face, the touch of Maryann wiping my cheek at the airport, the touch of the salt water on my cheeks when I swam with Vitorino, the touch of warm Portuguese bread on my tongue, the touch of my feet barely hitting the dance floor, these touches would stay with me forever.

Paulino and I flew away that afternoon. The Cape Verdean tradition when saying goodbye is that the one who is leaving should not have tears (lagrimas,) it makes the ones left behind feel sad. I had been taught by an expert, my man. Not a tear came, neither from Paulino or me. I saw Vitorino's car huddled by the side of a hill away from the airport. He stood beside the car, not moving but silently saying goodbye. He had the pipe I bought for him in Mali in his hand, raised it on high, and nodded. The women of the tin shack town waved white handkerchiefs as our prop plane flew away from their world. The tears of Paulino and Deana were not on our cheeks but hidden in our hearts.

EPILOGUE

"The cure for anything is salt water; sweat, tears or the sea."

Isak Dinesen

Well, we had the "sweat," getting Paulino out of Cape Verde with his mother's blessings to begin a new life in America. The "tears" were in the hearts of all who said goodbye to us. The "sea," we left that soothing memory behind.

I had already tried all the usual ways to get Paulino adopted before bringing him back: adoption agencies, making visits to Portuguese and Cape Verdean churches, going on the radio, doing newspaper interviews, calling friends, calling in every chit outstanding. No takers for a Cape Verdean little boy who was almost five years old. I took him to my Peace Corps office every day. Then someone told me about Bright Horizons, a day care center started by Returned Peace Corps Volunteers. I called, told them about Paulino, and they took him after my former husband Bill did a thorough medical check-up on him and signed the necessary papers for admittance to the center.

No luck with leads and I was getting panicked. Paulino only had a two month visa. Our Peace Corps New England office administrative officer, Ann Burnett, asked how the hunt was going, I said I was discouraged. Ann told me that her sister, Martha Beach, was looking to adopt a child but had four criteria that had to be met. The child must be between five and seven, be a boy, Roman Catholic, and speak a romance language. Bingo! I called her sister and brother in law in Salt Lake City and told them Paulino's story. They were interested but could not afford to fly out to Boston to see him.

I thought "OK, plan B." I called Garber Travel and asked my travel agent what Mr. Garber's private line was. She balked. I told her the Paulino/JFK/Peace Corps story. She gave me the number but said, "His secretary Rose will never let you through." I gave it a try and it must have been my lucky day: Mr. Garber answered his own telephone yelling "Where is Rose, where is Rose, my phone is ringing." I quickly told him the Paulino/JFK/Peace Corps story. "What do you want from me?" he said. "I need two free round trip tickets to Salt Lake City." He growled, "Where do you work?" I told him and he hung up.

I was stunned, thought I was doing a good selling story. The phone rang in the PC office two seconds later and I heard, "Yes Mr. Garber, Mrs. Gallagher does work here." I got on the phone, "when can you leave?" "In 48 hours". "Ok, come and pick up the tickets tomorrow." "Thank you Mr. Gerber." "No Gerber is the baby food. I am Garber, the travel man." "Oh, I am so sorry." I took Paulino to meet Mr. Garber the next day, Paulino was given a Garber hat, a hug and off we went to Salt Lake City.

Martha and Dan Beach met us at the plane, with their older adopted son, Jose. Their welcoming smiles, their gracious manner towards Paulino and their kindness to the two of us impressed me. For the next four days, Martha and I huddled together like two old friends, one questioning, one answering. On Sunday afternoon, I took Paulino for a long walk. I told him I would leave him there with the Beach family and would call him on the phone Monday night with my decision about his adoption. I told him he must not cry and to be brave.

We went to the airport, I cried, Martha cried, Jose held the hand of the little boy who clung to him. I wept in the plane, the Continental Airline stewardess asked to see my ticket, and when we landed at Denver, a grey haired gentleman in a Continental uniform came up to me and said he would take me to my next flight bound for Boston.

The stewardess awakened me, and asked me if I wanted something to eat. I said no, waved her away. I was in the window seat, no one was in the middle seat and a man with wing tipped shoes had the aisle seat. "She will have one chicken as I will, two white wines, please." He pulled the tray down for the middle seat, cut my meat, handed me the white wine and put my food tray on my table top, told me to drink the wine. I did and he got me another wine. I drank it down, ate the dinner, and then fell asleep. The stewardess awakened me four hours later, "Mrs. Gallagher, we are in Boston." I turned to thank Mr. Wing Tips, but he had left. He never got to hear the story about Paulino.

I called Martha Monday morning and said; "You are the best family for Paulino." She said "thank you", and Paulino became a member of their family. He was 4 ¾ years old, he is now 22 years old and married his college class mate, Talitha Story. Paulino was fortunate, the Beach family was fortunate, I was fortunate... and this all came about from the fortunate Isles, Cape Verde.

THE END

"The child's one chance to grow properly in mind and body should be shielded from the mistakes, misfortunes and malignancies of the adult world. This protection should have a first call on society's concerns and capacities so it can be maintained in bad times as well as good" from UNICEF'S 1994 report, "The Progress of Nations".

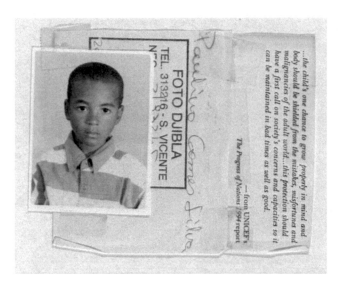

Paulino Gomes Silva

Vitorino and Diane, 1994

Paulino and Diane, 1994

Paulino and Diane, 1994

Paulino Beach, June 2003 High school graduation

Paulino at Diane's 70th birthday party, 2006

Paulino and Diane at his wedding in 2011

Dr. Ed Beard and Paulino- 1994

Cesaria Evora and Diane, Madrid, Spain 2010

About the Author

Diane Shugrue Gallagher, New York City born, now resides in Brookline, Massachusetts. Mother of four, Nana to two grandchildren, she works as the Nursing History and University archivist at the Gotlieb Archival Research Center at Boston University. A graduate of both Colby Sawyer College and Lesley University, she attended The Neighborhood Playhouse, School of the Theatre, NYC. Diane served as a volunteer in the Peace Corps, The Republic of Cape Verde, West Africa, at the age of 53. Diane serves on the Cape Verde Children's Coalition Advisory Board of Directors, on the Advisory Council of The Scottish Coalition, U.S.A. and is a long standing member of the Harvard Host Family Program. Her numerous awards include: Distinguished Alumni Award, Colby Sawyer College, United States President's Volunteer Award, The Lillian Carter Award, and was made an Honorary Member of the Sigma Theta Tau International Nursing Society.